Mathematics In Our World

Second Edition

Robert E. Eicholz

Phares G. O'Daffer

Charles R. Fleenor

⋏ Addison-Wesley Publishing Company

Menlo Park, California · Reading, Massachusetts · London · Amsterdam · Don Mills, Ontario · Sydney

Illustration Acknowledgments

Jim Boyer: 103

David Broad: 170-171

Dick Cole: 1, 20-21, 30-31, 46-47, 71, 102, 127, 146-147, 162-163, 172-173, 187, 214-215, 258-259, 274-275

Susan Jaekel: 235, 244-245, 254-255, 346, 347

Heather King: 28-29, 36-37, 56, 116-117, 141, 169, 192, 203, 216-217, 257, 300, 301, 325

Pat Maloney: 26-27, 64, 67, 71, 123, 125, 164-165, 182, 183, 235, 242, 243, 276-277, 313

Pat Marshall: 344A

Sal Murdocca: 187, 220-221, 266-267

Jim Murphy: 78-79

Sharleen Pedersen: 1, 33, 50-51, 54-55, 104-105

Judy Sakaguichi: 45

Wayne and Teresa Snyder: 194-195, 296-297, 306-307, 340, 341, 342

Bob Tamura: 19, 40-41, 48-49, 66, 74-75, 96-97, 120-121, 127, 136, 151, 152, 187, 231

Holly Zapp: 235, 239, 248-249, 285, 293, 304, 320, 337, 344, 345

Ivar Zapp: 330

Photograph Acknowledgments

The Bettman Archive: 111 right

*Elihu Blotnick:** 1 left and top center, 2, 4, 11, 12 top, 23, 24 both, 34 bottom, 38, 60 top right, 62 top left and top right, 64 all, 66, 71 top left and top right, 72 top, 76, 82-83 top, 87 bottom, 88 top, 94-95 top, 98-99 top, 106-107, 110, 113 all, 114 top right, 115, 118 all, 119, 127 center, 128 top, 138-139, 142 top right, 144, 148, 153, 154, 168, 208

Brown Brothers: 111 left

*Richard Crone:** 134-135 top

© *Walt Disney Productions:* 52-53

Joseph Doherty: 62 top center

John S. Flannery/Bruce Coleman Inc.: 132

*George B. Fry III:** 130-131, 161, 187 top left and top right, 188 both; 190-191, 200-201, 204, 206-207, 218, 224 top, 226 top, 235 top left and bottom right; 236 bottom left, 252, 262 left, 285 top right, bottom left and bottom right, 286, 294 both, 298, 299, 310, 312, 316 top, 324 all, 328, 332-333

*George Hall:** 1 top right, 62 bottom left

M. Philip Kahl: 210-211

Mark Meldgin: 230 top center

NASA: 198-199

The New York Public Library; Astor, Lenox and Tilden Foundations; Rare Book Division: 156

*Nick Pavloff:** 62 bottom center and bottom right

Sam C. Pierson, Jr./Van Cleve Photography: 42-43

*Bil Plummer:** 264

M. Woodbridge Williams, National Park Service, United States Department of the Interior: 127 bottom left, 158

Baron Wolman: 134-135 bottom

*Nikolay Zurek:** cover

*Photographs provided expressly for the publisher.

All other illustrations and photographs by Addison-Wesley staff.

Acknowledgments

Copyright © CN Tower Limited 1973., p. 46;

ISBN 0-201-16040-4

ABCDEFGHIJKL-DO-8543210

Contents

Addition and Subtraction
Place Value
Adding
Subtracting
Using Your Skills
Geometry (Basic Ideas)

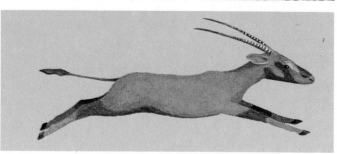

Addition and Subtraction

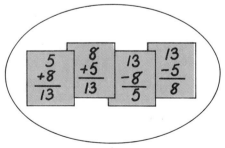

Fact Family

Show a fact family that uses the numbers 5 and 9.

If you forget a fact family, you can find it in one of these ways. Try to remember the facts.

1. Use counters.

A. $5 + 7 = n$ C. $12 - 7 = n$

B. $7 + 5 = n$ D. $12 - 5 = n$

2. Use the number line.

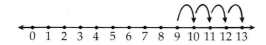

A. $9 + 4 = n$ C. $13 - 4 = n$

B. $4 + 9 = n$ D. $13 - 9 = n$

3. Use rods or strips.

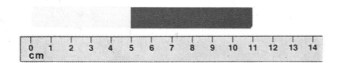

A. $5 + 6 = n$ C. $11 - 6 = n$

B. $6 + 5 = n$ D. $11 - 5 = n$

4. Use reasoning.

A—addend   S—sum

A. $8 + 8 = 16$, so $8 + 9 = n$

C. $\overset{A}{8} + \overset{A}{9} = \overset{S}{17}$, so $\overset{S}{17} - \overset{A}{9} = \overset{A}{n}$

B. $8 + 9 = 17$, so $9 + 8 = n$

D. $\overset{A}{9} + \overset{A}{8} = \overset{S}{17}$, so $\overset{S}{17} - \overset{A}{8} = \overset{A}{n}$

Addition facts

First spin: 7
Second spin: 8
Score: ?

$$\begin{array}{r} 7 \\ +\ 8 \\ \hline 15 \end{array}$$

The score is 15.

Add.

1. $\begin{array}{r}2\\+3\\\hline\end{array}$	2. $\begin{array}{r}3\\+4\\\hline\end{array}$	3. $\begin{array}{r}4\\+4\\\hline\end{array}$	4. $\begin{array}{r}5\\+0\\\hline\end{array}$	5. $\begin{array}{r}5\\+4\\\hline\end{array}$	6. $\begin{array}{r}6\\+3\\\hline\end{array}$	7. $\begin{array}{r}2\\+5\\\hline\end{array}$
5	*7*	*8*	*5*	*9*	*9*	*7*
8. $\begin{array}{r}8\\+1\\\hline\end{array}$	9. $\begin{array}{r}0\\+7\\\hline\end{array}$	10. $\begin{array}{r}5\\+3\\\hline\end{array}$	11. $\begin{array}{r}2\\+7\\\hline\end{array}$	12. $\begin{array}{r}4\\+5\\\hline\end{array}$	13. $\begin{array}{r}3\\+3\\\hline\end{array}$	14. $\begin{array}{r}2\\+6\\\hline\end{array}$
9	*7*	*8*	*9*	*9*	*6*	*8*
15. $\begin{array}{r}6\\+4\\\hline\end{array}$	16. $\begin{array}{r}5\\+5\\\hline\end{array}$	17. $\begin{array}{r}5\\+6\\\hline\end{array}$	18. $\begin{array}{r}7\\+3\\\hline\end{array}$	19. $\begin{array}{r}6\\+6\\\hline\end{array}$	20. $\begin{array}{r}6\\+5\\\hline\end{array}$	21. $\begin{array}{r}6\\+7\\\hline\end{array}$
10	*10*	*11*	*10*	*12*	*11*	*13*
22. $\begin{array}{r}8\\+2\\\hline\end{array}$	23. $\begin{array}{r}7\\+7\\\hline\end{array}$	24. $\begin{array}{r}7\\+6\\\hline\end{array}$	25. $\begin{array}{r}7\\+9\\\hline\end{array}$	26. $\begin{array}{r}8\\+8\\\hline\end{array}$	27. $\begin{array}{r}8\\+7\\\hline\end{array}$	28. $\begin{array}{r}8\\+9\\\hline\end{array}$
10	*14*	*13*	*16*	*16*	*15*	*17*
29. $\begin{array}{r}9\\+9\\\hline\end{array}$	30. $\begin{array}{r}9\\+8\\\hline\end{array}$	31. $\begin{array}{r}7\\+4\\\hline\end{array}$	32. $\begin{array}{r}8\\+3\\\hline\end{array}$	33. $\begin{array}{r}3\\+7\\\hline\end{array}$	34. $\begin{array}{r}6\\+9\\\hline\end{array}$	35. $\begin{array}{r}5\\+7\\\hline\end{array}$
18	*17*	*11*	*11*	*10*	*15*	*12*
36. $\begin{array}{r}8\\+5\\\hline\end{array}$	37. $\begin{array}{r}8\\+6\\\hline\end{array}$	38. $\begin{array}{r}9\\+4\\\hline\end{array}$	39. $\begin{array}{r}4\\+7\\\hline\end{array}$	40. $\begin{array}{r}6\\+8\\\hline\end{array}$	41. $\begin{array}{r}4\\+8\\\hline\end{array}$	42. $\begin{array}{r}5\\+9\\\hline\end{array}$
13	*14*	*13*	*11*	*14*	*12*	*14*

Add.

1. $\begin{array}{r} 6 \\ +7 \\ \hline \end{array}$ 13

2. $\begin{array}{r} 7 \\ +8 \\ \hline \end{array}$ 15

3. $\begin{array}{r} 4 \\ +7 \\ \hline \end{array}$ 11

4. $\begin{array}{r} 9 \\ +5 \\ \hline \end{array}$ 14

5. $\begin{array}{r} 5 \\ +7 \\ \hline \end{array}$ 12

6. $\begin{array}{r} 8 \\ +9 \\ \hline \end{array}$ 17

7. $\begin{array}{r} 4 \\ +8 \\ \hline \end{array}$ 12

8. $\begin{array}{r} 7 \\ +9 \\ \hline \end{array}$ 16

9. $\begin{array}{r} 5 \\ +8 \\ \hline \end{array}$ 13

10. $\begin{array}{r} 6 \\ +8 \\ \hline \end{array}$ 14

11. $\begin{array}{r} 7 \\ +5 \\ \hline \end{array}$ 12

12. $\begin{array}{r} 6 \\ +9 \\ \hline \end{array}$ 15

13. $\begin{array}{r} 4 \\ +9 \\ \hline \end{array}$ 13

14. $\begin{array}{r} 7 \\ +6 \\ \hline \end{array}$ 13

Solve the equations.

15. $7 + 5 = n$ 12

16. $8 + 4 = n$ 12

17. $9 + 6 = n$ 15

18. $7 + 8 = n$ 15

19. $6 + 8 = n$ 14

20. $8 + 3 = n$ 11

21. $9 + 5 = n$ 14

22. $6 + 5 = n$ 11

23. $7 + 9 = n$ 16

24. $4 + 6 = n$ 10

25. $9 + 2 = n$ 11

26. $3 + 6 = n$ 9

27. $0 + 5 = n$ 5

28. $1 + 9 = n$ 10

29. $9 + 9 = n$ 18

30. $6 + 7 = n$ 13

31. $n + 4 = 5$ 1

32. $n + 3 = 5$ 2

33. $n + 3 = 7$ 4

34. $n + 5 = 10$ 5

35. $n + 9 = 17$ 8

36. $n + 7 = 15$ 8

37. $n + 4 = 13$ 9

38. $n + 8 = 17$ 9

39. First spin: 9
Second spin: 7
Score: ?

☆ 40. Make up a spinner
game. Play it with
a friend.

We're as close as
any numbers that you
have ever seen.

Add both of us together
and you should get
fifteen.

Who are we?

More practice, page 348

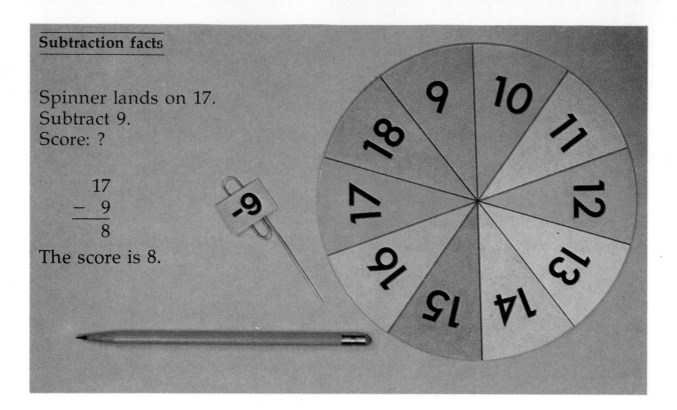

Subtraction facts

Spinner lands on 17.
Subtract 9.
Score: ?

$$\begin{array}{r} 17 \\ -\ 9 \\ \hline 8 \end{array}$$

The score is 8.

Subtract.

1. $\begin{array}{r}5\\-2\\\hline\end{array}$ 3	2. $\begin{array}{r}7\\-3\\\hline\end{array}$ 4	3. $\begin{array}{r}4\\-0\\\hline\end{array}$ 4	4. $\begin{array}{r}9\\-6\\\hline\end{array}$ 3	5. $\begin{array}{r}7\\-5\\\hline\end{array}$ 2	6. $\begin{array}{r}8\\-2\\\hline\end{array}$ 6	7. $\begin{array}{r}9\\-4\\\hline\end{array}$ 5
8. $\begin{array}{r}8\\-7\\\hline\end{array}$ 1	9. $\begin{array}{r}9\\-2\\\hline\end{array}$ 7	10. $\begin{array}{r}9\\-5\\\hline\end{array}$ 4	11. $\begin{array}{r}8\\-3\\\hline\end{array}$ 5	12. $\begin{array}{r}8\\-0\\\hline\end{array}$ 8	13. $\begin{array}{r}7\\-1\\\hline\end{array}$ 6	14. $\begin{array}{r}7\\-7\\\hline\end{array}$ 0
15. $\begin{array}{r}10\\-6\\\hline\end{array}$ 4	16. $\begin{array}{r}11\\-6\\\hline\end{array}$ 5	17. $\begin{array}{r}12\\-5\\\hline\end{array}$ 7	18. $\begin{array}{r}16\\-8\\\hline\end{array}$ 8	19. $\begin{array}{r}18\\-9\\\hline\end{array}$ 9	20. $\begin{array}{r}14\\-7\\\hline\end{array}$ 7	
21. $\begin{array}{r}12\\-9\\\hline\end{array}$ 3	22. $\begin{array}{r}16\\-9\\\hline\end{array}$ 7	23. $\begin{array}{r}17\\-8\\\hline\end{array}$ 9	24. $\begin{array}{r}13\\-7\\\hline\end{array}$ 6	25. $\begin{array}{r}12\\-7\\\hline\end{array}$ 5	26. $\begin{array}{r}12\\-8\\\hline\end{array}$ 4	
27. $\begin{array}{r}13\\-5\\\hline\end{array}$ 8	28. $\begin{array}{r}14\\-8\\\hline\end{array}$ 6	29. $\begin{array}{r}16\\-7\\\hline\end{array}$ 9	30. $\begin{array}{r}17\\-9\\\hline\end{array}$ 8	31. $\begin{array}{r}15\\-6\\\hline\end{array}$ 9	32. $\begin{array}{r}15\\-9\\\hline\end{array}$ 6	
33. $\begin{array}{r}14\\-5\\\hline\end{array}$ 9	34. $\begin{array}{r}14\\-9\\\hline\end{array}$ 5	35. $\begin{array}{r}13\\-8\\\hline\end{array}$ 5	36. $\begin{array}{r}13\\-6\\\hline\end{array}$ 7	37. $\begin{array}{r}13\\-9\\\hline\end{array}$ 4	38. $\begin{array}{r}15\\-7\\\hline\end{array}$ 8	

Subtract.

1. 16
    − 9
    ‾‾‾

2. 15
    − 8
    ‾‾‾

3. 17
    − 8
    ‾‾‾

4. 15
    − 7
    ‾‾‾

5. 13
    − 9
    ‾‾‾

6. 14
    − 7
    ‾‾‾

7. 16
    − 8
    ‾‾‾

8. 14
    − 9
    ‾‾‾

9. 13
    − 4
    ‾‾‾

10. 18
    − 9
    ‾‾‾

11. 13
    − 8
    ‾‾‾

12. 13
    − 7
    ‾‾‾

13. 17
    − 9
    ‾‾‾

14. 14
    − 6
    ‾‾‾

15. 15
    − 9
    ‾‾‾

16. 14
    − 8
    ‾‾‾

17. 16
    − 7
    ‾‾‾

18. 13
    − 5
    ‾‾‾

Solve the equations.

19. $10 - 8 = n$
20. $13 - 5 = n$
21. $14 - 8 = n$
22. $15 - 7 = n$

23. $16 - 9 = n$
24. $12 - 4 = n$
25. $12 - 9 = n$
26. $13 - 6 = n$

27. $13 - 8 = n$
28. $14 - 6 = n$
29. $14 - 5 = n$
30. $15 - 6 = n$

31. $16 - 7 = n$
32. $18 - 9 = n$
33. $17 - 9 = n$
34. $14 - 9 = n$

35. Spinner lands on 13.
    Subtract 8.
    Score: ?

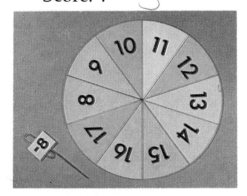

Draw a figure like this:

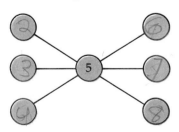

Put 2, 3, 4, 6, 7, and 8
in the circles so that
the sum along each line
is 15. Use each number
just once.

☆ 36. Try some spinner
    subtractions.
    How many can you
    do right in 60 seconds?

More practice, page 349

Column addition

You score 5 on the first dart,
3 on the next, and 7 on the last.
What is your total score?

Finding the answer

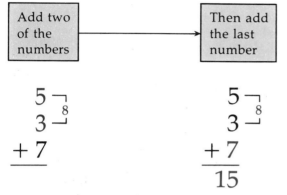

| Add two of the numbers | → | Then add the last number |

$$\begin{array}{r} 5 \\ 3 \\ +7 \\ \hline \end{array}\quad 8$$

$$\begin{array}{r} 5 \\ 3 \\ +7 \\ \hline 15 \end{array}\quad 8$$

Your total score is 15.

Find the sums.

1.
$$\begin{array}{r} 3 \\ 4 \\ +2 \\ \hline \end{array}$$

2.
$$\begin{array}{r} 6 \\ 3 \\ +1 \\ \hline \end{array}$$

3.
$$\begin{array}{r} 4 \\ 2 \\ +4 \\ \hline \end{array}$$

4.
$$\begin{array}{r} 5 \\ 2 \\ +3 \\ \hline \end{array}$$

5.
$$\begin{array}{r} 4 \\ 2 \\ +3 \\ \hline \end{array}$$

6.
$$\begin{array}{r} 2 \\ 3 \\ +1 \\ \hline \end{array}$$

7.
$$\begin{array}{r} 5 \\ 3 \\ +1 \\ \hline \end{array}$$

8.
$$\begin{array}{r} 4 \\ 3 \\ +5 \\ \hline \end{array}$$

9.
$$\begin{array}{r} 4 \\ 2 \\ +7 \\ \hline \end{array}$$

10.
$$\begin{array}{r} 5 \\ 3 \\ +9 \\ \hline \end{array}$$

11.
$$\begin{array}{r} 6 \\ 3 \\ +3 \\ \hline \end{array}$$

12.
$$\begin{array}{r} 4 \\ 4 \\ +9 \\ \hline \end{array}$$

13.
$$\begin{array}{r} 3 \\ 2 \\ +9 \\ \hline \end{array}$$

14.
$$\begin{array}{r} 4 \\ 5 \\ +6 \\ \hline \end{array}$$

Find the sums. Look for tens.

15.
$$\begin{array}{r} 4 \\ 6 \\ +7 \\ \hline \end{array}$$

16.
$$\begin{array}{r} 5 \\ 3 \\ +7 \\ \hline \end{array}$$

17.
$$\begin{array}{r} 2 \\ 4 \\ +8 \\ \hline \end{array}$$

18.
$$\begin{array}{r} 9 \\ 8 \\ +1 \\ \hline \end{array}$$

19.
$$\begin{array}{r} 6 \\ 4 \\ +3 \\ \hline \end{array}$$

20.
$$\begin{array}{r} 3 \\ 9 \\ +7 \\ \hline \end{array}$$

21.
$$\begin{array}{r} 6 \\ 8 \\ +2 \\ \hline \end{array}$$

Solve.

1. $5 + 2 + 1 = n$ 2. $3 + 4 + 2 = n$

3. $6 + 3 + 1 = n$ 4. $8 + 2 + 4 = n$

5. $6 + 3 + 4 = n$ 6. $7 + 2 + 6 = n$

7. $7 + 8 + 2 = n$ 8. $9 + 6 + 1 = n$

9. $8 + 4 + 3 = n$ 10. $9 + 7 + 3 = n$

Add. Look for tens.

11.	12.	13.	14.	15.
9	2	5	3	5
1	8	2	4	6
7	3	7	7	3
$+\ 2$	$+\ 3$	$+\ 3$	$+\ 2$	$+\ 5$

16. What is the score for these three darts?

17. What is the score for these four darts?

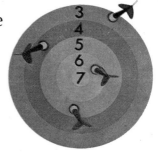

Guess this sum.
Write your guess.

$1 + 2 + 3 + 4 + 5 + 6 + 7 + 8 + 9 + 10 + 11 +$
    $12 + 13 + 14 + 15 + 16 + 17 + 18 + 19 = n$

Find the exact sum.
Was your guess more or less?

Answers for Self-check   1. 10   2. 14   3. 15   4. 17   5. 15   6. 9   7. 11   8. 5   9. 9   10. 8   11. 5
12. 9   13. 5   14. 17   15. 5   16. 16

More practice, page 350

Self-check

Add.

1. 4
   $+6$

2. 9
   $+5$

3. 8
   $+7$

4. 9
   $+8$

5. 5
   4
   $+6$

6. 3
   1
   $+5$

7. 2
   3
   $+6$

Subtract.

8. 11
   -6

9. 17
   -8

10. 15
    -7

11. 14
    -9

12. 13
    -4

13. 12
    -7

Solve.

14. $8 + 9 = n$

15. $12 - 7 = n$

16. $3 + 6 + 7 = n$

Answers for Self-check—page 9

Test

Add.

1. 6
   $+7$

2. 8
   $+4$

3. 9
   $+6$

4. 3
   $+8$

5. 2
   4
   $+7$

6. 3
   5
   $+9$

7. 4
   3
   $+6$

Subtract.

8. 12
   -5

9. 13
   -8

10. 14
    -8

11. 15
    -9

12. 16
    -8

13. 17
    -9

Solve.

14. $9 + 7 = n$

15. $13 - 5 = n$

16. $2 + 5 + 8 = n$

The 15 Game

Try the 15 Game with a classmate.

Rules

1. One player uses the odd digits: 1, 3, 5, 7, 9. The other player uses the even digits: 2, 4, 6, 8.

2. The player with odd digits goes first. Players then take turns writing one of their digits in a square. Each digit can be used only once.

3. The winner is the player who can write a digit that gives a sum of 15 for any complete row, column, or diagonal.

4. If more than one game is played, players take turns using the odd and even digits.

Here are some finished games.

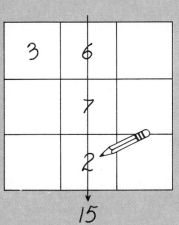

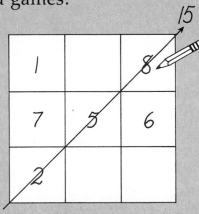

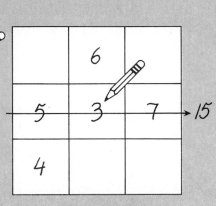

The even-digit player wins this game.

The even-digit player wins this game.

The odd-digit player wins this game.

Place Value

Getting started

What pieces would you use
to show the number 324?

flat
(hundred)

long
(ten)

unit
(one)

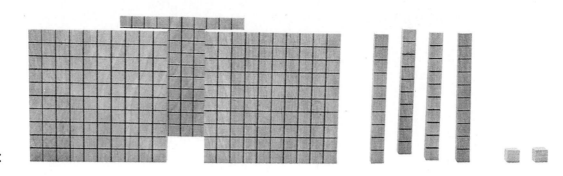

We see:

We think: 3 hundreds   4 tens   2 ones

We write: 342

We say: three hundred forty-two

Give the number.

1.

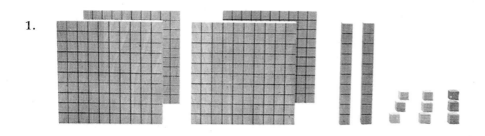

2.

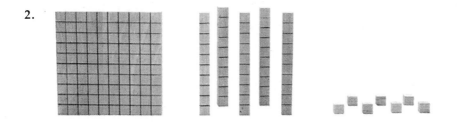

3.

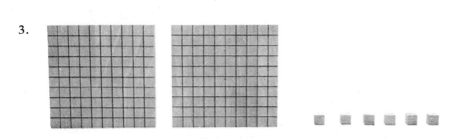

We see: 347

We think:

| How many hundreds? 3 | How many tens? 4 | How many ones? 7 |

Write the numeral for each ▕▊.

672

1. ▕▊ hundreds
2. ▕▊ tens
3. ▕▊ ones

563

4. ▕▊ ones
5. ▕▊ tens
6. ▕▊ hundreds

297

7. ▕▊ tens
8. ▕▊ ones
9. ▕▊ hundreds

480

10. ▕▊ hundreds
11. ▕▊ tens
12. ▕▊ ones

503

13. ▕▊ tens
14. ▕▊ ones
15. ▕▊ hundreds

78

16. ▕▊ ones
17. ▕▊ tens
18. ▕▊ hundreds

900

19. ▕▊ hundreds
20. ▕▊ tens
21. ▕▊ ones

164

22. ▕▊ hundred
23. ▕▊ tens
24. ▕▊ ones

986

25. ▕▊ hundreds
26. ▕▊ tens
27. ▕▊ ones

Write each numeral as in the examples.

Examples: 237 = 200 + 30 + 7   508 = 500 + 8   360 = 300 + 60

☆ 1. 627   ☆ 2. 348   ☆ 3. 794   ☆ 4. 836   ☆ 5. 98

☆ 6. 999   ☆ 7. 337   ☆ 8. 168   ☆ 9. 72   ☆ 10. 744

☆ 11. 608   ☆ 12. 703   ☆ 13. 509   ☆ 14. 860   ☆ 15. 230

☆ 16. 570   ☆ 17. 967   ☆ 18. 42   ☆ 19. 738   ☆ 20. 209

Write the numeral for each sum.

☆ 21. 300 + 40 + 2   ☆ 22. 600 + 70 + 5   ☆ 23. 900 + 30 + 7

☆ 24. 400 + 80 + 6   ☆ 25. 800 + 10 + 8   ☆ 26. 500 + 60 + 3

☆ 27. 400 + 50   ☆ 28. 700 + 60   ☆ 29. 800 + 20

☆ 30. 900 + 8   ☆ 31. 800 + 70 + 4   ☆ 32. 400 + 2

☆ 33. 200 + 90 + 1   ☆ 34. 500 + 80 + 6   ☆ 35. 50 + 8

☆ 36. 700 + 8   ☆ 37. 300 + 60 + 3   ☆ 38. 800 + 7

☆ 39. 600 + 60 + 6   ☆ 40. 40 + 9   ☆ 41. 900 + 80 + 2

Place 10 coins in a triangular shape.

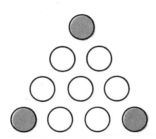

Then make it look like this

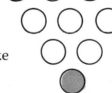

by moving **only** the coins at the corners.

Thousands, hundreds, tens, and ones

We see:

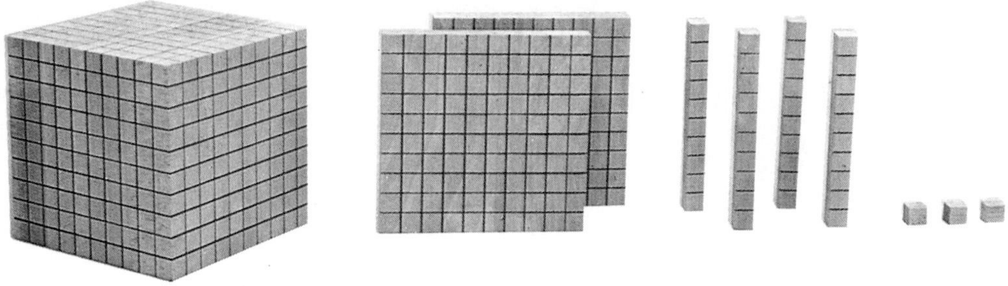

We write: 1243

We say: one thousand two hundred forty-three

Write the numeral.

1.

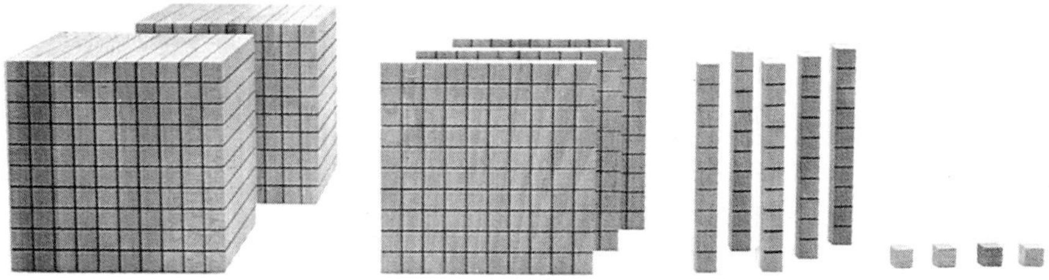

2.

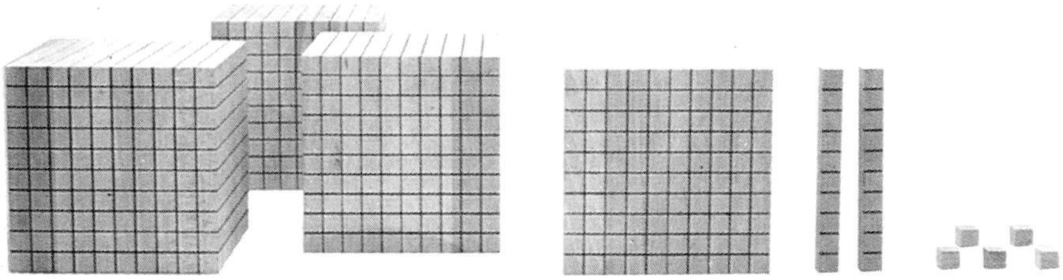

3.

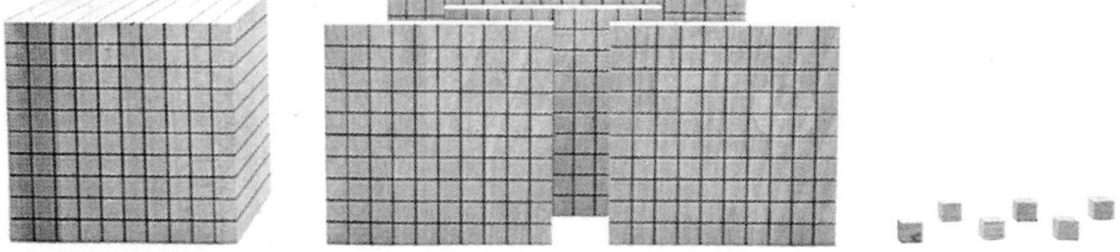

Write the numeral for each ▥.

Example:

4372
- 4 thousands
- 3 hundreds
- 7 tens
- 2 ones

2654
1. ▥ thousands
2. ▥ hundreds
3. ▥ tens
4. ▥ ones

8791
5. ▥ ones
6. ▥ tens
7. ▥ hundreds
8. ▥ thousands

6470
9. ▥ thousands
10. ▥ hundreds
11. ▥ tens
12. ▥ ones

7305
13. ▥ hundreds
14. ▥ thousands
15. ▥ ones
16. ▥ tens

9800
17. ▥ ones
18. ▥ tens
19. ▥ hundreds
20. ▥ thousands

Example:

19 856
- 19 thousands
- 8 hundreds
- 5 tens
- 6 ones

52 768
21. ▥ thousands
22. ▥ hundreds
23. ▥ tens
24. ▥ ones

60 294
25. ▥ thousands
26. ▥ hundreds
27. ▥ tens
28. ▥ ones

Write each numeral as in the example.

Example: 5327 = 5000 + 300 + 20 + 7

☆ 29. 2375   ☆ 30. 9676   ☆ 31. 5620

☆ 32. 5027   ☆ 33. 6708   ☆ 34. 4002

☆ 35. 3800   ☆ 36. 4763   ☆ 37. 9678

I'm a special number,
With 3 digits and no more.
Increase me by just one,
And the digit count is 4.

Who am I?

Reading and writing numerals

What is the score?

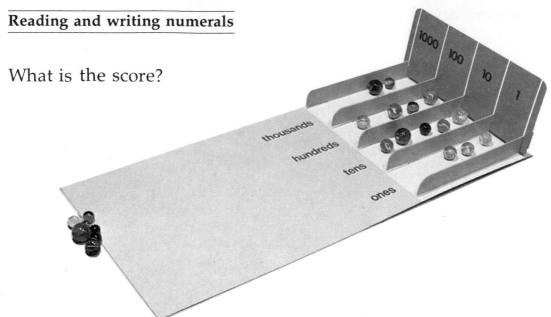

We write: 2453

We say: two thousand four hundred fifty-three

Read these numerals.

1. Mass of a car:
   1965
   kilograms

2. A year's pay:
   8650
   dollars

3. Number of children
   in a school:
   957
   children

4. Cost of a TV:
   325
   dollars

5. Length of the
   St. Lawrence Seaway:
   3777
   kilometers

6. Number of minutes
   in a day:
   1440
   minutes

7. How long a light
   bulb will last:
   1050
   hours

8. Mass of the
   Liberty Bell:
   943
   kilograms

9. Number of fans
   at a game:
   34 851
   people

Write the numerals.

Example:
Hawaii's highest volcano:
four thousand
two hundred five
meters

Answer: 4205

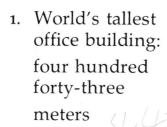

1. World's tallest
   office building:
   four hundred
   forty-three
   meters *443*

2. World's tallest
   tower:
   six hundred
   forty-six
   meters *646*

3. World's longest
   wall:
   two thousand
   four hundred ten
   kilometers
   2,410

4. World's longest
   river:
   six thousand
   seven hundred
   thirty-eight
   kilometers
   6,738

5. World's highest
   mountain:
   eight thousand
   eight hundred
   forty-eight
   meters
   8,848

6. World's deepest well:
   two thousand
   two hundred
   thirty-one
   meters
   2,231

I'm one more ten than 90.
10 tens in all, you see.
My first letter is an H,
My last one is a D.

Who am I? *Hundred*

Comparing numbers

Chicago to New York City:
1351 km
Chicago to Montreal: 1339 km

Which is farther?

Finding the answer

Look at the thousands' digits	Look at the hundreds' digits	Look at the tens' digits	Look at the ones' digits
1351	1351	1351	The tens are different. You need not look at the ones.
1339	1339	1339	
same	same	5 is greater	

We write: 1351 > 1339

It is farther to New York City.

Other examples

5392 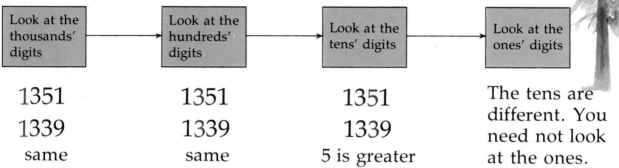 5389   2749 ● 2801   34 617 ● 35 578
5392 > 5389   2749 < 2801   34 617 < 35 578

Read: 5392 is greater than 5389.

Use > or < to compare the two numbers.

1. 256 ● 356   2. 437 ● 457   3. 5876 ● 4876

4. 946 ● 964   5. 3572 ● 3486   6. 7300 ● 7030

7. 8237 ● 8537   8. 6438 ● 6442   9. 6976 ● 6867

10. 9436 ● 9600   11. 3479 ● 3469   12. 8527 ● 8372

Give the greater number.

1. Tree heights:
   Douglas fir—7600 cm
   Redwood—8200 cm

2. Waterfall heights:
   Silver Strand—357 m
   Takakkow—380 m

3. Yearly pay:
   Zoo keeper—$8785
   Typist—$8595

4. Animal masses:
   Work horse—976 kg
   Race horse—475 kg

5. Travel:
   Los Angeles to Ottawa—4959 km
   Los Angeles to Boston—4910 km

6. Mountain heights:
   Mount McKinley—6194 m
   Mount Logan—6050 m

Practicing your skills

Add or subtract.

1. $\begin{array}{r} 9 \\ +8 \\ \hline \end{array}$
2. $\begin{array}{r} 8 \\ +9 \\ \hline \end{array}$
3. $\begin{array}{r} 17 \\ -8 \\ \hline \end{array}$
4. $\begin{array}{r} 17 \\ -9 \\ \hline \end{array}$
5. $\begin{array}{r} 6 \\ +7 \\ \hline \end{array}$
6. $\begin{array}{r} 7 \\ +6 \\ \hline \end{array}$

7. $\begin{array}{r} 13 \\ -7 \\ \hline \end{array}$
8. $\begin{array}{r} 13 \\ -6 \\ \hline \end{array}$
9. $\begin{array}{r} 8 \\ 3 \\ +4 \\ \hline \end{array}$
10. $\begin{array}{r} 9 \\ 4 \\ +2 \\ \hline \end{array}$
11. $\begin{array}{r} 8 \\ 2 \\ +7 \\ \hline \end{array}$
12. $\begin{array}{r} 5 \\ 4 \\ +6 \\ \hline \end{array}$

Write the numeral.

1.

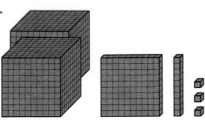

	592		5876
2. ▥ hundreds		5. ▥ thousands	
3. ▥ tens		6. ▥ hundreds	
4. ▥ ones		7. ▥ tens	
		8. ▥ ones	

Write > or < for each ▧ .

9. 680 ▧ 639   10. 3862 ▧ 3823   11. 2076 ▧ 2087

12. Write the numeral: four thousand nine hundred fifty-three

Answers for Self-check—page 21

Test

Write the numeral.

1.

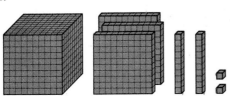

	687		7634
2. ▥ hundreds		5. ▥ thousands	
3. ▥ tens		6. ▥ hundreds	
4. ▥ ones		7. ▥ tens	
		8. ▥ ones	

Write > or < for each ▧ .

9. 839 ▧ 849   10. 7403 ▧ 7393   11. 891 ▧ 895

12. Write the numeral: six thousand two hundred seventy-eight

The Place Value Tally Game

Tape or write the following numerals on a small cube.

1000 on one face

100 on one face

10 on two faces

1 on two faces

Rules:

1. Each player tosses the cube 10 times.

2. Each player keeps count of the other's score.

3. The player with the highest score for the 10 tosses wins.

Adding

Give the total number
of hundreds, tens, and
ones for this chart.

When you can,
trade for a ten.

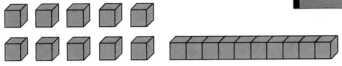

10 ones   for   1 ten

Hundreds	Tens	Ones
3	2	8
1	4	5

Total

Give the totals. Make trades when you can.

Example:

	Hundreds	Tens	Ones
		3	6
		5	9
Total		8	15
		9	5

Think: 15 ones
Trade 10 ones for a ten.
Have 5 ones left, 1 more ten.
Answer: 9 tens and 5 ones

1.

	Hundreds	Tens	Ones
		2	4
		6	8
Total		?	?

2.

	Hundreds	Tens	Ones
		2	3
		5	9
Total		?	?

3.

	Hundreds	Tens	Ones
	1	5	6
	3	2	7
Total	?	?	?

4.

	Hundreds	Tens	Ones
	5	9	1
	2	6	8
Total	?	?	?

Hint: Trade for a hundred.
Have 10 less tens, 1 more hundred.

Adding 2-digit numbers

Perry's family had a garage sale.
They sold 35 items in the morning
and 27 items in the afternoon.
How many items did they sell that day?

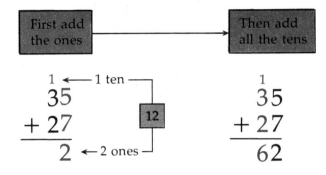

Finding the answer

First add the ones	→	Then add all the tens

$$
\begin{array}{r}
\overset{1}{3}5 \\
+\ 27 \\
\hline
2
\end{array}
$$

1 ← 1 ten
12
2 ones

$$
\begin{array}{r}
\overset{1}{3}5 \\
+\ 27 \\
\hline
62
\end{array}
$$

They sold 62 items.

Other examples

$$
\begin{array}{r}
\overset{1}{6}9 \\
+\ 36 \\
\hline
105
\end{array}
\qquad
\begin{array}{r}
\overset{1}{9}7 \\
+\ 58 \\
\hline
155
\end{array}
\qquad
\begin{array}{r}
80 \\
+\ 90 \\
\hline
170
\end{array}
\qquad
\begin{array}{r}
\overset{1}{5}9 \\
+\ \ 6 \\
\hline
65
\end{array}
\qquad
\begin{array}{r}
34 \\
+\ 25 \\
\hline
59
\end{array}
$$

Add.

1. $\begin{array}{r} 62 \\ +\ 53 \\ \hline \end{array}$
2. $\begin{array}{r} 54 \\ +\ 35 \\ \hline \end{array}$
3. $\begin{array}{r} 51 \\ +\ 76 \\ \hline \end{array}$
4. $\begin{array}{r} 80 \\ +\ 42 \\ \hline \end{array}$
5. $\begin{array}{r} 52 \\ +\ 28 \\ \hline \end{array}$
6. $\begin{array}{r} 39 \\ +\ 25 \\ \hline \end{array}$

7. $\begin{array}{r} 78 \\ +\ 50 \\ \hline \end{array}$
8. $\begin{array}{r} 38 \\ +\ 6 \\ \hline \end{array}$
9. $\begin{array}{r} 54 \\ +\ 9 \\ \hline \end{array}$
10. $\begin{array}{r} 49 \\ +\ 75 \\ \hline \end{array}$
11. $\begin{array}{r} 80 \\ +\ 60 \\ \hline \end{array}$
12. $\begin{array}{r} 69 \\ +\ 43 \\ \hline \end{array}$

13. $\begin{array}{r} 85 \\ +\ 37 \\ \hline \end{array}$
14. $\begin{array}{r} 26 \\ +\ 90 \\ \hline \end{array}$
15. $\begin{array}{r} 24 \\ +\ 18 \\ \hline \end{array}$
16. $\begin{array}{r} 79 \\ +\ 33 \\ \hline \end{array}$
17. $\begin{array}{r} 54 \\ +\ 22 \\ \hline \end{array}$
18. $\begin{array}{r} 48 \\ +\ 56 \\ \hline \end{array}$

Add.

Example:

```
   1
   3 5
   5 8
 + 4 6
 ─────
 1 3 9
```

1. 61	**2.** 74	**3.** 27	**4.** 37	**5.** 28
39	34	48	26	16
+ 27	+ 37	+ 86	+ 16	+ 37

6. 46	**7.** 57	**8.** 59	**9.** 37
38	63	48	95
+ 27	+ 45	+ 67	+ 48

10. 26	**11.** 82	**12.** 43	**13.** 74
54	67	94	59
+ 99	+ 79	+ 87	+ 62

14. 83	**15.** 36	**16.** 29
76	47	78
+ 48	+ 59	+ 67

LAMP SHADE 75¢

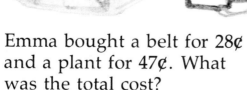

Book 29¢

FISH BOWL 38¢

BELT 28¢

PURSE 19¢

17. Emma bought a belt for 28¢ and a plant for 47¢. What was the total cost?

☆ **18.** What two items could you buy for a total cost of exactly 76¢?

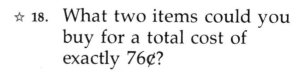

Guess which sum is larger.

Evens: $2 + 4 + 6 + 8 + 10 + 12 + 14 + 16 + 18 + 20 + 22 + 24 + 26 + 28 + 30 = n$
Odds: $1 + 3 + 5 + 7 + 9 + 11 + 13 + 15 + 17 + 19 + 21 + 23 + 25 + 27 + 29 = n$

Check your guess. Which is larger? How much larger?

More practice, page 351

Finding larger sums

Ray's class sold 564 tickets for the play on Friday. They sold 389 tickets for the play on Saturday.

How many tickets in all?

Finding the answer

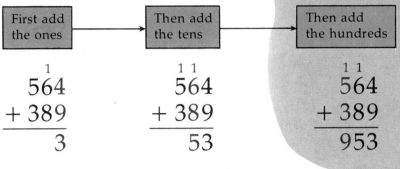

First add the ones	Then add the tens	Then add the hundreds
$\overset{1}{564}$	$\overset{1\ 1}{564}$	$\overset{1\ 1}{564}$
$+389$	$+389$	$+389$
$\overline{3}$	$\overline{53}$	$\overline{953}$

They sold 953 tickets in all.

Other examples

$$\overset{1\ 1}{378} \quad \overset{1}{407} \quad \overset{1}{987} \quad \overset{1\ 1\ 1}{4376}$$
$$+459 \quad +674 \quad +890 \quad +2789$$
$$\overline{837} \quad \overline{1081} \quad \overline{1877} \quad \overline{7165}$$

Add.

1. 314
    + 488

2. 368
    + 529

3. 234
    + 557

4. 486
    + 293

5. 273
    + 654

6. 932
    + 365

7. 842
    + 451

8. 608
    + 591

9. 723
    + 672

10. 545
    + 823

11. 457
    + 783

12. 594
    + 468

13. 675
    + 967

14. 798
    + 264

15. 376
    + 846

Find the sums.

1.	67 + 384	2.	648 + 57	3.	209 + 902	4.	765 + 896
5.	362 + 47	6.	952 + 8	7.	409 + 104	8.	792 + 64
9.	836 + 90	10.	3526 + 2349	11.	4367 + 3571	12.	1843 + 6752
13.	5874 + 953	14.	1789 + 5457	15.	2846 + 6478	16.	3627 + 96
17.	243 42 + 176	18.	956 874 + 65	19.	789 526 + 214	20.	444 35 + 6323

21. Sold 349 tickets to the first basketball game. Sold 267 tickets to the second game. How many tickets in all?

☆ 22. Find how many people went to each of two plays or other events at your school. Find the total number of people for both.

Copy and complete these Magic Wheels.
The three numbers in each line of a wheel should give the same sum. In the example, the sum is 9.

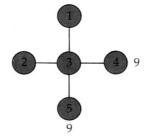

Example

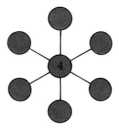

Use the numbers 1 through 7.

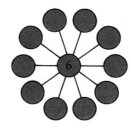

Use the numbers 1 through 11.

More practice, page 352

Writing addition problems

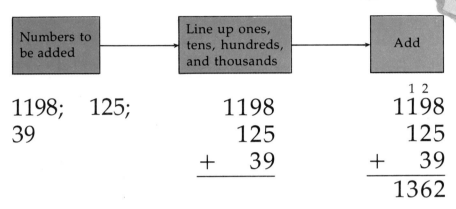

Ann picked three things she wished she could buy from newspaper ads.

How much for all three?

Finding the answer

Numbers to be added	→	Line up ones, tens, hundreds, and thousands	→	Add

1198;   125;   39

```
  1198
   125
+   39
```

```
 1 2
  1198
   125
+   39
  1362
```

Ann's items cost $1362.

Other examples

358;   9;   64

```
 1 2
  358
    9
+  64
  431
```

860;   1047;   18

```
  1 1
   860
  1047
+   18
  1925
```

Add each group of numbers.

1. 9;   67;   234

2. 12;   146;   987

3. 30;   157;   1096

4. 235;   19;   6

5. 42;   9;   357

6. 596;   302;   8

7. 1596;   12;   7

8. 56;   1372;   478

9. 9;   17;   2096

10. 78;   226;   1890

11. 7;   409;   18

12. 1347;   30;   609

Find each sum.

1. $65 + 942 + 8 = n$
2. $9 + 471 + 24 = n$
3. $563 + 407 + 29 = n$
4. $18 + 7 + 109 = n$
5. $968 + 1264 + 27 = n$
6. $5836 + 274 + 86 = n$
7. $98 + 89 + 7642 = n$
8. $3080 + 967 + 15 = n$
9. $2047 + 3896 + 77 = n$
10. $9 + 78 + 167 + 4296 = n$

11. How much for all three?
    Houseboat—$8698
    Color TV—$465
    Clock radio—$36

☆ 12. Look at some ads. Choose 3 things you would like to buy.
    How much for all three?

The sum of the numbers in each row, column, and diagonal of this Magic Square is 34. The sum of the numbers in the shaded part is also 34!
How many other groups of 4 numbers can you find that have a sum of 34?

16	2	3	13
5	11	10	8
9	7	6	12
4	14	15	1

Answers for Self-check   1. 65   2. 96   3. 134   4. 784   5. 673   6. 1387   7. 720   8. 1524   9. 9041   10. 7662   11. 22   12. 117   13. 1089   14. 7567   15. 4388   16. 5357   17. 1445   18. 6030

Self-check

Find the sums.

1. 56 + 9	**2.** 69 + 27	**3.** 85 + 49	**4.** 536 + 248	**5.** 374 + 299

6. 835 + 552	**7.** 457 + 263	**8.** 576 + 948	**9.** 5432 + 3609	**10.** 4768 + 2894

11. 8 9 + 5	**12.** 24 56 + 37	**13.** 462 379 + 248	**14.** 1234 2747 + 3586	**15.** 38 456 + 3894

16. 28 + 376 + 4953   **17.** 1024 + 367 + 54   **18.** 387 + 29 + 5614

Answers for Self-check—page 31

Test

Find the sums.

1. 86 + 9	**2.** 94 + 37	**3.** 639 + 77	**4.** 974 + 469	**5.** 594 + 278

6. 538 + 722	**7.** 459 + 367	**8.** 674 + 839	**9.** 4507 + 2743	**10.** 2795 + 5687

11. 9 6 + 7	**12.** 38 76 + 85	**13.** 587 342 + 679	**14.** 5379 1865 + 2348	**15.** 4658 377 + 29

16. 426 + 48 + 3579   **17.** 4128 + 45 + 302   **18.** 29 + 875 + 2341

Sum Riddle!

Why did the mother horse drink lots of orange juice and stay in bed all day?

To find out why,

1. First find the sums, then look for your answers in the message-maker box below.

2. Each time you see the answer to a problem, write the letter of that problem.

Problems

A.	397 + 468	B.	965 + 394	C.	802 + 999	D.	156 + 944
E.	687 + 39	H.	344 + 666	I.	497 + 3068	L.	5964 + 3872
O.	4379 + 2801	S.	3724 + 568	T.	8345 + 655	U.	3762 + 5689

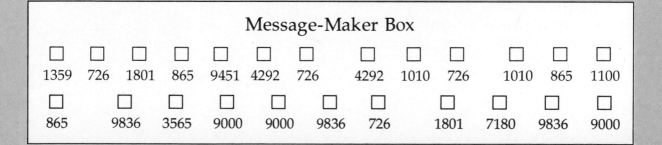

Message-Maker Box

☐	☐	☐	☐	☐	☐	☐	☐	☐	☐	☐	☐	☐
1359	726	1801	865	9451	4292	726	4292	1010	726	1010	865	1100

☐	☐	☐	☐	☐	☐	☐	☐	☐	☐	☐
865	9836	3565	9000	9000	9836	726	1801	7180	9836	9000

Subtracting

Getting started

Give the number
of pieces left.

When you need to,
you can trade a ten.

	Hundreds	Tens	Ones
Start with	4	6	3
Take away	1	2	6
Pieces Left			

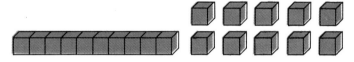

1 ten   for   10 ones

Give the number of pieces left.

Example:

	Hundreds	Tens	Ones
Start with 62		5 ~~6~~	12 ~~2~~
Take away 38		3	8
Pieces Left		2	4

{ Need more ones.
Trade a ten.
Have 1 less ten,
10 more ones.

Answer: 2 tens and 4 ones

1.

	Hundreds	Tens	Ones
Start with		7	4
Take away		4	6
Pieces Left		?	?

2.

	Hundreds	Tens	Ones
Start with		6	1
Take away		3	5
Pieces Left		?	?

3.

	Hundreds	Tens	Ones
Start with	5	8	5
Take away	2	3	7
Pieces Left	?	?	?

4.

	Hundreds	Tens	Ones
Start with	7	3	8
Take away	2	7	3
Pieces Left	?	?	?

Subtracting 2-digit numbers

Erica's usual pulse: 74 beats in 1 minute

Her pulse after running in place
for 10 seconds: 92 beats in 1 minute

What is the difference?

Finding the answer

You need more ones	→	Trade a ten	→	Subtract the ones	→	Subtract the tens

$$
\begin{array}{r} 92 \\ -74 \\ \hline ? \end{array}
\qquad
\begin{array}{r} {}^{8\ 12}\!\!\not{92} \\ -74 \\ \hline \end{array}
\qquad
\begin{array}{r} {}^{8\ 12}\!\!\not{92} \\ -74 \\ \hline 8 \end{array}
\qquad
\begin{array}{r} {}^{8\ 12}\!\!\not{92} \\ -74 \\ \hline 18 \end{array}
$$

The difference is 18 beats per minute.

Other examples

$$
\begin{array}{r} {}^{7\ 10}\!\!\not{80} \\ -36 \\ \hline 44 \end{array}
\qquad
\begin{array}{r} {}^{4\ 12}\!\!\not{52} \\ -45 \\ \hline 7 \end{array}
\qquad
\begin{array}{r} {}^{7\ 15}\!\!185 \\ -\ 49 \\ \hline 136 \end{array}
\qquad
\begin{array}{r} {}^{1\ 16}\!\!126 \\ -\ 58 \\ \hline 68 \end{array}
$$

Subtract.

1. $\begin{array}{r}32\\-14\\\hline\end{array}$	2. $\begin{array}{r}56\\-29\\\hline\end{array}$	3. $\begin{array}{r}40\\-25\\\hline\end{array}$	4. $\begin{array}{r}64\\-37\\\hline\end{array}$	5. $\begin{array}{r}72\\-38\\\hline\end{array}$	6. $\begin{array}{r}85\\-59\\\hline\end{array}$
7. $\begin{array}{r}76\\-68\\\hline\end{array}$	8. $\begin{array}{r}98\\-29\\\hline\end{array}$	9. $\begin{array}{r}65\\-38\\\hline\end{array}$	10. $\begin{array}{r}92\\-54\\\hline\end{array}$	11. $\begin{array}{r}77\\-58\\\hline\end{array}$	12. $\begin{array}{r}80\\-49\\\hline\end{array}$

Find the differences.

1.　52
　 − 18

2.　76
　 − 27

3.　83
　 − 54

4.　67
　 − 39

5.　71
　 − 46

6.　257
　 − 39

7.　174
　 − 58

8.　260
　 − 49

9.　483
　 − 69

10.　621
　 − 22

11.　192
　 − 49

12.　375
　 − 29

13.　452
　 − 47

14.　974
　 − 35

15.　883
　 − 64

16.　158
　 − 79

17.　147
　 − 84

18.　126
　 − 77

19.　170
　 − 96

20.　225
　 − 48

21.　317
　 − 58

22.　265
　 − 79

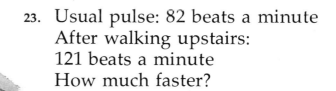

23. Usual pulse: 82 beats a minute
After walking upstairs:
121 beats a minute
How much faster?

☆ 24. Check your pulse.
Then check the pulse of
someone at least ten years
older than you.
How much difference?

Try to find the pattern and
give the next four numbers.

1, 0, 2, 0, 3, 0, . . .
12, 23, 34, 45, . . .
3, 1, 1, 6, 1, 1, 9, 1, 1, . . .

Think !

More practice, page 352A and page 353

Subtracting larger numbers

Height of Guy's sister: 160 cm
Height of the world's tallest woman: 231 cm
How much shorter is Guy's sister?

Finding the answer

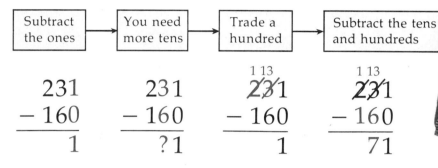

Subtract the ones	You need more tens	Trade a hundred	Subtract the tens and hundreds
$\begin{array}{r} 231 \\ -160 \\ \hline 1 \end{array}$	$\begin{array}{r} 231 \\ -160 \\ \hline ?1 \end{array}$	$\begin{array}{r} {}^{1\,13}2\cancel{3}1 \\ -160 \\ \hline 1 \end{array}$	$\begin{array}{r} {}^{1\,13}2\cancel{3}1 \\ -160 \\ \hline 71 \end{array}$

Guy's sister is 71 cm shorter.

Other examples

$\begin{array}{r} {}^{5\,12}8\cancel{6}\cancel{2} \\ -435 \\ \hline 427 \end{array}$
$\qquad$
$\begin{array}{r} {}^{5\,12}\cancel{6}\cancel{2}8 \\ -573 \\ \hline 55 \end{array}$
$\qquad$
$\begin{array}{r} {}^{8\,14\,13}\cancel{9}\cancel{5}\cancel{3} \\ -278 \\ \hline 675 \end{array}$

Subtract.

1. $\begin{array}{r} 981 \\ -\ 52 \\ \hline \end{array}$
2. $\begin{array}{r} 454 \\ -135 \\ \hline \end{array}$
3. $\begin{array}{r} 692 \\ -367 \\ \hline \end{array}$
4. $\begin{array}{r} 581 \\ -293 \\ \hline \end{array}$
5. $\begin{array}{r} 885 \\ -546 \\ \hline \end{array}$

6. $\begin{array}{r} 745 \\ -263 \\ \hline \end{array}$
7. $\begin{array}{r} 526 \\ -431 \\ \hline \end{array}$
8. $\begin{array}{r} 814 \\ -355 \\ \hline \end{array}$
9. $\begin{array}{r} 968 \\ -699 \\ \hline \end{array}$
10. $\begin{array}{r} 456 \\ -\ 87 \\ \hline \end{array}$

Subtract.

1. 562
    − 325

2. 847
    − 373

3. 834
    − 463

4. 754
    − 267

5. 820
    − 312

6. 438
    − 59

7. 465
    − 208

8. 714
    − 257

9. 976
    − 397

10. 421
    − 275

11. 615
    − 328

12. 547
    − 259

13. 326
    − 147

14. 818
    − 639

15. 772
    − 586

Example:

```
    4 13
  5̶3̶8 9
− 1 6 5 2
  3 7 3 7
```

16. 5379
    − 2835

17. 7456
    − 3724

18. 6275
    − 3761

19. 4172
    − 1536

20. 7258
    − 3429

21. 8149
    − 5372

22. 9258
    − 2784

23. 6723
    − 2586

24. 7146
    − 3498

25. 5164
    − 3247

26. 4876
    − 1975

27. 8355
    − 5366

28. 6529
    − 4538

29. 9427
    − 6648

30. Joe's height: 148 cm
    World's tallest man: 272 cm
    How much shorter is Joe?

☆ 31. Measure your height in
    centimeters.
    How much taller than you
    is the world's tallest man?
    the world's tallest woman?

Start with seven thousand.
Add four hundred three.
Then subtract eleven.
This will give you me.

Who am I?

More practice, page 353A

Subtraction—zeros in the middle

There are 508 marbles in
the jar. Rosa guessed 339.
By how many did she miss?

Finding the answer

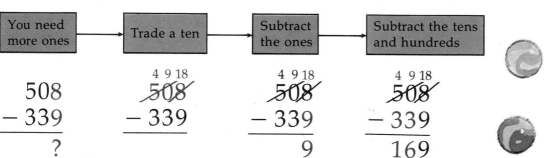

You need more ones	Trade a ten	Subtract the ones	Subtract the tens and hundreds

$$
\begin{array}{r} 508 \\ -\ 339 \\ \hline ? \end{array}
\qquad
\begin{array}{r} {}^{4\ 9\ 18}\\ \cancel{508} \\ -\ 339 \\ \hline \end{array}
\qquad
\begin{array}{r} {}^{4\ 9\ 18}\\ \cancel{508} \\ -\ 339 \\ \hline 9 \end{array}
\qquad
\begin{array}{r} {}^{4\ 9\ 18}\\ \cancel{508} \\ -\ 339 \\ \hline 169 \end{array}
$$

Rosa missed by 169.

Other examples

$$
\begin{array}{r} {}^{5\ 9\,12}\\ 8\cancel{602} \\ -\ 5168 \\ \hline 3434 \end{array}
\qquad
\begin{array}{r} {}^{8\ 9\,13}\\ \cancel{903} \\ -\ \ 78 \\ \hline 825 \end{array}
$$

Subtract.

1.	$\begin{array}{r}705\\-256\end{array}$	2.	$\begin{array}{r}306\\-148\end{array}$	3.	$\begin{array}{r}502\\-217\end{array}$	4.	$\begin{array}{r}607\\-438\end{array}$	5.	$\begin{array}{r}903\\-657\end{array}$
6.	$\begin{array}{r}506\\-358\end{array}$	7.	$\begin{array}{r}403\\-156\end{array}$	8.	$\begin{array}{r}204\\-126\end{array}$	9.	$\begin{array}{r}5602\\-3138\end{array}$	10.	$\begin{array}{r}3406\\-1298\end{array}$

Subtract.

1. 5704
    − 2365

2. 8602
    − 5157

3. 9504
    − 7368

4. 4302
    − 1189

5. 6508
    − 399

Example:

    7 9 14
    8̸0̸4̸7
    − 2583
    5464

6. 7036
    − 4392

7. 6058
    − 2175

8. 5039
    − 2467

9. 4081
    − 3594

Example:

    7 9 9 13
    8̸0̸0̸3̸
    − 4378
    3625

10. 6003
    − 2346

11. 8002
    − 5686

12. 7005
    − 3268

13. 9004
    − 4976

14. 5001
    − 2351

15. 8704
    − 2496

16. 5039
    − 1954

17. 9806
    − 3743

18. 3006
    − 2798

19. 8703
    − 2946

20. 6027
    − 2542

21. 5904
    − 3917

22. 3605
    − 2718

23. 7006
    − 5429

24. The vase holds 703 beans. Jill guessed 485. Missed by how many?

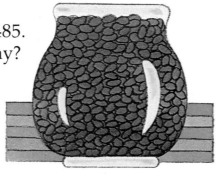

☆ 25. Fill a jar with things you choose. Have your classmates guess how many. Make a chart to show how close their guesses were.

Discover the pattern. Then find the next four numbers.

367, 734, 1101, 1468, . . .

More practice, page 353B

Subtraction—more zeros

On opening day 8700 people went to the fair. The next day 7375 people went. How many more people went on opening day?

Finding the answer

You need more ones	→	Trade a ten	→	Subtract

$$\begin{array}{r} 8700 \\ -7375 \\ \hline ? \end{array} \qquad \begin{array}{r} {}^{6\;9\;10} \\ 8\cancel{700} \\ -7375 \\ \hline \end{array} \qquad \begin{array}{r} {}^{6\;9\;10} \\ 8\cancel{700} \\ -7375 \\ \hline 1325 \end{array}$$

1325 more people went on opening day.

Other examples

$$\begin{array}{r} {}^{11} \\ {}^{6\;\cancel{7}\;9\;10} \\ \cancel{7200} \\ -4649 \\ \hline 2551 \end{array} \qquad \begin{array}{r} {}^{7\;9\;10} \\ \cancel{8009} \\ -3526 \\ \hline 4483 \end{array}$$

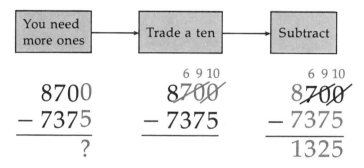

Subtract.

1. $\begin{array}{r}4600\\-1265\end{array}$	2. $\begin{array}{r}5900\\-3627\end{array}$	3. $\begin{array}{r}6700\\-4296\end{array}$	4. $\begin{array}{r}8500\\-5872\end{array}$	5. $\begin{array}{r}9500\\-3641\end{array}$
6. $\begin{array}{r}3200\\-2367\end{array}$	7. $\begin{array}{r}4005\\-1627\end{array}$	8. $\begin{array}{r}8000\\-2946\end{array}$	9. $\begin{array}{r}6002\\-3640\end{array}$	10. $\begin{array}{r}9003\\-5796\end{array}$

Subtract.

1.	83 − 56	2.	843 − 465	3.	501 − 403	4.	626 − 428
5.	704 − 238	6.	873 − 329	7.	700 − 96	8.	603 − 295
9.	5075 − 3489	10.	8302 − 6574	11.	3119 − 2758	12.	9006 − 7349
13.	4604 − 2735	14.	7056 − 4258	15.	6830 − 3745	16.	8529 − 7539

17. 4-H Club show:
Prize hog—221 kg
Prize bull—1200 kg
How much heavier
was the bull?

18. Rides:
Ferris wheel—1310 cm high
Giant slide—615 cm high
How much higher was the
ferris wheel?

Which of these figures can
you draw without lifting
your pencil from the paper
and without tracing back
over any lines?

(Two can be done. One cannot.)

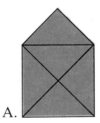

A.

B.   C.

Answers for Self-check   1. 33   2. 47   3. 143   4. 524   5. 806   6. 331   7. 473   8. 594   9. 331
10. 266   11. 537   12. 6626   13. 4425   14. 6226   15. 4775   16. 122   17. 1679   18. 1012

More practice, page 354 and page 354A

Self-check

Subtract.

1. 57
    − 24

2. 83
    − 36

3. 175
    − 32

4. 580
    − 56

5. 865
    − 59

6. 458
    − 127

7. 827
    − 354

8. 942
    − 348

9. 601
    − 270

10. 623
    − 357

11. 804
    − 267

12. 8172
    − 1546

13. 7302
    − 2877

14. 6723
    − 497

15. 9200
    − 4425

16. 420 − 298

17. 7006 − 5327

18. 2705 − 1693

Answers for Self-check—page 43

Test

Find the differences.

1. 93
    − 56

2. 82
    − 65

3. 763
    − 38

4. 920
    − 65

5. 914
    − 76

6. 395
    − 183

7. 617
    − 466

8. 837
    − 538

9. 707
    − 690

10. 514
    − 329

11. 830
    − 259

12. 9032
    − 4658

13. 8264
    − 685

14. 7005
    − 3528

15. 6100
    − 4327

16. 402 − 265

17. 8076 − 7217

18. 3900 − 1890

Magic Squares

Is this a Magic Square?
It is if the sums A through H are all the same!
Check and see.

Copy the squares and fill in the missing numbers to make each of these a Magic Square. Give the Magic Sum for each.

1.

5	8	▥
6	6	6
▥	4	7

2.

6	▥	6
▥	7	7
8	▥	8

3.

4	8	9
▥	7	▥
▥	▥	▥

Using Your Skills

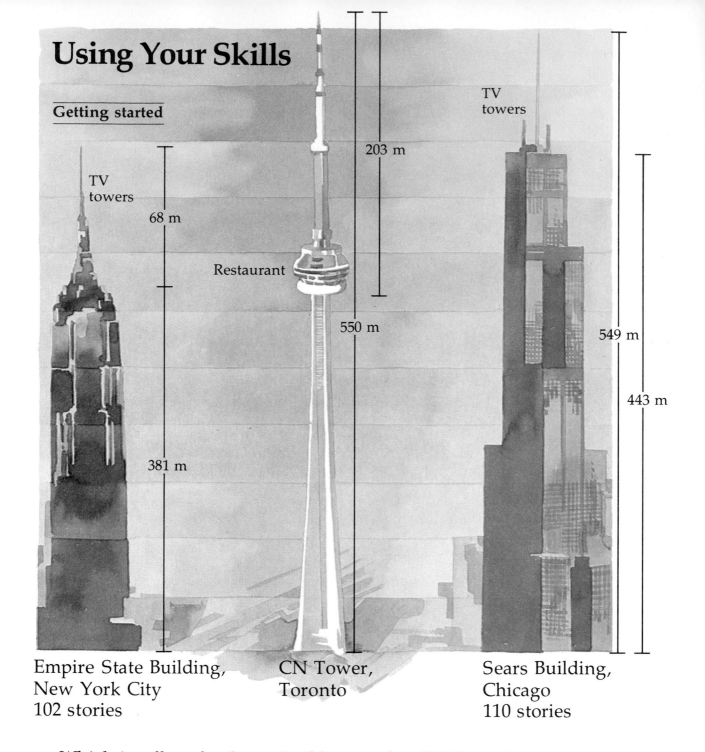

TV towers

68 m

TV towers

203 m

Restaurant

550 m

549 m

443 m

381 m

Empire State Building,
New York City
102 stories

CN Tower,
Toronto

Sears Building,
Chicago
110 stories

1. Which is taller, the Sears Building or the CN Tower?

2. How many more stories has the Sears Building than the Empire State Building?

3. What other problems about these buildings can you make up and solve?

The John Hancock Center in Chicago
is 337 m tall. If a 99-m TV tower
is put on top, how tall will the
building be with the tower?

Solving the problem

1. Read carefully to find
   the facts.

   Building: 337 m
   Tower: 99 m

2. Look for the question.

   How tall
   altogether?

3. Decide what to do.

   337 and 99 more
   Add.

4. Find the answer.

   $$\begin{array}{r} \overset{1\ 1}{3\,3\,7} \\ +\ \ 99 \\ \hline 436 \end{array}$$

5. Read again. Does your
   answer make sense?

   436 m seems
   about right.

Try this one.

The World Trade Center
in New York City is 411 m tall.
The RCA Building is 259 m tall.
How much taller is the
World Trade Center?

School time

1. Hours awake:
   Before school—2 hours
   In school—8 hours
   After school—5 hours
   How many hours?

2. Years in school:
   Elementary school—6 years
   Junior High School—3 years
   High School—3 years
   College—4 years
   How many years?

3. Spelling lesson: 23 minutes
   Math lesson: 38 minutes
   Reading lesson: 45 minutes
   How many minutes?

4. Days in a year: 365
   Days in school: 179
   How many days not in school?

5. School days before
   New Year's: 79
   School days after
   New Year's: 104
   How many school days?

6. Weeks in a year: 52
   Weeks in school: 36
   How many weeks not
   in school?

7. Vacation time:
   November—3 days
   December—14 days
   April—7 days
   How many days?

8. Hours in a month: 744
   Hours in school: 156
   How many hours not
   in school?

9. Have 40 minutes for lunch.
   Take 25 minutes to eat.
   How much time left over?

10. Math test: 23 minutes
    Spelling test: 14 minutes
    How many more minutes
    for math?

11. Took 22 minutes to walk
    to school.
    Took 16 minutes
    to walk home.
    How much longer to walk
    to school?

12. Reading:
    First story—25 minutes
    Second story—38 minutes
    Third story—44 minutes
    How long for all three?

Speeds

1. How much faster is the antelope than the deer?

4. Which animal is fastest? How much faster than the giraffe is the fastest animal?

2. Which animal is slowest? How much faster than the slowest animal is the gazelle?

5. How much faster is the kangaroo than the jackrabbit?

3. How much faster is the cheetah than the gazelle?

6. How much faster is the red fox than the rhinoceros?

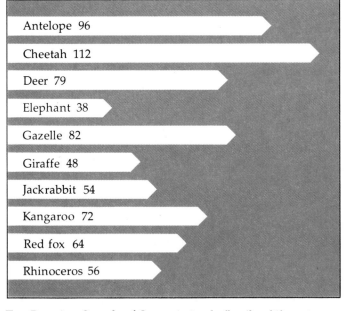

Animal	Speed
Antelope	96
Cheetah	112
Deer	79
Elephant	38
Gazelle	82
Giraffe	48
Jackrabbit	54
Kangaroo	72
Red fox	64
Rhinoceros	56

Top Running Speeds of Some Animals (km/h—kilometers per hour)

7. Which bird flies fastest? How much faster is the fastest bird than the fastest animal?

8. How much faster is the golden eagle than the homing pigeon?

10. An ostrich can run 72 km/h. How much faster is this than the flying speed of the pelican?

11. How much faster is the vulture than the great horned owl?

9. How much faster than the wild turkey is the canvasback?

☆ 12. Which bird's flying speed is 114 km/h faster than the slowest animal's running speed?

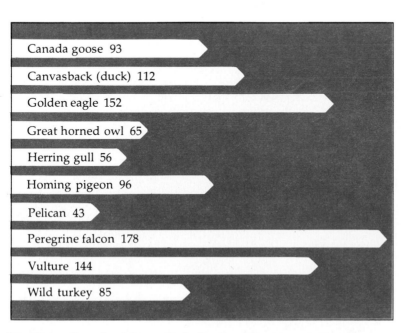

Canada goose 93

Canvasback (duck) 112

Golden eagle 152

Great horned owl 65

Herring gull 56

Homing pigeon 96

Pelican 43

Peregrine falcon 178

Vulture 144

Wild turkey 85

Top Flying Speeds of Some Birds (km/h—kilometers per hour)

Rounding numbers

Walt Disney World, in Florida, opened in 1971.
There are many exciting things to see and do.
In one of the parades, 43 people
march in funny animal costumes.
How many is that to the nearest ten?

Finding the answer

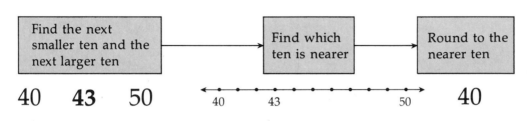

40   **43**   50

40   43   50

40

That is 40 people to the nearest ten.

Other examples

160   **168**   170

160   168   170

Answer: 170

70   **75**   80

70   75   80

When a number is halfway
between, round up.

Answer: 80

Choose the nearest ten.

1. 50 **53** 60   2. 60 **69** 70   3. 40 **45** 50

4. 80 **84** 90   5. 120 **125** 130   6. 150 **156** 160

Round to the nearest ten.

7. 42   8. 53   9. 64   10. 26   11. 37   12. 48

13. 96   14. 18   15. 159   16. 241   17. 85   18. 365

Choose the nearest hundred.

Examples:

300 **324** 400

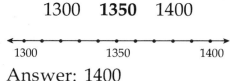
300   324   400

Answer: 300

1300 **1350** 1400

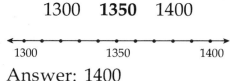
1300   1350   1400

Answer: 1400

1. 400 **415** 500   2. 700 **792** 800

3. 400 **450** 500   4. 200 **286** 300

5. 2100 **2198** 2200 6. 1200 **1224** 1300

Round to the nearest hundred.

7. 218   8. 479   9. 536   10. 875

11. 340   12. 782   13. 128   14. 250

15. 6460   16. 1855   17. 5234   18. 6394

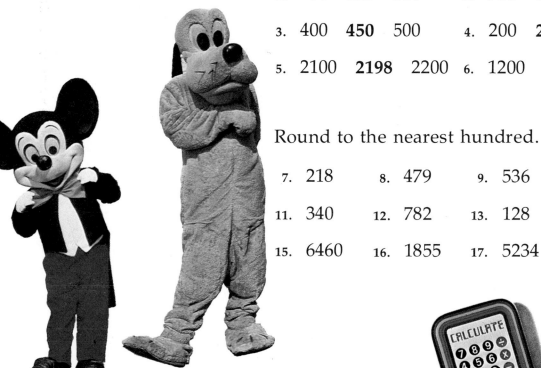

© Walt Disney Productions

19. 685 people went through Gate 3 in the first hour. How many to the nearest ten?

20. 448 people went through in the next hour. How many to the nearest hundred?

Estimate this sum. (Make the best guess you can. You may want to round the numbers.)

```
   498
   506
   587   Check your estimate.
   412
 + 475
```

How much greater or less than the actual sum was your estimate?

Animal	Mass
Wolf	74 kg*
Cheetah	53 kg
Emperor penguin	47 kg
Baby giraffe	38 kg

Smaller Animals

*kilograms

Animal	Mass
Buffalo	795 kg
Moose	666 kg
Bear	378 kg
Tiger	202 kg
Lion	164 kg
Deer	122 kg

Medium-size Animals

Round to the nearest ten and find the answers.

Example:

About how much heavier is the wolf than the baby giraffe?

Solution:

$$\begin{array}{r} 70 \\ -\ 40 \\ \hline 30 \end{array}$$

About 30 kg heavier

1. About how much heavier is the wolf than the emperor penguin?

2. Estimate the mass of the baby giraffe after it has gained 38 kg.

3. About how much is the total mass of the three lightest animals?

4. About how much heavier is the buffalo than the moose?

5. About how much heavier is the tiger than the lion?

6. About how much is the total mass of the lion, the bear, and the moose?

7. Estimate the total mass of the four lightest animals.

Animal	Mass
Elephant	4052 kg
Hippopotamus	3527 kg
Rhinoceros	2268 kg
Newborn blue whale	1865 kg

Larger Animals

Round to the nearest hundred and find the answers.

Example:

About how much heavier is
the buffalo than the bear?

Solution:

```
  800
- 400
-----
  400
```

About 400 kg heavier

8. Estimate the mass of
the buffalo, bear, and
moose together.

9. About how much heavier
is the hippopotamus
than the bear?

10. About how much heavier is
the elephant than the
hippopotamus?

11. Estimate the total mass
of the three heaviest animals.

12. About how much heavier is
the elephant than the
rhinoceros?

13. About how much heavier is
the newborn blue whale than
the buffalo?

☆ 14. About how much greater is the
mass of the elephant and the
rhinoceros together than the
mass of the hippopotamus?

More practice, page 355, Set A

Money sums and differences

Jeff bought this flashlight and battery.

Did he make out the check for the correct amount?

$5.98
(including tax)

$1.75
(including tax)

Finding the answer

Add or subtract as with whole numbers	→	Write as dollars and cents

$$\begin{array}{r} {}^{1}\ {}^{1}\\ \$\ 5.98 \\ +\ 1.75 \\ \hline 7\ 73 \end{array}$$

$$\begin{array}{r} \$\ 5.98 \\ +\ 1.75 \\ \hline \$\ 7.73 \end{array}$$

MIDTOWN BANK
142
March 31 1976
Pay to the order of Top Hardware Store $7.73
Seven and 73/100 _____ Dollars
For Camping supplies
1420233 155918
Jeff Camper

The check is made out for the correct amount.

Other examples

$$\begin{array}{r} {}^{1}\ {}^{1}\\ \$\ \ 3.69 \\ +\ 24.74 \\ \hline \$\ 28.43 \end{array}$$

$$\begin{array}{r} {}^{8}\ {}^{15}\\ \$\ 9.\cancel{95} \\ -\ 2.58 \\ \hline \$\ 7.37 \end{array}$$

$$\begin{array}{r} {}^{4}\ {}^{9}\ {}^{10}\\ \$\ \cancel{5.00} \\ -\ 1.79 \\ \hline \$\ 3.21 \end{array}$$

Find the total amounts.

1. $\begin{array}{r} \$\ 3.49 \\ +\ 2.50 \\ \hline \end{array}$

2. $\begin{array}{r} \$\ 6.45 \\ +\ 8.27 \\ \hline \end{array}$

3. $\begin{array}{r} \$\ 4.35 \\ +\ 0.79 \\ \hline \end{array}$

4. $\begin{array}{r} \$\ 15.95 \\ +\ \ 3.49 \\ \hline \end{array}$

5. $\begin{array}{r} \$\ 0.89 \\ +\ 0.98 \\ \hline \end{array}$

6. $\begin{array}{r} \$\ 24.95 \\ +\ \ 8.75 \\ \hline \end{array}$

7. $\begin{array}{r} \$\ \ 1.56 \\ 12.98 \\ +\ \ 0.89 \\ \hline \end{array}$

8. $\begin{array}{r} \$\ 9.75 \\ 1.47 \\ +\ 0.98 \\ \hline \end{array}$

Find the differences in the amounts.

1. $ 3.98
   − 2.25

2. $ 4.75
   − 3.49

3. $ 5.00
   − 2.95

4. $ 8.75
   − 8.49

5. $ 12.98
   − 9.69

6. $ 10.00
   − 6.50

7. $ 10.00
   − 6.98

8. $ 5.00
   − 3.75

9. $ 20.00
   − 15.49

10. $ 9.75
    − 8.98

Solve.

11. How much for both?

$2.75 $1.98

12. How much for both?

$9.95 $12.98

13. How much more for the 18-piece set?

$17.49 $15.98

14. Could you buy both with $25? If so, how much change should you get back?

$6.49 $18.35

☆ 15. Suppose you have $20 to spend. Choose 3 things you would like to buy from a newspaper ad. Give the total cost.

☆ 16. Choose 2 things to buy. Use a piece of paper and "print a check." Make out the check for the total amount and sign it.

Answers for Self-check   1. 253 km   2. $7.44   3. 60   4. 40   5. 170   6. 900   7. 400   8. 1300
9. About 20 kg   10. About 2500

More practice, page 355, Set B

Self-check

Solve the problems.

1. New York to Boston: 347 km
   New York to Montreal: 600 km
   How much further to Montreal?

2. Flashlight: $4.95
   Camping book: $2.49
   How much for both?

Round to the nearest ten.

3. 58   4. 35   5. 167

Round to the nearest hundred.

6. 876   7. 442   8. 1296

☆ 9. Round to the nearest ten and find the answer.

Wolf's mass: 71 kg
Cheetah's mass: 53 kg
About how much heavier is the wolf?

☆ 10. Round to the nearest hundred and find the answer.

Fans at Friday's game: 1178
Fans at Saturday's game: 1335
About how many fans altogether?

Answers for Self-check—page 57

Test

Solve the problems.

1. Park to library: 506 m
   Library to bakery: 236 m
   How many meters?

2. Jean bought a book for $3.69.
   Jack bought one for $5.73.
   How much more did Jack pay?

Round to the nearest ten.

3. 67   4. 23   5. 125

Round to the nearest hundred.

6. 789   7. 232   8. 2357

☆ 9. Round to the nearest ten and find the answer.

Carmen has 63¢.
Maury has 28¢.
About how much in all?

☆ 10. Round to the nearest hundred and find the answer.

Hudson School: 1281 students
Hamilton School: 843 students
About how many more at Hudson?

The Greatest Sum Game

1. Draw a large circle and make a spinner board like this. Use a paper clip as a pointer.

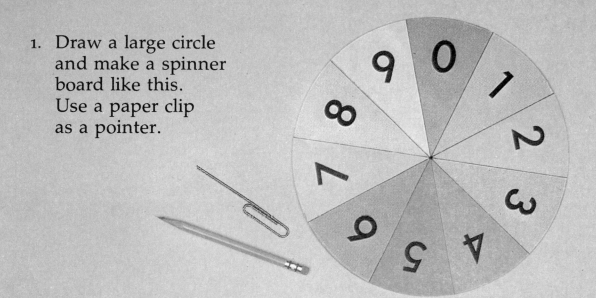

2. Draw an addition grid for each player.

Rico's grid   Beth's grid

3. Spin the spinner.

   Each player writes the spinner number in any one of the spaces in the top two rows of his or her grid.

Rico's grid   Beth's grid

4. After 6 spinner numbers are written on the grid, the winner is the person who has the greatest sum.

   Who won this game?

Rico's grid   Beth's grid

The Least Difference Game is very much like the Greatest Sum Game. Can you figure out how to play it?

Geometry (basic ideas)

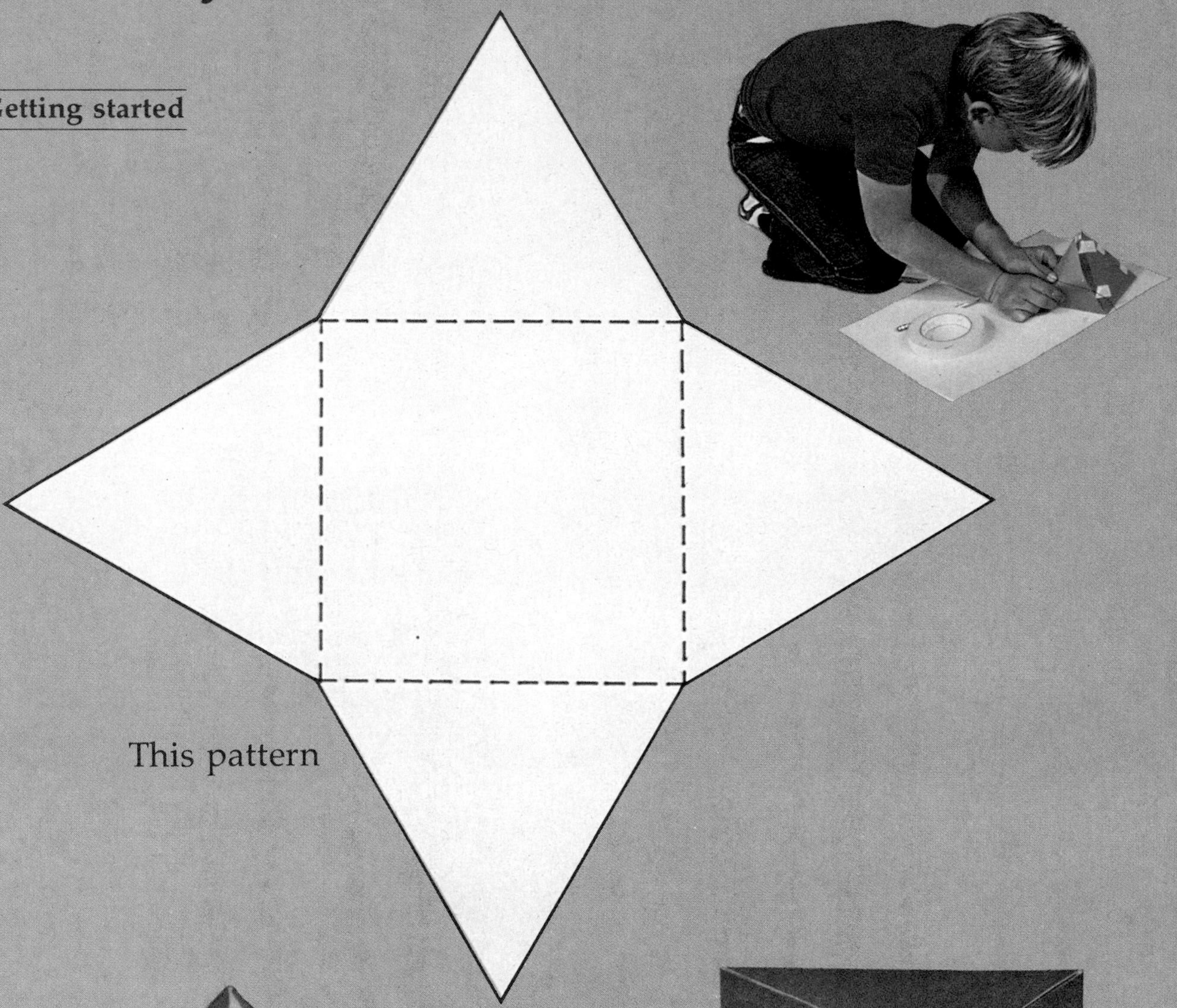

This pattern

can be folded

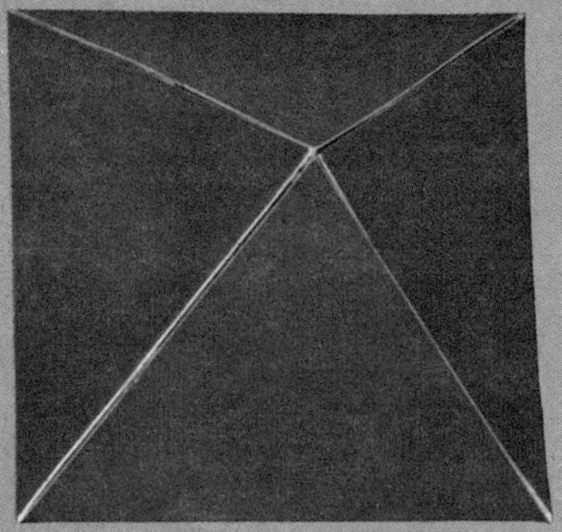

to make a square pyramid.

Trace the pattern and make the pyramid.

1.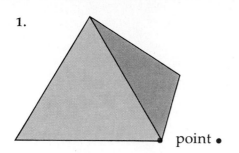

point •

Each corner of the pyramid has a point.

How many corners does your pyramid have?

2.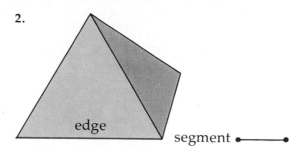

segment •——•

Each edge of the pyramid is a segment.

How many edges does your pyramid have?

3.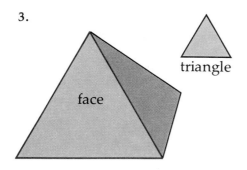

triangle

Some faces of a pyramid have a triangle shape.

How many triangle faces does your pyramid have?

4.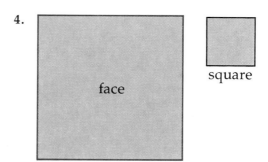

square

You can turn the pyramid so that a square face shows.

How many square faces does your pyramid have?

5. When two edges come together at a corner, an angle is formed.

How many angles of each kind does your pyramid have?

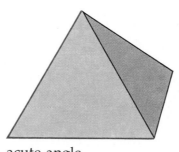

acute angle

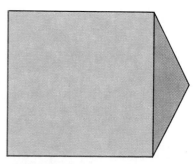

right angle

Polygons

Many objects are shaped like polygons.

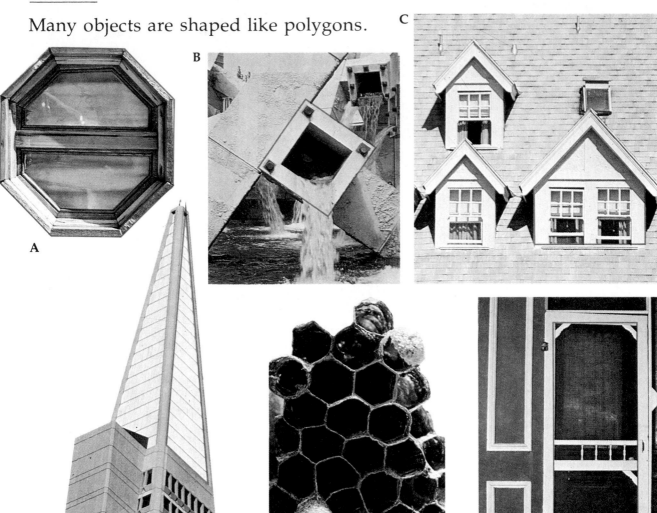

A B C D E F

Give the letter of the picture above that shows the polygon.

1.   triangle—3 sides

2.   square—4 equal sides

3.   pentagon—5 sides

4.   hexagon—6 sides

5.   octagon—8 sides

6.   rectangle—4 sides,
4 right angles

Strips are used to show some polygons in the figures below. Give the number of sides and the name of each polygon.

1.

2.

3.

4.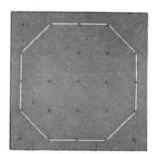

5.

6.

Give the number of sides and the name of each polygon below.

7.

8.

9.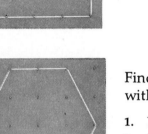

10.

Find each sum quickly without pencil and paper.

1. $1 + 5 + 9$
2. $1 + 2 + 5 + 8 + 9$
3. $1 + 2 + 3 + 5 + 7 + 8 + 9$
4. $1 + 50 + 99$
5. $1 + 2 + 50 + 98 + 99$

Polygons and angles

Each polygon has angles.

A right angle

Less than a
right angle

Greater than a
right angle

For each picture, tell if the angle is a **right angle,**
less than a right angle, or **greater than** a right angle.

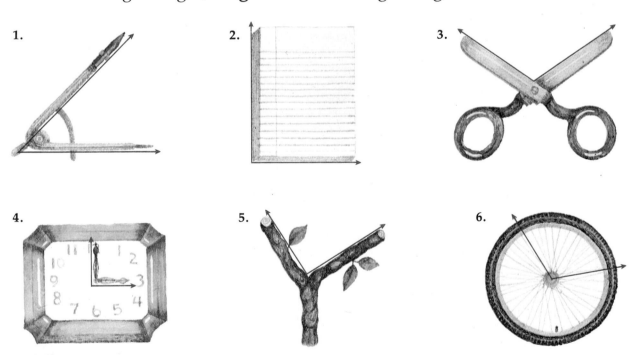

1.

2.

3.

4.

5.

6.

Tell how many right angles each polygon has.

1.
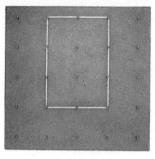
rectangle

2.
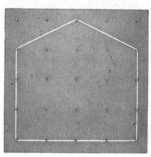
pentagon

3.
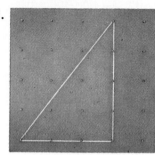
right triangle

For each polygon, tell if the angles are **right angles,**
less than right angles, or **greater than** right angles.

4.
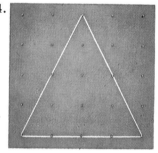
triangle

5.
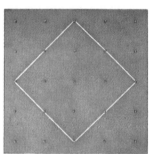
square

6.
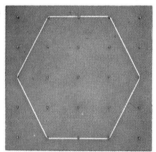
hexagon

Practicing your skills

Add or subtract.

1.	345	2.	583	3.	873	4.	2475	5.	409
	+ 527		− 269		+ 98		+ 798		− 175

6.	196	7.	1370	8.	1689	9.	500	10.	862
	+ 478		− 539		+ 2432		− 145		− 198

To draw a circle, you can

use a compass or make your own "circle drawer."

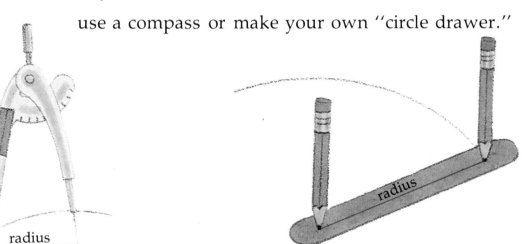

radius

radius

Use one of these ways to draw a circle
with a radius as long as each segment.

1. radius _____

2. radius _____

3. radius _____

4. radius _____

A 66-cm bike has tires with a diameter of 66 cm.

A 4-cm pipe has a diameter of 4 cm.

A 1-cm bolt has a diameter of 1 cm.

The diameter is double the radius.

Give the radius or diameter.

1.

Bracelet:
Radius—3 cm
Diameter—||||| cm

2.

Fan:
Diameter—50 cm
Radius—||||| cm

3.

Ring:
Diameter—2 cm
Radius—||||| cm

4.

Birdbath:
Diameter—80 cm
Radius—||||| cm

5.

Dog collar:
Radius—12 cm
Diameter—||||| cm

6.

Basketball hoop:
Radius—23 cm
Diameter—||||| cm

Answers for Self-check   1. hexagon   2. square   3. triangle   4. pentagon   5. A   6. C   7. B
8. (construction)   9. 6 cm   10. 8 cm

Self-check

Give the name of each polygon.

1. 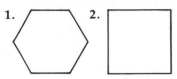 2.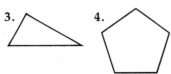

triangle—3 sides
square—4 equal sides
rectangle—4 sides, all
   right angles

pentagon—5 sides
hexagon—6 sides
octagon—8 sides

3. 4.

5. Which angle is a right angle?
6. Which is greater than a right angle?
7. Which is less than a right angle?

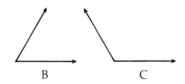

☆ 8. Draw a circle with this radius. •————————•

☆ 9. What is the diameter of the circle you drew for exercise 8?

☆ 10. Bracelet: Radius—4 cm
              Diameter— ||||| cm

Answers for Self-check—page 67

Test

Give the name of each polygon. 1. 2. 3. 4.

5. Which angle is a right angle?
6. Which is greater than a right angle?
7. Which is less than a right angle?

☆ 8. Draw a circle with this radius. •——————————•

☆ 9. What is the diameter of the circle you drew in exercise 8?

☆ 10. Dinner plate: Radius—22 cm
                Diameter— ||||| cm

Jigsaw Polygons

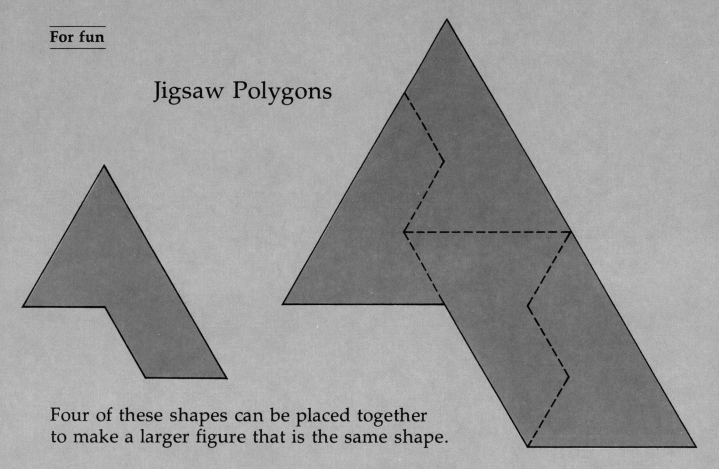

Four of these shapes can be placed together
to make a larger figure that is the same shape.

Trace and cut out four copies of these shapes.
Show that the four copies of each shape can
be used to make a larger figure of the same shape.

Level 17 review

Add or subtract.

1. 3
   + 7

2. 4
   + 8

3. 9
   + 6

4. 8
   + 9

5. 5
   3
   + 7

6. 2
   6
   + 9

7. 4
   1
   + 8

8. 11
   − 4

9. 16
   − 9

10. 14
    − 6

11. 12
    − 3

12. 18
    − 9

13. 13
    − 7

14. 42
    + 26

15. 28
    + 37

16. 259
    + 672

17. 817
    + 296

18. 329
    43
    + 2714

19. 36
    − 23

20. 46
    − 19

21. 390
    − 72

22. 507
    − 398

23. 8300
    − 6276

24. 389
    + 816

25. 604
    − 327

26. 3146
    + 868

27. 7053
    − 5164

28. 5917
    + 3483

29. 5 + 17 + 196

30. 607 + 489

31. 3200 − 1356

Write > or < for each ▦ .

32. 68 ▦ 77

33. 895 ▦ 905

34. 7928 ▦ 7899

Round to the nearest ten.

35. 54

36. 78

37. 44

38. 97

39. 228

40. 547

Round to the nearest hundred.

41. 88

42. 298

43. 412

44. 763

45. 1840

46. 3491

Level **18**

Multiplication
Division
Using Your Skills
Length and Perimeter

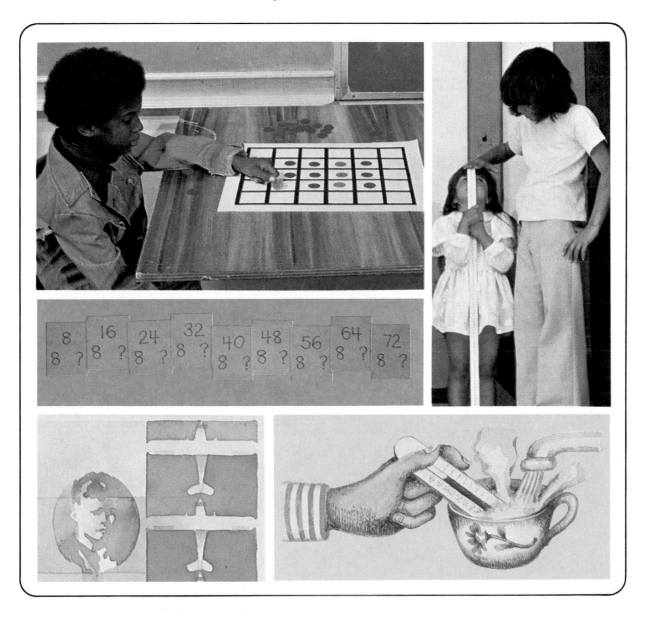

Multiplication Facts

Getting started

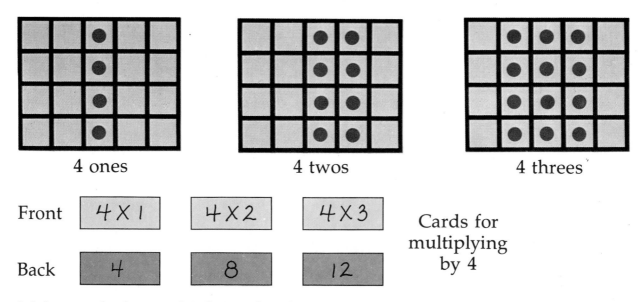

4 ones	4 twos	4 threes

Front   4 × 1   4 × 2   4 × 3

Cards for multiplying by 4

Back   4   8   12

Make cards for multiplying by 6.

Here is how Iris and Wes found
some facts they did not know.

Give the facts.

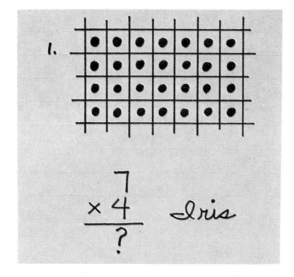

1.

$\begin{array}{r} 7 \\ \times 4 \\ \hline ? \end{array}$ Iris

2.
$\begin{array}{r} 9 \\ 9 \\ + 9 \\ \hline 27 \end{array}$ $\begin{array}{r} 9 \\ \times 3 \\ \hline ? \end{array}$

Wes

3. 4 fives are 20
   3 fives are 15
        so
   7 fives are 20+15

   $7 \times 5 = ?$

   Wes

4. $3 \times 8 = 24$
        so

   $8 \times 3 = ?$

   Iris

Make fact cards for the facts
you do not know.
Use the table on page 373.
Write the factors on the front.
Write the product on the back.

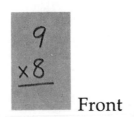 Front

 Back

The paper clip lands in 5.
Rule: Multiply by 2.
Score: ?

$$\begin{array}{r} 5 \\ \times 2 \\ \hline 10 \end{array}$$

The score is 10.

Find the products.

1. $\begin{array}{r}2\\ \times 0\\\hline\end{array}$	2. $\begin{array}{r}9\\ \times 0\\\hline\end{array}$	3. $\begin{array}{r}4\\ \times 0\\\hline\end{array}$	4. $\begin{array}{r}7\\ \times 0\\\hline\end{array}$	5. $\begin{array}{r}6\\ \times 0\\\hline\end{array}$	6. $\begin{array}{r}8\\ \times 0\\\hline\end{array}$	7. $\begin{array}{r}0\\ \times 0\\\hline\end{array}$
8. $\begin{array}{r}3\\ \times 1\\\hline\end{array}$	9. $\begin{array}{r}5\\ \times 1\\\hline\end{array}$	10. $\begin{array}{r}7\\ \times 1\\\hline\end{array}$	11. $\begin{array}{r}8\\ \times 1\\\hline\end{array}$	12. $\begin{array}{r}1\\ \times 1\\\hline\end{array}$	13. $\begin{array}{r}9\\ \times 1\\\hline\end{array}$	14. $\begin{array}{r}6\\ \times 1\\\hline\end{array}$
15. $\begin{array}{r}3\\ \times 2\\\hline\end{array}$	16. $\begin{array}{r}0\\ \times 2\\\hline\end{array}$	17. $\begin{array}{r}4\\ \times 2\\\hline\end{array}$	18. $\begin{array}{r}7\\ \times 2\\\hline\end{array}$	19. $\begin{array}{r}9\\ \times 2\\\hline\end{array}$	20. $\begin{array}{r}8\\ \times 2\\\hline\end{array}$	21. $\begin{array}{r}2\\ \times 2\\\hline\end{array}$
22. $\begin{array}{r}2\\ \times 3\\\hline\end{array}$	23. $\begin{array}{r}7\\ \times 3\\\hline\end{array}$	24. $\begin{array}{r}5\\ \times 3\\\hline\end{array}$	25. $\begin{array}{r}4\\ \times 3\\\hline\end{array}$	26. $\begin{array}{r}6\\ \times 3\\\hline\end{array}$	27. $\begin{array}{r}9\\ \times 3\\\hline\end{array}$	28. $\begin{array}{r}8\\ \times 3\\\hline\end{array}$

Multiply.

1. 3×3	2. 1×2	3. 5×0	4. 4×1	5. 6×2
6. 3×0	7. 2×3	8. 5×2	9. 1×0	10. 7×1
11. 4×2	12. 0×1	13. 8×3	14. 8×0	15. 6×3
16. 8×1	17. 9×3	18. 7×2	19. 4×3	20. 6×0

21. 1×2 22. 0×4 23. 2×8 24. 1×9 25. 3×7

26. 0×0 27. 3×6 28. 2×9 29. 2×8 30. 1×3

31. 3×5 32. 1×5 33. 3×9 34. 2×3 35. 2×2

36. Paper clip lands in 4.   Rule: Multiply by 3.
Score: ?

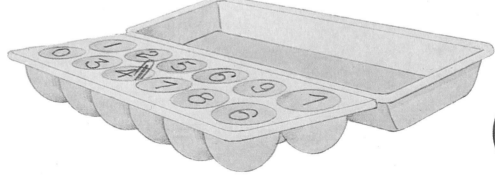

☆ 37. Play egg-carton multiplication
with a friend. Take turns.
The highest total score
for 10 throws wins.

Some people think
I'm tiresome as can be.
Whenever I'm a factor,
The product's also me.

Who am I?

Multiplying by 4 and 5

The spinner lands on 8.
Rule: Multiply by 5.
Score: ?

$$\begin{array}{r} 8 \\ \times\,5 \\ \hline 40 \end{array}$$

The score is 40.

Find the products.

1. $\begin{array}{r}5\\ \times4\\ \hline\end{array}$	2. $\begin{array}{r}1\\ \times4\\ \hline\end{array}$	3. $\begin{array}{r}2\\ \times4\\ \hline\end{array}$	4. $\begin{array}{r}7\\ \times4\\ \hline\end{array}$	5. $\begin{array}{r}6\\ \times4\\ \hline\end{array}$	6. $\begin{array}{r}0\\ \times4\\ \hline\end{array}$	7. $\begin{array}{r}4\\ \times4\\ \hline\end{array}$
8. $\begin{array}{r}9\\ \times4\\ \hline\end{array}$	9. $\begin{array}{r}8\\ \times4\\ \hline\end{array}$	10. $\begin{array}{r}7\\ \times4\\ \hline\end{array}$	11. $\begin{array}{r}2\\ \times4\\ \hline\end{array}$	12. $\begin{array}{r}3\\ \times4\\ \hline\end{array}$	13. $\begin{array}{r}6\\ \times4\\ \hline\end{array}$	14. $\begin{array}{r}0\\ \times4\\ \hline\end{array}$
15. $\begin{array}{r}8\\ \times4\\ \hline\end{array}$	16. $\begin{array}{r}1\\ \times4\\ \hline\end{array}$	17. $\begin{array}{r}5\\ \times4\\ \hline\end{array}$	18. $\begin{array}{r}3\\ \times4\\ \hline\end{array}$	19. $\begin{array}{r}9\\ \times4\\ \hline\end{array}$	20. $\begin{array}{r}7\\ \times4\\ \hline\end{array}$	21. $\begin{array}{r}4\\ \times4\\ \hline\end{array}$
22. $\begin{array}{r}2\\ \times5\\ \hline\end{array}$	23. $\begin{array}{r}4\\ \times5\\ \hline\end{array}$	24. $\begin{array}{r}3\\ \times5\\ \hline\end{array}$	25. $\begin{array}{r}6\\ \times5\\ \hline\end{array}$	26. $\begin{array}{r}8\\ \times5\\ \hline\end{array}$	27. $\begin{array}{r}1\\ \times5\\ \hline\end{array}$	28. $\begin{array}{r}7\\ \times5\\ \hline\end{array}$
29. $\begin{array}{r}5\\ \times5\\ \hline\end{array}$	30. $\begin{array}{r}9\\ \times5\\ \hline\end{array}$	31. $\begin{array}{r}0\\ \times5\\ \hline\end{array}$	32. $\begin{array}{r}2\\ \times5\\ \hline\end{array}$	33. $\begin{array}{r}5\\ \times5\\ \hline\end{array}$	34. $\begin{array}{r}4\\ \times5\\ \hline\end{array}$	35. $\begin{array}{r}8\\ \times5\\ \hline\end{array}$
36. $\begin{array}{r}3\\ \times5\\ \hline\end{array}$	37. $\begin{array}{r}4\\ \times5\\ \hline\end{array}$	38. $\begin{array}{r}1\\ \times5\\ \hline\end{array}$	39. $\begin{array}{r}9\\ \times5\\ \hline\end{array}$	40. $\begin{array}{r}0\\ \times5\\ \hline\end{array}$	41. $\begin{array}{r}7\\ \times5\\ \hline\end{array}$	42. $\begin{array}{r}6\\ \times5\\ \hline\end{array}$

Multiply.

1. 4×2 2. 4×5 3. 4×9 4. 4×0 5. 4×3

6. 4×6 7. 4×8 8. 4×7 9. 4×1 10. 4×4

11. 5×2 12. 5×6 13. 5×5 14. 5×9 15. 5×3

16. 5×8 17. 5×4 18. 5×7 19. 5×0 20. 5×1

Practice for speed. Multiply as quickly as you can.

21. $\begin{array}{r} 3 \\ \times 4 \\ \hline \end{array}$
22. $\begin{array}{r} 2 \\ \times 4 \\ \hline \end{array}$
23. $\begin{array}{r} 8 \\ \times 4 \\ \hline \end{array}$
24. $\begin{array}{r} 5 \\ \times 4 \\ \hline \end{array}$
25. $\begin{array}{r} 6 \\ \times 4 \\ \hline \end{array}$
26. $\begin{array}{r} 8 \\ \times 5 \\ \hline \end{array}$
27. $\begin{array}{r} 9 \\ \times 5 \\ \hline \end{array}$

28. $\begin{array}{r} 0 \\ \times 5 \\ \hline \end{array}$
29. $\begin{array}{r} 4 \\ \times 5 \\ \hline \end{array}$
30. $\begin{array}{r} 6 \\ \times 5 \\ \hline \end{array}$
31. $\begin{array}{r} 7 \\ \times 4 \\ \hline \end{array}$
32. $\begin{array}{r} 7 \\ \times 5 \\ \hline \end{array}$
33. $\begin{array}{r} 9 \\ \times 4 \\ \hline \end{array}$
34. $\begin{array}{r} 5 \\ \times 5 \\ \hline \end{array}$

35. $\begin{array}{r} 1 \\ \times 4 \\ \hline \end{array}$
36. $\begin{array}{r} 1 \\ \times 5 \\ \hline \end{array}$
37. $\begin{array}{r} 0 \\ \times 4 \\ \hline \end{array}$
38. $\begin{array}{r} 2 \\ \times 5 \\ \hline \end{array}$
39. $\begin{array}{r} 4 \\ \times 4 \\ \hline \end{array}$
40. $\begin{array}{r} 3 \\ \times 5 \\ \hline \end{array}$
41. $\begin{array}{r} 9 \\ \times 5 \\ \hline \end{array}$

42. The spinner lands on 9.
Rule: Multiply by 4.
Score: ?

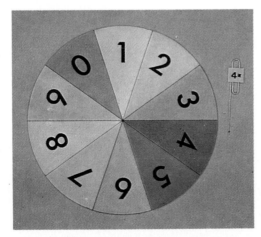

Ann's age is 4 times Bill's.
Fred's age is twice Bill's.
The sum of their ages is 21.
How old is each child?

Begin by making a trial guess.

☆ 43. Try some spinner multiplications.
How many can you do right
in 60 seconds?

More practice, page 356, Set A

Multiplying by 6

The cube shows 8.
Rule: Multiply by 6.
Score: ?

$$\begin{array}{r} 8 \\ \times\,6 \\ \hline 48 \end{array}$$

The score is 48.

Find these products.

Use the table on page 373 to check your answers.
Try to remember the facts.

Find the products.

1. $\begin{array}{r} 2 \\ \times\,6 \\ \hline \end{array}$	2. $\begin{array}{r} 5 \\ \times\,6 \\ \hline \end{array}$	3. $\begin{array}{r} 1 \\ \times\,6 \\ \hline \end{array}$	4. $\begin{array}{r} 3 \\ \times\,6 \\ \hline \end{array}$	5. $\begin{array}{r} 7 \\ \times\,6 \\ \hline \end{array}$	6. $\begin{array}{r} 4 \\ \times\,6 \\ \hline \end{array}$	7. $\begin{array}{r} 8 \\ \times\,6 \\ \hline \end{array}$
8. $\begin{array}{r} 6 \\ \times\,6 \\ \hline \end{array}$	9. $\begin{array}{r} 9 \\ \times\,6 \\ \hline \end{array}$	10. $\begin{array}{r} 0 \\ \times\,6 \\ \hline \end{array}$	11. $\begin{array}{r} 4 \\ \times\,6 \\ \hline \end{array}$	12. $\begin{array}{r} 3 \\ \times\,6 \\ \hline \end{array}$	13. $\begin{array}{r} 5 \\ \times\,6 \\ \hline \end{array}$	14. $\begin{array}{r} 7 \\ \times\,6 \\ \hline \end{array}$
15. $\begin{array}{r} 2 \\ \times\,6 \\ \hline \end{array}$	16. $\begin{array}{r} 6 \\ \times\,6 \\ \hline \end{array}$	17. $\begin{array}{r} 1 \\ \times\,6 \\ \hline \end{array}$	18. $\begin{array}{r} 9 \\ \times\,6 \\ \hline \end{array}$	19. $\begin{array}{r} 8 \\ \times\,6 \\ \hline \end{array}$	20. $\begin{array}{r} 3 \\ \times\,6 \\ \hline \end{array}$	21. $\begin{array}{r} 6 \\ \times\,6 \\ \hline \end{array}$
22. $\begin{array}{r} 4 \\ \times\,6 \\ \hline \end{array}$	23. $\begin{array}{r} 7 \\ \times\,6 \\ \hline \end{array}$	24. $\begin{array}{r} 2 \\ \times\,6 \\ \hline \end{array}$	25. $\begin{array}{r} 8 \\ \times\,6 \\ \hline \end{array}$	26. $\begin{array}{r} 5 \\ \times\,6 \\ \hline \end{array}$	27. $\begin{array}{r} 9 \\ \times\,6 \\ \hline \end{array}$	28. $\begin{array}{r} 0 \\ \times\,6 \\ \hline \end{array}$

Multiply.

1. 6 × 3   2. 6 × 2   3. 6 × 5   4. 6 × 7   5. 6 × 8

6. 6 × 4   7. 6 × 1   8. 6 × 0   9. 6 × 9   10. 6 × 7

11. 6 × 5   12. 6 × 8   13. 6 × 2   14. 6 × 6   15. 6 × 9

16. 1 × 6   17. 0 × 6   18. 3 × 6   19. 4 × 6   20. 5 × 6

Practice for speed.

21.	22.	23.	24.	25.	26.
3 × 6	8 × 4	7 × 6	7 × 5	2 × 6	6 × 6

27.	28.	29.	30.	31.
9 × 0	9 × 6	3 × 1	7 × 3	8 × 6

32.	33.	34.	35.	36.
6 × 4	9 × 2	5 × 6	8 × 5	4 × 6

37.	38.	39.	40.	41.
0 × 6	1 × 6	7 × 4	4 × 5	9 × 4

42. The cube shows 9.
Rule: Multiply by 6.
Score: ?

☆ 43. Mark 4, 5, 6, 7, 8, 9 on the faces of a cube. Roll the cube. Multiply the number by 6. How long does it take to fill in this table?

×	4	5	6	7	8	9
6	▥	▥	▥	▥	▥	▥

$$3 \times 2 \times 2 \times 2$$
$$6 \times 4$$
$$24$$

This is a "tree" for 24.
Can you make a "tree" for 36?

Multiplying by 7

The card is **7 × 6.**
What number should
you cover?

$$\begin{array}{r} 6 \\ \times\,7 \\ \hline 42 \end{array}$$

You should cover 42.

Find these products.

$$\begin{array}{ccccccccc} \frac{0}{\times 7} & \frac{1}{\times 7} & \frac{2}{\times 7} & \frac{3}{\times 7} & \frac{4}{\times 7} & \frac{5}{\times 7} & \frac{6}{\times 7} & \frac{7}{\times 7} & \frac{8}{\times 7} & \frac{9}{\times 7} \end{array}$$

Use the table on page 373 to check your answers.

Find the products.

1. $\begin{array}{r} 4 \\ \times\,7 \\ \hline \end{array}$
2. $\begin{array}{r} 9 \\ \times\,7 \\ \hline \end{array}$
3. $\begin{array}{r} 2 \\ \times\,7 \\ \hline \end{array}$
4. $\begin{array}{r} 0 \\ \times\,7 \\ \hline \end{array}$
5. $\begin{array}{r} 5 \\ \times\,7 \\ \hline \end{array}$
6. $\begin{array}{r} 8 \\ \times\,7 \\ \hline \end{array}$
7. $\begin{array}{r} 1 \\ \times\,7 \\ \hline \end{array}$

8. $\begin{array}{r} 3 \\ \times\,7 \\ \hline \end{array}$
9. $\begin{array}{r} 8 \\ \times\,7 \\ \hline \end{array}$
10. $\begin{array}{r} 6 \\ \times\,7 \\ \hline \end{array}$
11. $\begin{array}{r} 2 \\ \times\,7 \\ \hline \end{array}$
12. $\begin{array}{r} 4 \\ \times\,7 \\ \hline \end{array}$
13. $\begin{array}{r} 3 \\ \times\,7 \\ \hline \end{array}$
14. $\begin{array}{r} 9 \\ \times\,7 \\ \hline \end{array}$

15. $\begin{array}{r} 6 \\ \times\,7 \\ \hline \end{array}$
16. $\begin{array}{r} 7 \\ \times\,7 \\ \hline \end{array}$
17. $\begin{array}{r} 8 \\ \times\,7 \\ \hline \end{array}$
18. $\begin{array}{r} 9 \\ \times\,7 \\ \hline \end{array}$
19. $\begin{array}{r} 3 \\ \times\,7 \\ \hline \end{array}$
20. $\begin{array}{r} 1 \\ \times\,7 \\ \hline \end{array}$
21. $\begin{array}{r} 4 \\ \times\,7 \\ \hline \end{array}$

Multiply.

1. 7×2 2. 7×6 3. 7×1 4. 7×7 5. 7×3

6. 7×0 7. 7×9 8. 7×5 9. 7×8 10. 7×5

11. 7×4 12. 7×3 13. 7×2 14. 7×6 15. 7×9

16. 7×8 17. 7×4 18. 7×7 19. 7×1 20. 7×8

21. 7×4 22. 7×5 23. 7×6 24. 7×9 25. 7×0

Practice for speed.

26. $\begin{array}{r} 3 \\ \times 7 \\ \hline \end{array}$ 27. $\begin{array}{r} 7 \\ \times 6 \\ \hline \end{array}$ 28. $\begin{array}{r} 8 \\ \times 7 \\ \hline \end{array}$ 29. $\begin{array}{r} 4 \\ \times 6 \\ \hline \end{array}$ 30. $\begin{array}{r} 0 \\ \times 7 \\ \hline \end{array}$ 31. $\begin{array}{r} 5 \\ \times 7 \\ \hline \end{array}$ 32. $\begin{array}{r} 8 \\ \times 5 \\ \hline \end{array}$

33. $\begin{array}{r} 6 \\ \times 7 \\ \hline \end{array}$ 34. $\begin{array}{r} 9 \\ \times 5 \\ \hline \end{array}$ 35. $\begin{array}{r} 9 \\ \times 7 \\ \hline \end{array}$ 36. $\begin{array}{r} 5 \\ \times 7 \\ \hline \end{array}$ 37. $\begin{array}{r} 6 \\ \times 4 \\ \hline \end{array}$ 38. $\begin{array}{r} 7 \\ \times 7 \\ \hline \end{array}$ 39. $\begin{array}{r} 9 \\ \times 4 \\ \hline \end{array}$

40. $\begin{array}{r} 1 \\ \times 7 \\ \hline \end{array}$ 41. $\begin{array}{r} 2 \\ \times 7 \\ \hline \end{array}$ 42. $\begin{array}{r} 8 \\ \times 6 \\ \hline \end{array}$ 43. $\begin{array}{r} 6 \\ \times 7 \\ \hline \end{array}$ 44. $\begin{array}{r} 5 \\ \times 6 \\ \hline \end{array}$ 45. $\begin{array}{r} 3 \\ \times 5 \\ \hline \end{array}$ 46. $\begin{array}{r} 4 \\ \times 7 \\ \hline \end{array}$

47. What other factor on this card would let you say "Combo" and win the game?

Try these:

$120 - 12 + 3 = n$
$1230 - 123 + 4 = n$
$12\,340 - 1234 + 5 = n$
$123\,450 - 12\,345 + 6 = n$

What is interesting about the answers?

Write and solve the equation that would come next.

☆ 48. Make some Combo cards and play Combo with your classmates. You may want to use a timer.

Multiplying by 8

The bean bag lands on 3.
Rule: Multiply by 8.
Score: ?

$$\begin{array}{r} 3 \\ \times\,8 \\ \hline 24 \end{array}$$

The score is 24.

Find these products.

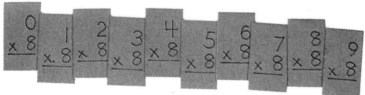

Use the table on page 373 to check your answers.

Find the products.

1. $\begin{array}{r}2\\ \times 8\\ \hline\end{array}$	2. $\begin{array}{r}3\\ \times 8\\ \hline\end{array}$	3. $\begin{array}{r}8\\ \times 8\\ \hline\end{array}$	4. $\begin{array}{r}9\\ \times 8\\ \hline\end{array}$	5. $\begin{array}{r}6\\ \times 8\\ \hline\end{array}$	6. $\begin{array}{r}5\\ \times 8\\ \hline\end{array}$	7. $\begin{array}{r}4\\ \times 8\\ \hline\end{array}$
8. $\begin{array}{r}7\\ \times 8\\ \hline\end{array}$	9. $\begin{array}{r}1\\ \times 8\\ \hline\end{array}$	10. $\begin{array}{r}9\\ \times 8\\ \hline\end{array}$	11. $\begin{array}{r}6\\ \times 8\\ \hline\end{array}$	12. $\begin{array}{r}8\\ \times 8\\ \hline\end{array}$	13. $\begin{array}{r}0\\ \times 8\\ \hline\end{array}$	14. $\begin{array}{r}5\\ \times 8\\ \hline\end{array}$
15. $\begin{array}{r}1\\ \times 8\\ \hline\end{array}$	16. $\begin{array}{r}8\\ \times 8\\ \hline\end{array}$	17. $\begin{array}{r}4\\ \times 8\\ \hline\end{array}$	18. $\begin{array}{r}2\\ \times 8\\ \hline\end{array}$	19. $\begin{array}{r}5\\ \times 8\\ \hline\end{array}$	20. $\begin{array}{r}3\\ \times 8\\ \hline\end{array}$	21. $\begin{array}{r}7\\ \times 8\\ \hline\end{array}$
22. $\begin{array}{r}9\\ \times 8\\ \hline\end{array}$	23. $\begin{array}{r}2\\ \times 8\\ \hline\end{array}$	24. $\begin{array}{r}7\\ \times 8\\ \hline\end{array}$	25. $\begin{array}{r}3\\ \times 8\\ \hline\end{array}$	26. $\begin{array}{r}4\\ \times 8\\ \hline\end{array}$	27. $\begin{array}{r}0\\ \times 8\\ \hline\end{array}$	28. $\begin{array}{r}6\\ \times 8\\ \hline\end{array}$

Multiply.

1. 8×3 2. 8×5 3. 8×8 4. 8×1

5. 8×4 6. 8×6 7. 8×2 8. 8×7

9. 8×9 10. 8×4 11. 8×1 12. 8×6

13. 8×0 14. 8×7 15. 8×3 16. 8×9

17. 8×6 18. 8×5 19. 8×4 20. 8×0

Practice for speed.

21. $\begin{array}{r} 5 \\ \times 8 \\ \hline \end{array}$ 22. $\begin{array}{r} 6 \\ \times 7 \\ \hline \end{array}$ 23. $\begin{array}{r} 9 \\ \times 8 \\ \hline \end{array}$ 24. $\begin{array}{r} 4 \\ \times 7 \\ \hline \end{array}$ 25. $\begin{array}{r} 6 \\ \times 8 \\ \hline \end{array}$ 26. $\begin{array}{r} 8 \\ \times 8 \\ \hline \end{array}$ 27. $\begin{array}{r} 9 \\ \times 6 \\ \hline \end{array}$

28. $\begin{array}{r} 8 \\ \times 7 \\ \hline \end{array}$ 29. $\begin{array}{r} 7 \\ \times 6 \\ \hline \end{array}$ 30. $\begin{array}{r} 4 \\ \times 8 \\ \hline \end{array}$ 31. $\begin{array}{r} 3 \\ \times 8 \\ \hline \end{array}$ 32. $\begin{array}{r} 8 \\ \times 5 \\ \hline \end{array}$ 33. $\begin{array}{r} 5 \\ \times 8 \\ \hline \end{array}$ 34. $\begin{array}{r} 9 \\ \times 5 \\ \hline \end{array}$

35. $\begin{array}{r} 4 \\ \times 6 \\ \hline \end{array}$ 36. $\begin{array}{r} 9 \\ \times 7 \\ \hline \end{array}$ 37. $\begin{array}{r} 6 \\ \times 6 \\ \hline \end{array}$ 38. $\begin{array}{r} 7 \\ \times 7 \\ \hline \end{array}$

39. Bean bag lands on 6.
Rule: Multiply by 8.
Score: ?

Start with   0
Add 18 $\begin{array}{r} + 18 \\ \hline 18 \end{array}$
Add 18 $\begin{array}{r} + 18 \\ \hline 36 \\ \vdots \end{array}$

Guess what the sum will be when nineteen 18's are added.

Check your guess.

☆ 40. Play the bean-bag multiplication game with a friend. Take turns. Highest total score for 10 throws wins.

Multiplying by 9

The cubes show 6 and 9.

On which number should
you put the checker?

$$\begin{array}{r} 6 \\ \times\,9 \\ \hline 54 \end{array}$$

You should put
the checker on 54.

16	20	24	25
28	30	32	35
36	40	42	45
48	49	54	56
63	64	72	81

Find these products.

Use the table on page 373 to check your answers.

Find the products.

1. $\begin{array}{r} 2 \\ \times\,9 \\ \hline \end{array}$
2. $\begin{array}{r} 5 \\ \times\,9 \\ \hline \end{array}$
3. $\begin{array}{r} 8 \\ \times\,9 \\ \hline \end{array}$
4. $\begin{array}{r} 0 \\ \times\,9 \\ \hline \end{array}$
5. $\begin{array}{r} 3 \\ \times\,9 \\ \hline \end{array}$
6. $\begin{array}{r} 1 \\ \times\,9 \\ \hline \end{array}$
7. $\begin{array}{r} 6 \\ \times\,9 \\ \hline \end{array}$

8. $\begin{array}{r} 4 \\ \times\,9 \\ \hline \end{array}$
9. $\begin{array}{r} 7 \\ \times\,9 \\ \hline \end{array}$
10. $\begin{array}{r} 5 \\ \times\,9 \\ \hline \end{array}$
11. $\begin{array}{r} 9 \\ \times\,9 \\ \hline \end{array}$
12. $\begin{array}{r} 6 \\ \times\,9 \\ \hline \end{array}$
13. $\begin{array}{r} 3 \\ \times\,9 \\ \hline \end{array}$
14. $\begin{array}{r} 8 \\ \times\,9 \\ \hline \end{array}$

15. $\begin{array}{r} 1 \\ \times\,9 \\ \hline \end{array}$
16. $\begin{array}{r} 4 \\ \times\,9 \\ \hline \end{array}$
17. $\begin{array}{r} 3 \\ \times\,9 \\ \hline \end{array}$
18. $\begin{array}{r} 7 \\ \times\,9 \\ \hline \end{array}$
19. $\begin{array}{r} 2 \\ \times\,9 \\ \hline \end{array}$
20. $\begin{array}{r} 9 \\ \times\,9 \\ \hline \end{array}$
21. $\begin{array}{r} 6 \\ \times\,9 \\ \hline \end{array}$

Practice for speed.

1. 9×5 2. 9×0 3. 9×8 4. 7×9 5. 4×9

6. 9×6 7. 1×9 8. 3×7 9. 8×5 10. 6×8

11. 7×6 12. 8×8 13. 6×5 14. 9×9

15. 4×8 16. 7×7 17. 5×7

18. 6×4 19. 9×3 20. 6×6

21. 8×7 22. 7×4

23. The cubes show 8 and 9.
    Which number should you cover?

16	20	24	25	28	30	32	35	36	40
42	45	48	49	54	56	63	64	72	81

Find this 5-step sum.

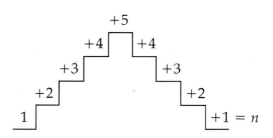

Find this product: $5 \times 5 = n$

What did you find?
What do you think the 8-step sum is? Check your guess.

☆ 24. Make a chart like the one in exercise 23. Put the numerals 4, 5, 6, 7, 8, 9 on two cubes. Roll the cubes and multiply. Cover the product on your chart. How long does it take to cover all the numbers?

Answers for Self-check   1. 6   2. 7   3. 12   4. 16   5. 30   6. 0   7. 15   8. 24   9. 56   10. 54   11. 35
12. 27   13. 16   14. 48   15. 64   16. 63   17. 18   18. 72   19. 42   20. 81   21. 20   22. 24   23. 49   24. 0
25. 36   26. 14   27. 25   28. 21

More practice, page 356, Set B

Self-check

Find the products.

1. $\begin{array}{r} 2 \\ \times 3 \\ \hline \end{array}$ *6*

2. $\begin{array}{r} 7 \\ \times 1 \\ \hline \end{array}$ *7*

3. $\begin{array}{r} 3 \\ \times 4 \\ \hline \end{array}$ *12*

4. $\begin{array}{r} 8 \\ \times 2 \\ \hline \end{array}$ *16*

5. $\begin{array}{r} 6 \\ \times 5 \\ \hline \end{array}$ *30*

6. $\begin{array}{r} 0 \\ \times 9 \\ \hline \end{array}$ *0*

7. $\begin{array}{r} 3 \\ \times 5 \\ \hline \end{array}$ *15*

8. $\begin{array}{r} 4 \\ \times 6 \\ \hline \end{array}$ *24*

9. $\begin{array}{r} 8 \\ \times 7 \\ \hline \end{array}$ *56*

10. $\begin{array}{r} 6 \\ \times 9 \\ \hline \end{array}$ *54*

11. $\begin{array}{r} 5 \\ \times 7 \\ \hline \end{array}$ *35*

12. $\begin{array}{r} 9 \\ \times 3 \\ \hline \end{array}$ *27*

13. $\begin{array}{r} 4 \\ \times 4 \\ \hline \end{array}$ *16*

14. $\begin{array}{r} 6 \\ \times 8 \\ \hline \end{array}$ *48*

15. $\begin{array}{r} 8 \\ \times 8 \\ \hline \end{array}$ *64*

16. $\begin{array}{r} 9 \\ \times 7 \\ \hline \end{array}$ *63*

17. $\begin{array}{r} 3 \\ \times 6 \\ \hline \end{array}$ *18*

18. $\begin{array}{r} 8 \\ \times 9 \\ \hline \end{array}$ *72*

19. 6×7 *42*

20. 9×9 *81*

21. 5×4 *20*

22. 3×8 *24*

23. 7×7 *49*

24. 0×8 *0*

25. 4×9 *36*

26. 2×7 *14*

27. 5×5 *25*

28. 7×3 *21*

Answers for Self-check—page 85

Test

Find the products.

1. $\begin{array}{r} 3 \\ \times 6 \\ \hline \end{array}$ *18*

2. $\begin{array}{r} 4 \\ \times 4 \\ \hline \end{array}$ *16*

3. $\begin{array}{r} 7 \\ \times 2 \\ \hline \end{array}$ *14*

4. $\begin{array}{r} 5 \\ \times 6 \\ \hline \end{array}$ *30*

5. $\begin{array}{r} 1 \\ \times 9 \\ \hline \end{array}$ *9*

6. $\begin{array}{r} 3 \\ \times 8 \\ \hline \end{array}$ *24*

7. $\begin{array}{r} 6 \\ \times 7 \\ \hline \end{array}$ *42*

8. $\begin{array}{r} 9 \\ \times 5 \\ \hline \end{array}$ *45*

9. $\begin{array}{r} 4 \\ \times 0 \\ \hline \end{array}$ *0*

10. $\begin{array}{r} 9 \\ \times 3 \\ \hline \end{array}$ *27*

11. $\begin{array}{r} 8 \\ \times 6 \\ \hline \end{array}$ *48*

12. $\begin{array}{r} 7 \\ \times 7 \\ \hline \end{array}$ *49*

13. $\begin{array}{r} 5 \\ \times 8 \\ \hline \end{array}$ *40*

14. $\begin{array}{r} 9 \\ \times 6 \\ \hline \end{array}$ *54*

15. $\begin{array}{r} 6 \\ \times 2 \\ \hline \end{array}$ *12*

16. $\begin{array}{r} 3 \\ \times 5 \\ \hline \end{array}$ *15*

17. $\begin{array}{r} 7 \\ \times 3 \\ \hline \end{array}$ *21*

18. $\begin{array}{r} 7 \\ \times 9 \\ \hline \end{array}$ *63*

19. 8×4 *32*

20. 5×5 *25*

21. 7×8 *56*

22. 6×0 *0*

23. 4×3 *12*

24. 9×9 *81*

25. 4×9 *36*

26. 9×2 *18*

27. 6×6 *36*

28. 5×7 *35*

Multiplication Concentration

Play this game with a friend.

Make two cards like this for
each of these facts.

6 × 7 = 42   8 × 9 = 72
6 × 8 = 48   6 × 6 = 36
6 × 9 = 54   7 × 7 = 49
7 × 8 = 56   8 × 8 = 64
7 × 9 = 63   9 × 9 = 81

Rules:

1. Mix the cards.
   Lay them facedown.

2. Take turns.
   Turn up 1 factors card and
   1 product card at each turn.

3. If the product and factors
   cards match, keep them.

4. If they do not match, put them
   back facedown where they were.

5. Play until all cards have
   been matched.

The player with the most cards wins.

Division

12 counters
4 in each row
? rows

Getting started

How many rows can you make?

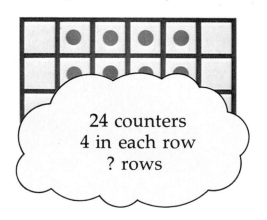

24 counters
4 in each row
? rows

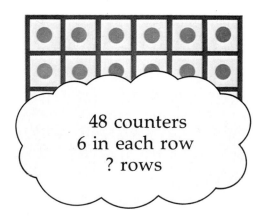

48 counters
6 in each row
? rows

How many rows of 5 can you make with 35 counters?

Example

We see:

We think
about missing factors.

We write
a division equation.

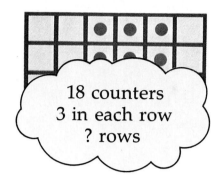

18 counters
3 in each row
? rows

factor   factor   product
$n \times 3 = 18$

$18 \div 3 = 6$
The quotient is 6.

Copy and finish the division equations.

1.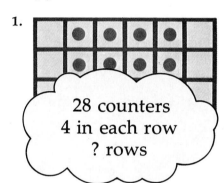

28 counters
4 in each row
? rows

$n \times 4 = 28$

$28 \div 4 = n$

2.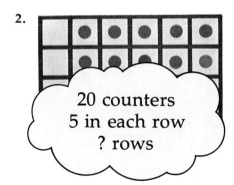

20 counters
5 in each row
? rows

$n \times 5 = 20$

$20 \div 5 = n$

3.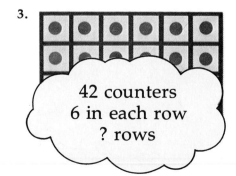

42 counters
6 in each row
? rows

$n \times 6 = 42$

$42 \div 6 = n$

Multiplication and division fact families

These fact family numbers can help you solve these equations.

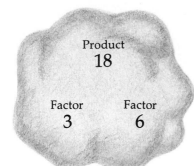

$$3 \times 6 = n \qquad n = 18$$
$$6 \times 3 = n \qquad n = 18$$
$$18 \div 6 = n \qquad n = 3$$
$$18 \div 3 = n \qquad n = 6$$

Use the fact family numbers to solve the fact family equations.

1. $5 \times 3 = n$

$3 \times 5 = n$

$15 \div 3 = n$

$15 \div 5 = n$

2. $3 \times 4 = n$

$4 \times 3 = n$

$12 \div 4 = n$

$12 \div 3 = n$

3. $2 \times 8 = n$

$8 \times 2 = n$

$16 \div 8 = n$

$16 \div 2 = n$

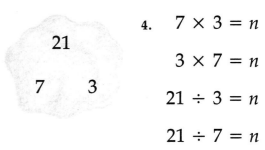

4. $7 \times 3 = n$

$3 \times 7 = n$

$21 \div 3 = n$

$21 \div 7 = n$

5. $4 \times 8 = n$

$8 \times 4 = n$

$32 \div 8 = n$

$32 \div 4 = n$

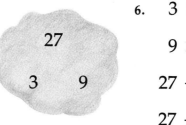

6. $3 \times 9 = n$

$9 \times 3 = n$

$27 \div 9 = n$

$27 \div 3 = n$

Solve the fact family equations.

1. $5 \times 2 = n$
   $2 \times 5 = n$
   $10 \div 2 = n$
   $10 \div 5 = n$

2. $3 \times 8 = n$
   $8 \times 3 = n$
   $24 \div 8 = n$
   $24 \div 3 = n$

3. $4 \times 7 = n$
   $7 \times 4 = n$
   $28 \div 7 = n$
   $28 \div 4 = n$

4. $6 \times 4 = n$
   $4 \times 6 = n$
   $24 \div 4 = n$
   $24 \div 6 = n$

5. $4 \times 5 = n$
   $5 \times 4 = n$
   $20 \div 5 = n$
   $20 \div 4 = n$

6. $5 \times 6 = n$
   $6 \times 5 = n$
   $30 \div 6 = n$
   $30 \div 5 = n$

7. $4 \times 9 = n$
   $9 \times 4 = n$
   $36 \div 9 = n$
   $36 \div 4 = n$

8. $7 \times 5 = n$
   $5 \times 7 = n$
   $35 \div 5 = n$
   $35 \div 7 = n$

9. $3 \times 3 = n$
   $9 \div 3 = n$

10. $6 \times 6 = n$
    $36 \div 6 = n$

11. $5 \times 5 = n$
    $25 \div 5 = n$

12. $4 \times 4 = n$
    $16 \div 4 = n$

Practicing your skills

Add or subtract.

1. 287
   + 365

2. 429
   − 284

3. 502
   − 356

4. 469
   + 297

5. 541
   − 482

6. 728
   + 187

7. 800
   − 276

8. 740
   − 369

9. 523
   − 98

10. 499
    + 399

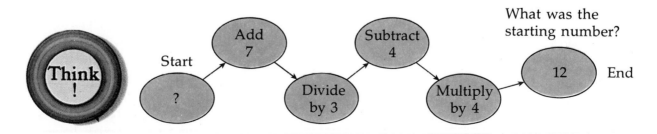

Think!

Start — ? → Add 7 → Divide by 3 → Subtract 4 → Multiply by 4 → 12 End

What was the starting number?

Dividing by 1, 2, and 3

The spinner lands on 18.
Rule: Divide by 2.
Quotient: ?
We think:

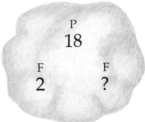

$18 \div 2 = n$

The missing factor is 9,
so the quotient is 9.

Find the quotients.

1. $16 \div 2 = n$

2. $15 \div 3 = n$

3. $9 \div 1 = n$

4. $24 \div 3 = n$

5. $12 \div 2 = n$

6. $21 \div 3 = n$

7. $7 \div 1 = n$

8. $27 \div 3 = n$

9. $8 \div 2 = n$

10. $12 \div 3 = n$

11. $18 \div 3 = n$

12. $14 \div 2 = n$

Divide.

1. $7 \div 1$ 2. $3 \div 1$ 3. $2 \div 1$ 4. $1 \div 1$ 5. $8 \div 1$

6. $9 \div 1$ 7. $5 \div 1$ 8. $4 \div 1$ 9. $6 \div 1$ 10. $0 \div 1$

11. $6 \div 2$ 12. $8 \div 2$ 13. $12 \div 2$ 14. $14 \div 2$ 15. $18 \div 2$

16. $10 \div 2$ 17. $4 \div 2$ 18. $2 \div 2$ 19. $16 \div 2$ 20. $0 \div 2$

21. $9 \div 3$ 22. $12 \div 3$ 23. $6 \div 3$ 24. $27 \div 3$ 25. $24 \div 3$

26. $18 \div 3$ 27. $21 \div 3$ 28. $15 \div 3$ 29. $3 \div 3$ 30. $0 \div 3$

Practice for speed.

31. $16 \div 2$ 32. $24 \div 3$ 33. $6 \div 1$ 34. $14 \div 2$ 35. $21 \div 3$

36. $27 \div 3$ 37. $18 \div 2$ 38. $15 \div 3$ 39. $9 \div 1$ 40. $8 \div 2$

41. $12 \div 2$ 42. $9 \div 3$ 43. $4 \div 1$ 44. $18 \div 3$ 45. $2 \div 2$

46. The spinner lands on 21.
Rule: Divide by 3.
Quotient: ?

☆ 47. Make up a spinner-quotients game and play it with a classmate. Use a spinner like this.

Do you see anything unusual about the rows and columns in this sum?

```
   13 128
   31 757
   17 133
 + 25 346
   87 364
```

Is the addition correct?

Dividing by 4 and 5

The bean bag lands on 35.

Rule: Divide by 5.

Quotient: ?

We think: $35 \div 5 = n$

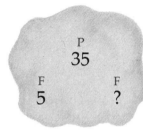

The missing factor is 7,
so $35 \div 5 = 7$.

Thinking about the
missing factor will
help you find the
quotients.

4	8	12	16	20	24	28	32	36
4 ?	4 ?	4 ?	4 ?	4 ?	4 ?	4 ?	4 ?	4 ?

5	10	15	20	25	30	35	40	45
5 ?	5 ?	5 ?	5 ?	5 ?	5 ?	5 ?	5 ?	5 ?

Find the quotients.

1. $12 \div 4$ 2. $20 \div 4$ 3. $8 \div 4$ 4. $4 \div 4$ 5. $36 \div 4$

6. $16 \div 4$ 7. $24 \div 4$ 8. $28 \div 4$ 9. $32 \div 4$ 10. $20 \div 4$

11. $24 \div 4$ 12. $0 \div 4$ 13. $32 \div 4$ 14. $36 \div 4$ 15. $28 \div 4$

16. $45 \div 5$ 17. $30 \div 5$ 18. $25 \div 5$ 19. $15 \div 5$ 20. $20 \div 5$

21. $35 \div 5$ 22. $45 \div 5$ 23. $40 \div 5$ 24. $5 \div 5$ 25. $30 \div 5$

26. $10 \div 5$ 27. $35 \div 5$ 28. $20 \div 5$ 29. $40 \div 5$ 30. $0 \div 5$

Divide.

1. $24 \div 4 = n$ 2. $15 \div 5 = n$

3. $20 \div 4 = n$ 4. $20 \div 5 = n$

5. $35 \div 5 = n$ 6. $16 \div 4 = n$

7. $28 \div 4 = n$ 8. $45 \div 5 = n$

9. $30 \div 5 = n$ 10. $8 \div 4 = n$

11. $24 \div 4 = n$ 12. $5 \div 5 = n$

13. $32 \div 4 = n$ 14. $40 \div 5 = n$ 15. $0 \div 4 = n$ 16. $12 \div 4 = n$

17. $10 \div 5 = n$ 18. $36 \div 4 = n$ 19. $4 \div 4 = n$ 20. $25 \div 5 = n$

The quotient $32 \div 4$ may also be written as $4\overline{)32}$.
Practice for speed.

21. $4\overline{)32}$ 22. $2\overline{)18}$ 23. $3\overline{)27}$ 24. $5\overline{)45}$ 25. $5\overline{)30}$

26. $4\overline{)28}$ 27. $3\overline{)24}$ 28. $2\overline{)16}$ 29. $4\overline{)12}$ 30. $5\overline{)25}$

31. $3\overline{)21}$ 32. $5\overline{)40}$ 33. $4\overline{)36}$ 34. $5\overline{)35}$ 35. $3\overline{)18}$

36. The bean bag lands on 28.
Rule: Divide by 4.
Quotient: ?

Make these:

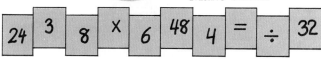

Use some to form an equation.

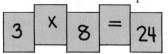

☆ 37. Play a division-bean-
bag game with a friend.
How many quotients can
you each get right in
10 tosses?

How many different equations
can you form? Write each one
on your paper.

More practice, page 357, Set A

Dividing by 6 and 7

The pencil goes through the hole at 28.

Rule: Divide by 7. Quotient: ?

We think:

$28 \div 7 = n$

P
28

F
7

F
?

The missing factor is 4, so $28 \div 7 = 4$.

Thinking about the missing factor will help you find the quotients.

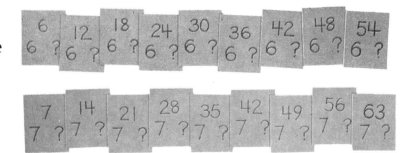

Find the quotients.

1. $30 \div 6$ 2. $42 \div 6$ 3. $18 \div 6$ 4. $24 \div 6$ 5. $12 \div 6$

6. $6 \div 6$ 7. $30 \div 6$ 8. $36 \div 6$ 9. $54 \div 6$ 10. $18 \div 6$

11. $0 \div 6$ 12. $24 \div 6$ 13. $48 \div 6$ 14. $36 \div 6$ 15. $12 \div 6$

16. $7 \div 7$ 17. $49 \div 7$ 18. $63 \div 7$ 19. $56 \div 7$ 20. $21 \div 7$

21. $28 \div 7$ 22. $14 \div 7$ 23. $35 \div 7$ 24. $42 \div 7$ 25. $63 \div 7$

26. $0 \div 7$ 27. $42 \div 7$ 28. $56 \div 7$ 29. $49 \div 7$ 30. $35 \div 7$

Divide.

1. $24 \div 6 = n$
2. $21 \div 7 = n$
3. $54 \div 6 = n$
4. $42 \div 7 = n$

5. $48 \div 6 = n$
6. $14 \div 7 = n$
7. $56 \div 7 = n$
8. $30 \div 6 = n$

9. $35 \div 7 = n$
10. $0 \div 6 = n$
11. $6 \div 6 = n$
12. $63 \div 7 = n$

13. $49 \div 7 = n$
14. $12 \div 6 = n$
15. $28 \div 7 = n$
16. $42 \div 6 = n$

17. $7 \div 7 = n$
18. $36 \div 6 = n$
19. $18 \div 6 = n$
20. $0 \div 7 = n$

Practice for speed.

21. $6\overline{)36}$
22. $7\overline{)42}$
23. $5\overline{)45}$
24. $4\overline{)28}$
25. $3\overline{)18}$

26. $6\overline{)48}$
27. $7\overline{)56}$
28. $2\overline{)16}$
29. $4\overline{)32}$
30. $6\overline{)30}$

31. $7\overline{)63}$
32. $5\overline{)40}$
33. $3\overline{)27}$
34. $6\overline{)54}$
35. $5\overline{)35}$

36. The pencil goes through the hole at 54.
Rule: Divide by 6.
Answer: ?

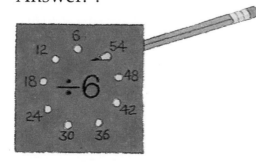

Start with   126
Subtract 18 $-$ 18
                    108
Subtract 18 $-$ 18
                     90
⋮   ⋮

Guess how many 18's you must subtract to reach 0. Try it.
How many 18's in 126?

☆ 37. Make some pencil-point-division cards. Use them with a classmate to practice dividing.

Dividing by 8 and 9

Division concentration:
Carmen turned up the **72 ÷ 9** card.
What quotient card should she
try to turn up?

We think: $72 \div 9 = n$

The missing factor
is 8, so $72 \div 9 = 8$.

P
72

F
9

F
?

She should try to
turn up the **8** card.

Thinking about the
missing factor will
help you find the
quotients.

Find the quotients.

1. $40 \div 8$	2. $16 \div 8$	3. $24 \div 8$	4. $32 \div 8$	5. $56 \div 8$
6. $48 \div 8$	7. $0 \div 8$	8. $72 \div 8$	9. $16 \div 8$	10. $8 \div 8$
11. $56 \div 8$	12. $40 \div 8$	13. $32 \div 8$	14. $72 \div 8$	15. $64 \div 8$
16. $27 \div 9$	17. $45 \div 9$	18. $36 \div 9$	19. $81 \div 9$	20. $54 \div 9$
21. $18 \div 9$	22. $0 \div 9$	23. $9 \div 9$	24. $63 \div 9$	25. $72 \div 9$
26. $36 \div 9$	27. $27 \div 9$	28. $54 \div 9$	29. $72 \div 9$	30. $63 \div 9$

Divide.

1. $32 \div 8 = n$ 2. $27 \div 9 = n$

3. $24 \div 8 = n$ 4. $18 \div 9 = n$

5. $36 \div 9 = n$ 6. $40 \div 8 = n$

7. $48 \div 8 = n$ 8. $9 \div 9 = n$

9. $56 \div 8 = n$ 10. $45 \div 9 = n$

11. $0 \div 9 = n$ 12. $16 \div 8 = n$

13. $8 \div 8 = n$ 14. $72 \div 9 = n$

15. $81 \div 9 = n$ 16. $54 \div 9 = n$

Practice for speed.

17. $9\overline{)45}$ 18. $7\overline{)56}$ 19. $8\overline{)40}$ 20. $6\overline{)54}$ 21. $8\overline{)32}$

22. $9\overline{)36}$ 23. $5\overline{)30}$ 24. $4\overline{)28}$ 25. $8\overline{)72}$ 26. $9\overline{)63}$

27. $8\overline{)64}$ 28. $7\overline{)42}$ 29. $6\overline{)48}$ 30. $7\overline{)63}$ 31. $9\overline{)81}$

32. What quotient card should you try to turn up?

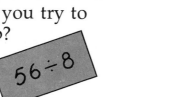

☆ 33. Make a set of cards for dividing by 9. Play a game of division concentration with a classmate.

Guess how many pennies you can place around another penny.

All pennies must touch each other.

Try it. How close was your guess? Would you guess the same for a quarter?

Answers for Self-check   1. 9   2. 24; 24; 4; 6   3. 7   4. 4   5. 8   6. 5   7. 3   8. 8   9. 7   10. 7   11. 3
12. 9   13. 6   14. 6   15. 9   16. 7   17. 8   18. 7   19. 7   20. 9

More practice, page 357, Set B

Self-check

1.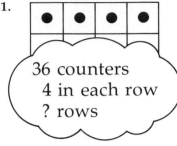

36 counters
4 in each row
? rows

2. Solve the fact family equations.

$4 \times 6 = n$

$6 \times 4 = n$

$24 \div 6 = n$

$24 \div 4 = n$

Find the quotients.

3. 42   6   ?

$42 \div 6 = n$

4. $36 \div 9 = n$

5. $56 \div 7 = n$

Divide.

6. $10 \div 2$ 7. $21 \div 7$ 8. $24 \div 3$ 9. $28 \div 4$ 10. $35 \div 5$

11. $18 \div 6$ 12. $63 \div 7$ 13. $48 \div 8$ 14. $54 \div 9$ 15. $72 \div 8$

16. $7\overline{)49}$ 17. $8\overline{)64}$ 18. $8\overline{)56}$ 19. $9\overline{)63}$ 20. $9\overline{)81}$

Answers for Self-check—page 99

Test

1.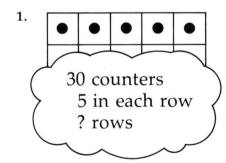

30 counters
5 in each row
? rows

2. Solve the fact family equations.

$5 \times 9 = n$

$9 \times 5 = n$

$45 \div 9 = n$

$45 \div 5 = n$

Find the quotients.

3. 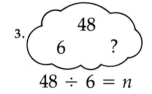 48   6   ?

$48 \div 6 = n$

4. $56 \div 8 = n$

5. $36 \div 4 = n$

Divide.

6. $27 \div 3$ 7. $32 \div 4$ 8. $40 \div 5$ 9. $30 \div 6$ 10. $36 \div 6$

11. $56 \div 8$ 12. $72 \div 8$ 13. $64 \div 8$ 14. $25 \div 5$ 15. $35 \div 7$

16. $6\overline{)42}$ 17. $7\overline{)49}$ 18. $7\overline{)56}$ 19. $9\overline{)81}$ 20. $5\overline{)45}$

Tangram Puzzle

Trace this square and the dotted lines. Then cut out the square and cut along the dotted lines. You should then have 5 triangles, 1 square, and 1 parallelogram.

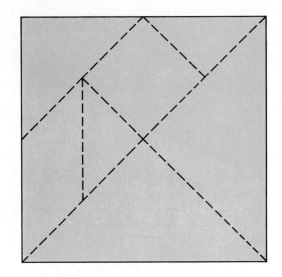

Can you put all 7 pieces together to make these figures?

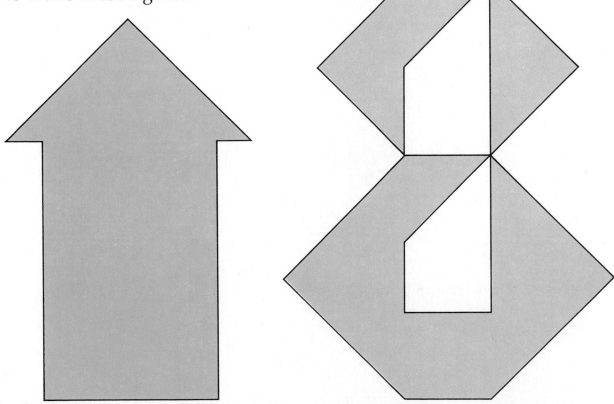

Using Your Skills

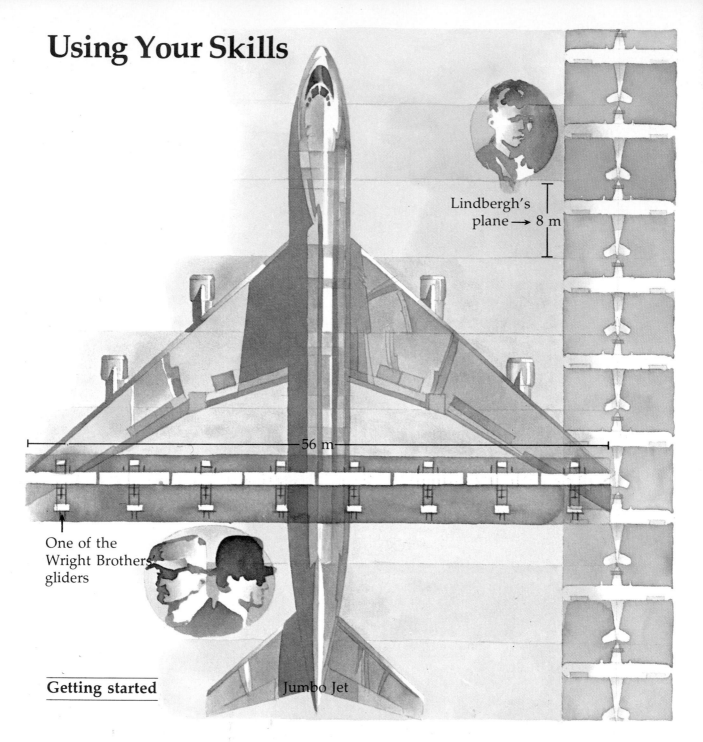

Lindbergh's
plane → 8 m

One of the
Wright Brothers
gliders

56 m

Jumbo Jet

Getting started

1. Lindbergh's plane is 8 m
   long. The jumbo jet is about how
   many times that long?

2. About how many meters
   long is the jumbo jet?

3. What other problems
   about these planes can
   you make up and solve?

Solving Problems

1. Read carefully to find the facts.

2. Look for the question.

3. Decide what to do. (+,−,×,÷).

4. Find the answer.

5. Read again.
   Does your answer make sense?

Try these.

1. Large plane: 374 people
   Smaller plane: 165 people
   How many more people
   in the large plane than
   in the smaller one?

2. First trip: 3840 km
   Second trip: 1280 km
   How many kilometers
   altogether?

3. 9 flights
   3 different crew members
   on each flight
   How many crew members
   in all?

4. 54 crew members
   Same number on each of
   9 planes
   How many on each plane?

Plant and animal records

1. Longest elephant: 9 m
   Longest jellyfish: 8 times
   as long as the elephant
   How long is the jellyfish?

2. Longest whale: 32 m
   Longest snake: whale's
   length divided by 4
   How long is the snake?

3. Long hen egg: 8 cm
   Longest fish egg: 32 cm
   The fish egg is how many
   times as long as the hen egg?

4. Tallest tree: 110 m
   Tallest fern: 24 m
   How much taller is the tree?

5. Fastest centipede: 6 km/h
   Fastest bat: 9 times as
   fast as the centipede
   How fast does the bat go?

6. Oldest turtle: 129 years
   Oldest elephant: 69 years
   How much older was the turtle?

7. Tallest sunflower: 5 m
   Tallest cactus: 15 m
   The cactus is how
   many times as tall as
   the sunflower?

8. Tallest bear: 3 m
   Tallest giraffe: 2 times
   as tall as the bear
   How tall is the giraffe?

9. Longest seaweed: 60 m
   Longest whale: 32 m
   How much longer is
   the seaweed?

10. Fastest penguin: 35 km/h
    Fastest sea lion: 41 km/h
    How much faster is the sea lion?

☆ 11. Tallest horse: 20 dm
      (decimeters)
      Shortest horse: 4 dm
      The tallest horse is how many
      times as tall as the shortest?

☆ 12. Heavy rabbit: 9 kg
      Heaviest kangaroo:
      2 kg less than 8 times
      as heavy as the rabbit
      How heavy is the kangaroo?

Coin collections

Some people collect coins because of their value. Not long ago, a special 1914D Lincoln head penny was sold for $45. Most people who collect coins also do it because they enjoy it. Many of them keep their coins in coin books.

1. In the coin book page below, how many pennies are in each row? How many rows are there? How many pennies in all?

2. In the page below, how many pennies are in each column? How many columns are there? How many pennies in all?

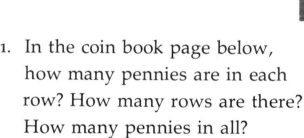

3. Sal collects pennies. He had 3 rows of Indian head pennies with 6 in each row. How many Indian head pennies did he have?

4. There are 3 pages in each of Della's coin books. She has 7 books. How many pages does she have altogether?

5. Alice has 36 dimes in one page of her coin book. There are 4 dimes in each row of the page. How many rows are there?

Liberty Dime

Indian Head Penny

Made in
Denver

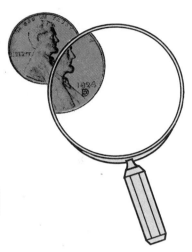

Large Cent—1851

6. Glen sold a 1924ᴅ penny
for $7.00. He sold a
1924s penny for $2.50.
How much more did he get
for the 1924ᴅ penny?

7. Robin had an 1851 Large
Cent that was worth $2.75.
She had a 1901 Indian head
penny that was worth $0.50.
How much were they worth
altogether?

8. Jim put 8 quarters in one coin
book. He put 4 times that
many dimes in another book.
How many dimes was that?

9. Helga had an 1891 Liberty
dime worth $2. How much
would 8 of these dimes be
worth?

10. One page of a coin book
has spaces for 7 rows of
dimes with 4 dimes in
each row. There are only
7 empty spaces. How many
dimes are already on the page?

⊛ **Factors and primes**

Here are the "product 12" equations. (There are 3 more if you change the order of the factors.)

$$
\begin{array}{ccc}
\text{F} & \text{F} & \text{P} \\
1 \times 12 & = & 12 \\
2 \times 6 & = & 12 \\
3 \times 4 & = & 12
\end{array}
$$

The factors of 12 are 1, 2, 3, 4, 6, and 12.

Copy and complete the equations.
Then list all the factors of the product.

1. $1 \times n = 18$

   $2 \times n = 18$

   $3 \times n = 18$

2. $1 \times n = 15$

   $3 \times n = 15$

3. $1 \times n = 13$

4. $1 \times n = 24$

   $2 \times n = 24$

   $3 \times n = 24$

   $4 \times n = 24$

5. $1 \times n = 32$

   $2 \times n = 32$

   $4 \times n = 32$

6. $1 \times n = 36$

   $2 \times n = 36$

   $3 \times n = 36$

   $4 \times n = 36$

   $6 \times n = 36$

7. $1 \times n = 16$

   $2 \times n = 16$

   $4 \times n = 16$

8. $1 \times n = 21$

   $3 \times n = 21$

9. $1 \times n = 30$

   $2 \times n = 30$

   $3 \times n = 30$

   $5 \times n = 30$

Solve the equations and list the factors of each product.

1. $1 \times n = 2$

2. $1 \times n = 3$

3. $1 \times n = 5$

Each product above has exactly 2 different factors.

> A number with exactly 2 different factors
> is called a **prime number.**

Solve these equations and list the factors.
Then tell whether the product is prime or not prime.

Examples:

$1 \times n = 5$

$1 \times 5 = 5$

Factors of 5: 1 and 5
5 is prime.

$1 \times n = 6$ $1 \times 6 = 6$

$2 \times n = 6$ $2 \times 3 = 6$

Factors of 6: 1, 2, 3, 6
6 is not prime.

4. $1 \times n = 7$

5. $1 \times n = 8$

$2 \times n = 8$

6. $1 \times n = 9$

$3 \times n = 9$

7. $1 \times n = 10$

$2 \times n = 10$

8. $1 \times n = 13$

9. $1 \times n = 14$

$2 \times n = 14$

10. $1 \times n = 19$

11. $1 \times n = 16$

$2 \times n = 16$

$4 \times n = 16$

12. $1 \times n = 23$

Flying—now and then

Would you like to be a pilot?
It is not easy to become a pilot.
You must study a great deal and
do many hours of practice flying.
You must be skillful in math and
science. Before you can fly one
of the planes that carry many
people, you must have flown
for at least 1500 hours.

Try these problems about pilots and planes.

1. Beginning pilot's school:
   9 weeks, 5 days a week
   How many days?

2. Flew 36 hours in 4 weeks.
   Flew the same number of
   hours each week.
   How many hours each week?

3. Engine control dials:
   5 dials for each engine
   4 engines
   How many dials?

4. Flight A: 8 hours
   Flight B: 6 hours
   Flight C: 4 hours
   Flight D: 7 hours
   How many hours?

5. Flying at 2750 m.
   Go up to 9300 m.
   How many meters higher is this?

6. 32 jet engines
   4 engines on each plane
   How many planes?

7. One of Earhart's early records:
A flight across the
United States in 17 hours
How many hours less than
a day is this?

8. First solo flight around
the world: 8 days
Jet flight around the
world: 2 days
How many times as long
did the first flight take?

9. Earhart's flight across
the Pacific Ocean in 1935:
1800 m high
Recent flight for a plane:
35 669 m high
How much higher was this?

10. Speed of the Wright Brothers'
flight in 1903: 56 km/h
Speed of a very fast bird:
178 km/h
How much faster is the bird?

Amelia Earhart set many new
records for flights over both
land and sea. Her bravery and
skill won her fame in her own
country and throughout the world.

In 1927 Charles Lindbergh
became the first person to fly
alone across the Atlantic Ocean.
This flight made him a hero
in many countries.

Answers for Self-check   1. 36   2. 9   3. 42   4. 6   5. 8   6. 21; 7   7. 1, 3, 7, 21   8. no

Self-check

Solve.

1. 9 jet airplanes
   4 engines per plane
   How many engines?

2. 54 cans of juice
   6 cans in each box
   How many boxes?

3. 6 weeks
   7 days per week
   How many days?

4. 48 pencils
   8 pencils in each box
   How many boxes?

5. 40 cookies
   5 cookies for each child
   How many children?

☆ 6. Solve these equations:

$$1 \times n = 21$$
$$3 \times n = 21$$

☆ 7. List all the factors of 21.

☆ 8. Is 21 a prime number?

Answers for Self-check—page 111

Test

Solve.

1. 24 marbles
   3 in each bag
   How many bags?

2. 4 boxes
   8 crayons per box
   How many crayons?

3. 36 players
   9 on each team
   How many teams?

4. Drove 367 km on Friday
   and 589 km on Saturday.
   How far altogether?

5. Had 42 pieces of candy.
   Gave 7 pieces away.
   How many pieces left?

☆ 6. Solve these equations:

$$1 \times n = 14$$
$$2 \times n = 14$$

☆ 7. List all the factors of 14.

☆ 8. Is 14 a prime number?

A Math Machine

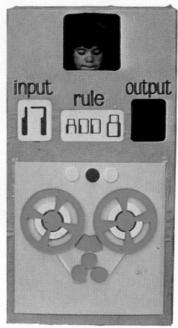

Find the output numbers.

	input	rule	output
1.	8	Multiply by 5	?
2.	24	Divide by 3	?
3.	6	Double it and add 1	?

Make up some rules of your own.
Give the input and output for each rule.

Length and Perimeter

Julio was surprised to find that Anna was 1 m tall.

Someone 1 m (meter) tall is 100 cm (centimeters) tall.

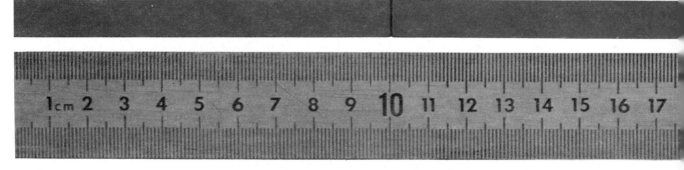

1. How many white rods in a line are needed for 1 m?

2. How many orange rods in a line are needed for 1 m?

1. What things in your classroom are about 1 m long?

2. Try to find something about 2 m long.

3. What things are about 1 m high?

4. Try to find something that is more than 5 m long.

5. Find some things that are less than 1 m long.
   Give their length in centimeters.

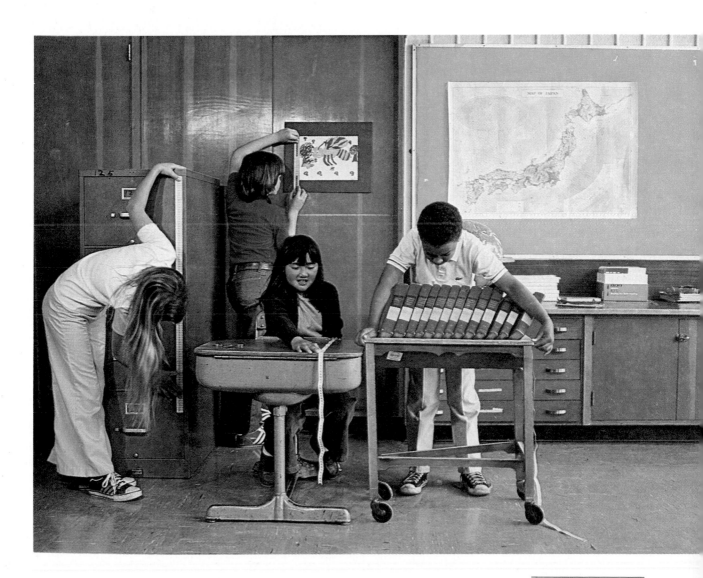

Sally and Ted worked together on a science project. The problems tell about some of the things they did.

Guess first. Then measure.

1. Sally and Ted cut a 12-cm board for the planter box. At which mark did they cut?

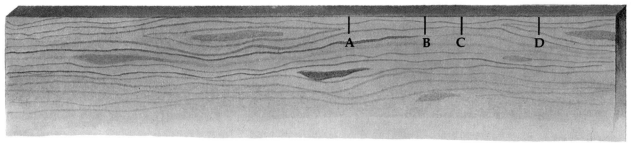

2. They used 3-cm nails to put the box together. Which one did they use?

A   B   C   D

3. They made a 6-cm stick to measure how deep the soil is. Which mark did they cut along?

4. They made 3-cm by 5-cm signs for the box. Which of these did they use?

Beans

Science
Project
How fast do
they grow?
Sally and Ted

Guess the height of each plant.
Then measure it to the nearest centimeter.

1.

2.

3.

4.

5.

6.

7.

8.

9.

Measuring with centimeters and meters

Carl found that a 1-m tape would wrap around his waist almost two times.

Marie found that the top of a meter stick came up to the under side of her arm.

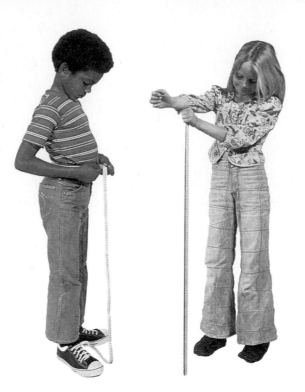

First estimate. Then measure.

1. Can you step 1 m?

4. Can you reach 2 m high?

2. What is your height in centimeters?
   Are you more or less than 1 m tall?

3. What is the length of your shoe?

5. What is your head size? (Use a string or a centimeter tape.)

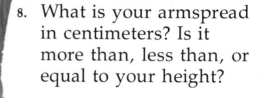

6. What is your neck size?

7. What size watch band would you wear?

8. What is your armspread in centimeters? Is it more than, less than, or equal to your height?

9. What is your waist size? (Use a string or a centimeter tape.)

☆ Activities for outside the classroom

10. How long does it take you to walk 100 meters?

Suppose a brick has a mass 8 kg more than half a brick. What is the mass of the brick?

11. How far can you throw a baseball?

Meters and kilometers

1 km (kilometer) is
1000 m (meters).

Copy and finish the tables.

1. You might walk 1 km in
   10 minutes.

   How far in 1 hour?

km	1	2	3			
minutes	10	20	30			60

2. You might ride a bike
   3 km in 10 minutes.

   How far in 1 hour?

km	3	6	9			
minutes	10	20	30			60

3. You might drive a car
   15 km in 10 minutes.

   How far in 1 hour?

km	15	30	45			
minutes	10	20	30			60

Use your tables from page 120 to answer these questions.

1. A 20-minute walk to the ranger station

   How far?

2. A 4-km walk

   How long will it take?

3. A 60-minute bike ride

   How far?

4. An 18-km bike path

   How long will the ride take?

5. 50 minutes to drive around the park

   How far?

6. 75 km to the park

   How long will the drive take?

Find the perimeter

Sara walks her dog on the sidewalk around the school every day.
How far do they walk?

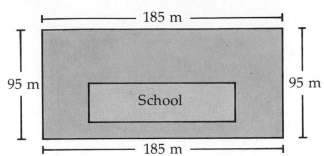

Finding the answer

Lengths of sides	→	Add	→	The distance around (perimeter)

95, 185,
95, 185

$$\begin{array}{r} \overset{3\,2}{95} \\ 185 \\ 95 \\ + 185 \\ \hline 560 \end{array}$$

560 m

Sara and her dog walk 560 m.

Find the perimeter.

1. How many centimeters of blue crepe paper will Sara need to make the border for this bulletin board?

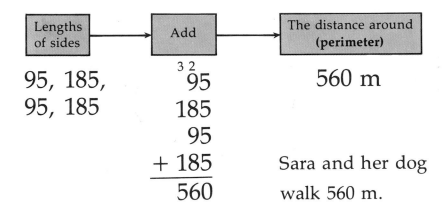

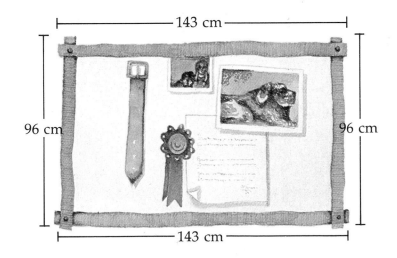

2. How many centimeters of crepe paper will she need for the picture?

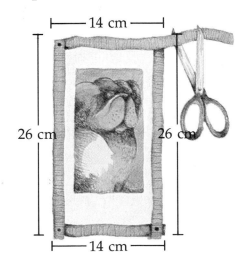

How many meters of fence are needed for each plan?

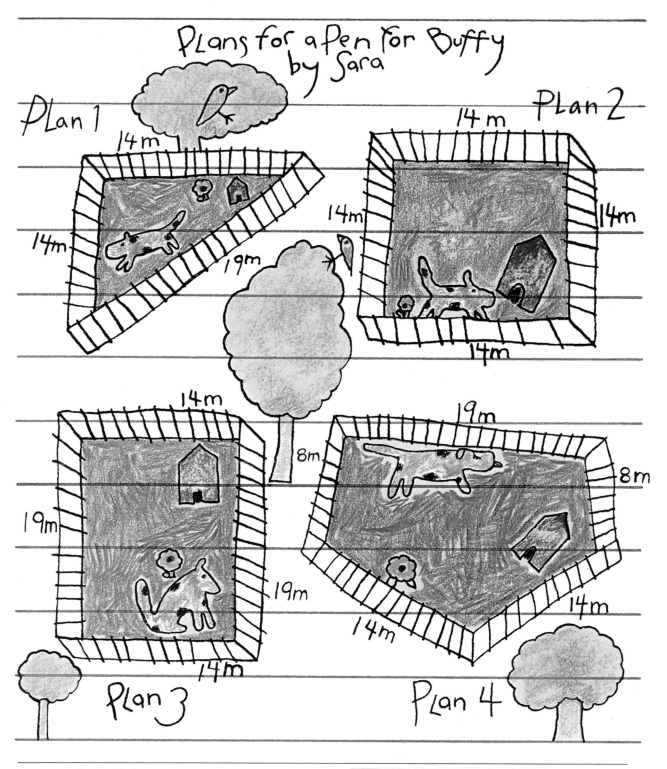

Plans for a Pen for Buffy
by Sara

Plan 1

14 m

14m

19m

Plan 2

14 m

14m

14m

14m

Plan 3

14 m

19m

19m

14m

8m

Plan 4

19m

8m

14m

14m

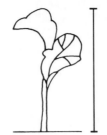

1. How long?

2. How high (to the nearest centimeter)?

3. How long is the segment below (to the nearest centimeter)?

4. Copy and finish the table.

km	30	60	90	▦	▦	▦
minutes	10	20	30	▦	▦	60

5. Find the perimeter.

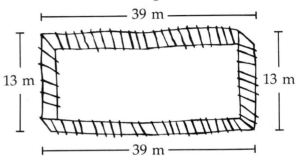

13 m   39 m   13 m   39 m

Answers for Self-check—page 123

Test

1. How long?

2. How high (to the nearest centimeter)?

3. How long is the segment below (to the nearest centimeter)?

4. Copy and finish the table.

km	12	24	36	▦	▦	▦
minutes	10	20	30	▦	▦	60

5. Find the perimeter.

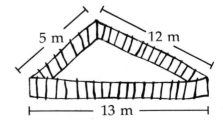

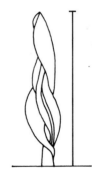

5 m   12 m   13 m

Experiments with a Celsius Thermometer

Take a guess!
Then check your guess.

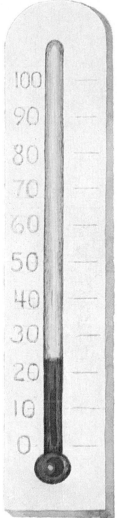

1. Hold the thermometer in a glass of cold water for 3 minutes.

   _?_ °C

3. Lay it on your desk for 3 minutes.

   _?_ °C

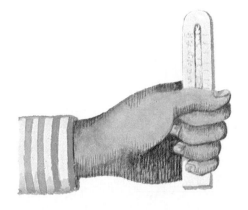

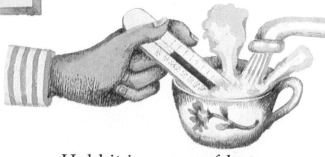

2. Wrap your hand around it for 3 minutes.

   _?_ °C

4. Hold it in a cup of hot faucet water for 3 minutes.

   _?_ °C

Level 18 Review

Multiply.

1. $\begin{array}{r} 9 \\ \times 2 \\ \hline \end{array}$
2. $\begin{array}{r} 3 \\ \times 4 \\ \hline \end{array}$
3. $\begin{array}{r} 6 \\ \times 3 \\ \hline \end{array}$
4. $\begin{array}{r} 5 \\ \times 1 \\ \hline \end{array}$
5. $\begin{array}{r} 3 \\ \times 2 \\ \hline \end{array}$
6. $\begin{array}{r} 4 \\ \times 4 \\ \hline \end{array}$
7. $\begin{array}{r} 5 \\ \times 3 \\ \hline \end{array}$

8. $\begin{array}{r} 4 \\ \times 5 \\ \hline \end{array}$
9. $\begin{array}{r} 8 \\ \times 3 \\ \hline \end{array}$
10. $\begin{array}{r} 6 \\ \times 2 \\ \hline \end{array}$
11. $\begin{array}{r} 9 \\ \times 0 \\ \hline \end{array}$
12. $\begin{array}{r} 9 \\ \times 3 \\ \hline \end{array}$
13. $\begin{array}{r} 6 \\ \times 4 \\ \hline \end{array}$
14. $\begin{array}{r} 3 \\ \times 3 \\ \hline \end{array}$

15. $\begin{array}{r} 3 \\ \times 7 \\ \hline \end{array}$
16. $\begin{array}{r} 7 \\ \times 5 \\ \hline \end{array}$
17. $\begin{array}{r} 6 \\ \times 6 \\ \hline \end{array}$
18. $\begin{array}{r} 4 \\ \times 7 \\ \hline \end{array}$
19. $\begin{array}{r} 5 \\ \times 8 \\ \hline \end{array}$
20. $\begin{array}{r} 8 \\ \times 6 \\ \hline \end{array}$
21. $\begin{array}{r} 9 \\ \times 5 \\ \hline \end{array}$

22. 9×4
23. 8×7
24. 9×8
25. 7×7
26. 6×9

Divide.

27. $8 \div 2$
28. $10 \div 5$
29. $21 \div 7$
30. $42 \div 6$
31. $30 \div 5$

32. $0 \div 7$
33. $25 \div 5$
34. $6 \div 1$
35. $18 \div 2$
36. $63 \div 9$

37. $8\overline{)40}$
38. $9\overline{)81}$
39. $7\overline{)28}$
40. $8\overline{)64}$
41. $7\overline{)56}$

Solve.

42. $5 \times 0 = n$
43. $7 \times 9 = n$
44. $27 \div 3 = n$
45. $48 \div 6 = n$

Special Products and Quotients
Multiplying by 1-Digit Factors
Multiplying by 2-Digit Factors
Using Your Skills
Graphs

Special Products and Quotients

Getting started

Give the number of units for each group.

4 tens   4 hundreds   4 thousands

Solve the equations.

1. 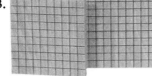 $2 \times 10 = n$

2.  $5 \times 10 = n$

3. 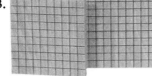 $2 \times 100 = n$

4.  $5 \times 100 = n$

5. 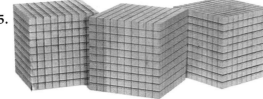 $3 \times 1000 = n$

6. 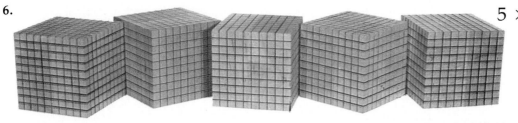 $5 \times 1000 = n$

Multiplying by 10 and 100

Picnic:
10 hot dog buns per package
24 packages
How many hot dog buns?

100 paper plates per package
12 packages
How many paper plates?

Finding the answer

To multiply a number by 10, write that number followed by 1 zero.

$$24 \times 10 = 240$$

There are 240 hot dog buns.

To multiply a number by 100, write that number followed by 2 zeros.

$$12 \times 100 = 1200$$

There are 1200 paper plates.

Other examples

$8 \times 10 = 80$
$30 \times 10 = 300$
$327 \times 10 = 3270$
$2449 \times 10 = 24\,490$

$8 \times 100 = 800$
$30 \times 100 = 3000$
$327 \times 100 = 32\,700$

Find the products.

1. 5×10
2. 6×10
3. 9×10
4. 3×10

5. 12×10
6. 37×10
7. 56×10
8. 246×10

9. 8×100
10. 7×100
11. 26×100
12. 15×100

13. 42×100
14. 246×10
15. 598×10
16. 329×10

Multiply.

1. 9×10　　2. 9×100　　3. 10×10　　4. 10×100

5. 99×10　　6. 100×10　　7. 5×100　　8. 100×6

9. 999×10　　10. 10×87　　11. 32×100　　12. 100×23

13. 10×346　　14. 100×29　　15. 5972×10　　16. 10×957

17. 30×10　　18. 10×400　　19. 100×7　　20. 90×100

21. 563×100　　22. 100×857　　23. 10×98　　24. 389×100

25. 100×340　　26. 560×10　　27. 10×780　　28. 1760×10

Solve the equations.

29. $8 \times n = 8$　　30. $8 \times n = 800$　　31. $23 \times n = 2300$

32. $8 \times n = 80$　　☆ 33. $9 \times n = 9000$　　☆ 34. $15 \times n = 15\,000$

35. 100 napkins
in a package
15 packages
How many napkins?

36. 25 sandwiches
10 ants on each sandwich
How many ants?

To multiply by me
Is as easy as can be.
That it's hard, I'll not pretend.
Just put zero on the end.

Who am I?

More practice, page 358, Set A

The Pyramid of the Sun, in Mexico, is about 60 m high. Mica Dam, in Canada, is 4 times that high. About how high is the dam?

Finding the answer

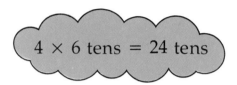

$$4 \times 60 = 24 \times 10$$
$$4 \times 60 = \mathbf{240}$$

The dam is about 240 m high.

Other examples	$8 \times 20 = 160$	$6 \times 400 = 2400$
	$5 \times 40 = 200$	$5 \times 600 = 3000$

Solve the equations.

1. $5 \times 30 = n$ 2. $8 \times 40 = n$ 3. $7 \times 60 = n$ 4. $9 \times 60 = n$

5. $8 \times 30 = n$ 6. $5 \times 60 = n$ 7. $3 \times 400 = n$ 8. $4 \times 700 = n$

9. $9 \times 300 = n$ 10. $6 \times 800 = n$ 11. $4 \times 900 = n$ 12. $7 \times 200 = n$

13. $8 \times 200 = n$ 14. $9 \times 70 = n$ 15. $8 \times 700 = n$ 16. $5 \times 800 = n$

17. $7 \times 500 = n$ 18. $8 \times 50 = n$ 19. $6 \times 600 = n$ 20. $9 \times 600 = n$

Multiply.

1. 3×6
2. 3×60
3. 4×5
4. 4×50

5. 5×3
6. 5×30
7. 5×300
8. 6×4

9. 6×40
10. 5×7
11. 5×70
12. 5×700

13. 3×8
14. 3×80
15. 3×800
16. 7×8

17. 7×80
18. 9×3
19. 9×30
20. 9×300

21. 4×30
22. 60×5
23. 7×70
24. 80×6

25. 50×9
26. 3×70
27. 60×6
28. 9×90

29. 4×200
30. 600×6
31. 8×800
32. 700×9

33. 600×7
34. 5×500
35. 7×400
36. 800×5

Solve.

☆ 37. $9000 \times 7 = n$
☆ 38. $630 = n \times 90$
☆ 39. $n \times 4000 = 36\,000$

☆ 40. $6 \times 4000 = n$
☆ 41. $6 \times n = 48\,000$
☆ 42. $54\,000 = n \times 6$

43. Ribbon Falls, in California, is about 8 times as high as the Pyramid of the Sun. About how high is Ribbon Falls?

Round each top number to the nearest hundred and find each product. Then estimate the sum of the products.

489	709	894
$\times 6$	$\times 7$	$\times 8$

Find the products above. Then find their sum. How far off was your estimate?

44. The Empire State Building is about 5 times as high as the Pyramid. How high is the Empire State Building?

More practice, page 358, Set B

Finding products like 60 × 20

Rainfall in Nevada: 20 cm a year
Rainfall on one of the Hawaiian islands:
60 times that much
This is how many centimeters a year?

Finding the answer

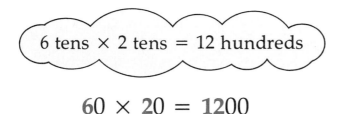

$$6 \text{ tens} \times 2 \text{ tens} = 12 \text{ hundreds}$$

$$60 \times 20 = 1200$$

This is 1200 cm a year.

Other examples

$30 \times 70 = 2100$ $80 \times 50 = 4000$

Solve the equations.

1. $80 \times 30 = n$
2. $90 \times 60 = n$
3. $40 \times 70 = n$

4. $60 \times 70 = n$
5. $30 \times 50 = n$
6. $40 \times 50 = n$

7. $90 \times 40 = n$
8. $20 \times 50 = n$
9. $30 \times 60 = n$

10. $70 \times 80 = n$
11. $90 \times 50 = n$
12. $40 \times 80 = n$

13. $30 \times 20 - n$
14. $70 \times 30 = n$
15. $80 \times 60 = n$

16. $70 \times 70 = n$
17. $50 \times 60 = n$
18. $90 \times 80 = n$

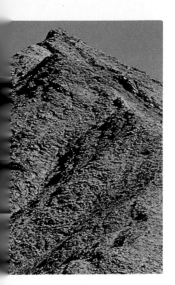

Multiply.

1. 60×20
2. 30×30
3. 30×20

4. 20×40
5. 10×60
6. 30×50

7. 70×20
8. 50×50
9. 60×30

10. 90×20
11. 90×80
12. 80×70

13. 80×40
14. 90×30
15. 70×40

16. 90×70
17. 60×40
18. 40×90

19. 60×80
20. 40×40
21. 60×90

22. 90×90
23. 50×60
24. 70×70

Example:
$60 \times 300 = 18\,000$

☆ 25. 30×800
☆ 26. 20×700

☆ 27. 40×400
☆ 28. 50×800
☆ 29. 60×900

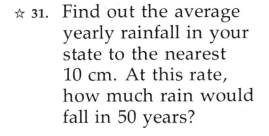

30. Near-record rainfall:
30 mm in one minute
At this rate, how much
rain in 60 minutes?

☆ 31. Find out the average
yearly rainfall in your
state to the nearest
10 cm. At this rate,
how much rain would
fall in 50 years?

Guess how many pennies
you need to make a
stack of pennies as
high as a penny standing
on its edge.

Check your guess. How close was it?

More practice, page 359, Set A

Estimating products

Tree farm:
38 young trees in a row
4 rows
About how many trees is this?

Finding the answer

about 40

4×38
$4 \times 40 = 160$

This is about 160 trees.

Other examples

6×76	39×23	7×498
$6 \times 80 = 480$	$40 \times 20 = 800$	$7 \times 500 = 3500$

Round the greater factor to the nearest ten and find the product.

1. 8×52 2. 5×98 3. 4×49 4. 7×72 5. 5×39

6. 4×28 7. 7×76 8. 2×27 9. 8×56 10. 6×78

11. 9×54 12. 6×43 13. 9×25 14. 8×23 15. 5×88

16. 3×92 17. 7×95 18. 6×47 19. 5×19 20. 4×32

Round both factors to the nearest ten
and find the product.

1. 48×61 2. 29×82 3. 91×47 4. 33×68 5. 74×36

6. 22×19 7. 41×93 8. 51×49 9. 65×79 10. 34×28

11. 47×68 12. 42×53 13. 28×58 14. 17×82 15. 64×89

Round the greater factor to the nearest
hundred and find the product.

16. 8×695 17. 3×289 18. 4×375 19. 2×513 20. 7×499

21. 6×321 22. 873×5 23. 298×9 24. 8×307 25. 3×525

26. 419×5 27. 7×278 28. 576×8 29. 190×9 30. 6×483

31. Planted 8 rows of new trees.
Put 96 trees in each row.
About how many trees in all?

☆ 32. Fill a paper cup with acorns
or other nuts. Guess how many
are in the cup. Use this guess
to estimate how many would be
in 8 cups. Then count the acorns
in the cup and multiply by 8.
How close was your estimate?

I'm quite close to one hundred three,
Closer still to ninety-eight.
Yet for both numbers I am used
When you want to estimate.

Who am I?

More practice, page 359, Set B

Finding special quotients

280 cars go through the
car wash in 7 hours.
How many cars go
through each hour?

Finding the answer

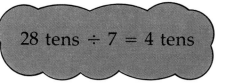

28 tens ÷ 7 = 4 tens

$$280 \div 7 = 40$$

40 cars go through each hour.

Other examples

$400 \div 5 = 80$ $470 \div 10 = 47$ $3500 \div 7 = 500$

Find the quotients.

1. $270 \div 3$	2. $320 \div 4$	3. $350 \div 7$	4. $450 \div 5$
5. $450 \div 10$	6. $420 \div 6$	7. $180 \div 3$	8. $560 \div 10$
9. $240 \div 3$	10. $180 \div 10$	11. $270 \div 9$	12. $810 \div 9$
13. $360 \div 4$	14. $630 \div 9$	15. $640 \div 8$	16. $720 \div 8$
17. $480 \div 6$	18. $210 \div 3$	19. $540 \div 6$	20. $490 \div 7$
21. $180 \div 2$	22. $720 \div 9$	23. $400 \div 5$	24. $360 \div 6$

Divide.

1. $4500 \div 9$ 2. $2100 \div 7$

3. $1600 \div 8$ 4. $1400 \div 7$

5. $1800 \div 3$ 6. $1200 \div 4$

7. $2700 \div 9$ 8. $2800 \div 4$

9. $3200 \div 8$ 10. $3600 \div 9$

11. $4000 \div 5$ 12. $4200 \div 6$

13. $4800 \div 8$ 14. $5400 \div 6$

15. $5600 \div 7$ 16. $6300 \div 9$

17. $7200 \div 8$ 18. $800 \div 2$

19. $1500 \div 3$ 20. $1600 \div 4$

Example:

$3600 \div 60 = 60$ ☆ 21. $5600 \div 80$ ☆ 22. $360 \div 90$ ☆ 23. $560 \div 70$

24. 420 cans of car wax
10 cans in each case
How many cases?

25. Need 5 cloths to polish a car.
Used 300 cloths.
How many cars?

The age of each "number person"
can be found by adding
the person's numbers.
How old is each?

Maude   Biff

More practice, page 360, Set A

Find the products.

1. 6×10 2. 56×10 3. 324×10 4. 5×100

5. 38×100 6. 10×54 7. 100×37 8. 8×60

9. 40×8 10. 300×7 11. 20×60 12. 80×70

Find the quotients.

13. $280 \div 4$ 14. $360 \div 9$ 15. $320 \div 10$ 16. $5600 \div 7$

Round the greater factor to nearest ten and find the product.

17. 59×7 18. 42×9 19. 36×8 20. 598×4

Answers for Self-check—page 139

Test

Find the products.

1. 8×10 2. 86×10 3. 24×100 4. 100×9

5. 6×70 6. 7×40 7. 800×6 8. 90×3

9. 40×20 10. 10×246 11. 60×30 12. 45×100

Find the quotients.

13. $480 \div 6$ 14. $120 \div 4$ 15. $540 \div 10$ 16. $7200 \div 8$

Round the greater factor to the nearest ten and find the product.

17. 89×4 18. 52×6 19. 75×3 20. 203×9

Estimation Activities

First make a guess. Then check your guess.
How close were your guesses?

1. How long a string
    will fit exactly
    around your waist?

2. Which is greater,
    your arm span or
    your height?

3. How many steps
    will it take you
    to walk from one
    end of your classroom
    to the other?

4. How many pennies
    does it take to cover
    a dollar bill?

5. What is the total mass
    of 5 of your math books?

6. How many pages are
    in your teacher's
    dictionary?

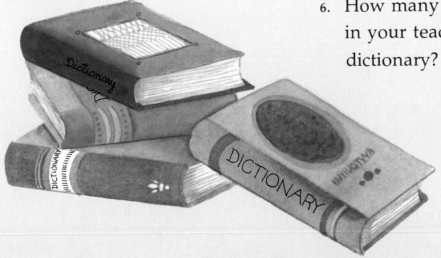

Multiplying by 1-Digit Factors

Make sets of cards like these.
Make a cube with the numerals
4 through 9 on its faces.

Mix the cards in each set and place them face down. Then
pick a card from each pile and roll the number cube. Multiply
each card number by the cube number. Add the two products.

Play the game with a friend. The highest total wins.

Give the total for each of these.

1.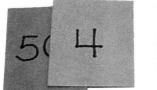

2.

3.

4.

5.

6.

7. Suppose you also picked a card from this set.

What would the total be for these?

Multiplying: one 2-digit factor

Anita worked at the animal care center 23 days in June.
She worked 8 hours each day.
How many hours did she work that month?

Finding the answer

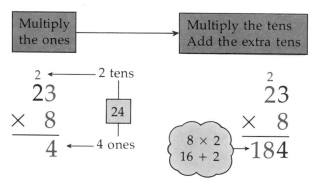

Anita worked 184 hours that month.

Other examples

$$\begin{array}{r} 32 \\ \times\ 4 \\ \hline 128 \end{array} \qquad \begin{array}{r} \scriptstyle 1 \\ 46 \\ \times\ 3 \\ \hline 138 \end{array} \qquad \begin{array}{r} \scriptstyle 4 \\ 15 \\ \times\ 8 \\ \hline 120 \end{array}$$

Find the products.

1. $\begin{array}{r} 23 \\ \times\ 2 \\ \hline \end{array}$
2. $\begin{array}{r} 31 \\ \times\ 5 \\ \hline \end{array}$
3. $\begin{array}{r} 52 \\ \times\ 4 \\ \hline \end{array}$
4. $\begin{array}{r} 43 \\ \times\ 3 \\ \hline \end{array}$
5. $\begin{array}{r} 56 \\ \times\ 1 \\ \hline \end{array}$
6. $\begin{array}{r} 25 \\ \times\ 3 \\ \hline \end{array}$

7. $\begin{array}{r} 17 \\ \times\ 4 \\ \hline \end{array}$
8. $\begin{array}{r} 49 \\ \times\ 2 \\ \hline \end{array}$
9. $\begin{array}{r} 37 \\ \times\ 3 \\ \hline \end{array}$
10. $\begin{array}{r} 36 \\ \times\ 7 \\ \hline \end{array}$
11. $\begin{array}{r} 43 \\ \times\ 8 \\ \hline \end{array}$
12. $\begin{array}{r} 74 \\ \times\ 8 \\ \hline \end{array}$

13. $\begin{array}{r} 54 \\ \times\ 7 \\ \hline \end{array}$
14. $\begin{array}{r} 76 \\ \times\ 5 \\ \hline \end{array}$
15. $\begin{array}{r} 94 \\ \times\ 6 \\ \hline \end{array}$
16. $\begin{array}{r} 37 \\ \times\ 9 \\ \hline \end{array}$
17. $\begin{array}{r} 48 \\ \times\ 7 \\ \hline \end{array}$
18. $\begin{array}{r} 79 \\ \times\ 8 \\ \hline \end{array}$

Multiply.

1. 37 × 9	2. 65 × 8	3. 39 × 6	4. 76 × 5	5. 94 × 6	6. 37 × 7
7. 34 × 3	8. 37 × 6	9. 54 × 5	10. 73 × 6	11. 32 × 3	12. 56 × 4
13. 79 × 5	14. 67 × 6	15. 84 × 7	16. 93 × 8	17. 46 × 9	18. 25 × 7
19. 48 × 7	20. 79 × 8	21. 58 × 4	22. 84 × 6	23. 78 × 8	24. 69 × 5
25. 97 × 7	26. 86 × 8	27. 57 × 9	28. 46 × 8	29. 92 × 5	30. 77 × 7

31. July work record:
Days at work—22
Hours each day—8
How many hours
for the month?

☆ 32. Choose a month and make a record of your hours in school.

School record for (Month)	
Days in school	?
Hours each day	?
Total hours	?

Draw a box around 9 numbers on a calendar.

S	M	T	W	TH	F	S
			1	2	3	4
5	6	7	8	9	10	11
12	13	14	15	16	17	18
19	20	21	22	23	24	25
26	27	28	29	30	31	

1. Add the numbers in the box.

2. Add 8 to the smallest number in the box.
Multiply this sum by 9.

Are the answers for 1 and 2 the same?
Do you think this will be true
for any 9 numbers you choose?

More practice, page 360, Set B

Multiplying: one 3-digit factor

Each car on a train has
162 seats. How many seats
would 7 cars have?

Finding the answer

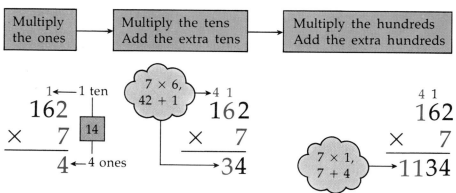

| Multiply the ones | → | Multiply the tens Add the extra tens | → | Multiply the hundreds Add the extra hundreds |

$1 \leftarrow 1$ ten

$$\begin{array}{r} 162 \\ \times\ \ 7 \\ \hline 4 \end{array}$$ 14 $\leftarrow$ 4 ones

$7 \times 6, 42 + 1 \rightarrow$ 4 1

$$\begin{array}{r} 162 \\ \times\ \ 7 \\ \hline 34 \end{array}$$

4 1

$7 \times 1, 7 + 4 \rightarrow$

$$\begin{array}{r} 162 \\ \times\ \ 7 \\ \hline 1134 \end{array}$$

7 cars would have 1134 seats.

Other examples

$$\begin{array}{r} 632 \\ \times\ \ \ 3 \\ \hline 1896 \end{array}$$
$$\begin{array}{r} {\scriptstyle 1} \\ 438 \\ \times\ \ \ 2 \\ \hline 876 \end{array}$$
$$\begin{array}{r} {\scriptstyle 3} \\ 982 \\ \times\ \ \ 4 \\ \hline 3928 \end{array}$$
$$\begin{array}{r} {\scriptstyle 4\ 3} \\ 796 \\ \times\ \ \ 5 \\ \hline 3980 \end{array}$$

Find the products.

1. $\begin{array}{r} 423 \\ \times\ \ 2 \\ \hline \end{array}$
2. $\begin{array}{r} 632 \\ \times\ \ 3 \\ \hline \end{array}$
3. $\begin{array}{r} 912 \\ \times\ \ 4 \\ \hline \end{array}$
4. $\begin{array}{r} 424 \\ \times\ \ 3 \\ \hline \end{array}$
5. $\begin{array}{r} 848 \\ \times\ \ 2 \\ \hline \end{array}$

6. $\begin{array}{r} 436 \\ \times\ \ 2 \\ \hline \end{array}$
7. $\begin{array}{r} 315 \\ \times\ \ 3 \\ \hline \end{array}$
8. $\begin{array}{r} 384 \\ \times\ \ 4 \\ \hline \end{array}$
9. $\begin{array}{r} 348 \\ \times\ \ 6 \\ \hline \end{array}$
10. $\begin{array}{r} 227 \\ \times\ \ 8 \\ \hline \end{array}$

Multiply.

1.	346 × 2	2.	278 × 3	3.	539 × 4	4.	687 × 5
5.	349 × 6	6.	563 × 9	7.	428 × 7	8.	967 × 8
9.	854 × 6	10.	323 × 4	11.	455 × 3	12.	638 × 5
13.	747 × 7	14.	923 × 9	15.	865 × 2	16.	725 × 3

Find the products. Multiply the shaded numbers first.

Example:

24 × 6 × 3

144 × 3 = 432

17. 47 × 5 × 3   18. 56 × 4 × 2   19. 25 × 7 × 4

20. 76 × 4 × 6   21. 36 × 8 × 4   22. 43 × 7 × 6

23. 86 × 5 × 3   24. 97 × 7 × 6   25. 8 × 56 × 9

26. A train is traveling
135 km/h. How far will
it travel in 9 hours?

27. One of the world's
   fastest trains: 199 km/h
Jet airliner: 5 times
   as fast as the train
How fast does the jet go?

Use graph paper and cut out a 5-square
figure like this.

The squares must touch each other along
a complete side. There are 12 different
5-square figures.

How many 5-square figures of different
shapes can you find and cut out?

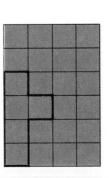

Multiplying with money

Goldfish cost $1.20 each.
Lou bought 6 of them.
How much did they cost?

Finding the answer

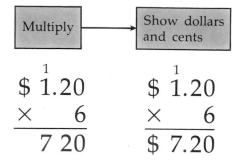

$$\begin{array}{r} \overset{1}{\$\ 1.20} \\ \times\quad 6 \\ \hline 7\ 20 \end{array} \qquad \begin{array}{r} \overset{1}{\$\ 1.20} \\ \times\quad 6 \\ \hline \$\ 7.20 \end{array}$$

They cost $7.20.

Other examples

$$\begin{array}{r} \overset{3}{\$\ 8.04} \\ \times\quad 9 \\ \hline \$72.36 \end{array} \qquad \begin{array}{r} \overset{2\ 3}{\$\ 4.35} \\ \times\quad 7 \\ \hline \$30.45 \end{array}$$

Find the products.

1. $ 4.60
   × 3

2. $ 3.80
   × 4

3. $ 5.20
   × 6

4. $ 3.50
   × 5

5. $ 6.90
   × 7

6. $ 6.08
   × 9

7. $ 3.07
   × 8

8. $ 5.05
   × 2

9. $ 6.04
   × 3

10. $ 7.06
    × 5

11. $ 4.36
    × 8

12. $ 2.98
    × 7

13. $ 5.66
    × 4

14. $ 8.87
    × 6

15. $ 9.95
    × 3

Multiply.

1. $ 4.67
   × 5

2. $ 9.82
   × 7

3. $ 6.01
   × 9

4. $ 3.42
   × 8

5. $ 6.50
   × 6

6. $ 2.99
   × 4

7. $ 4.63
   × 3

8. $ 9.45
   × 7

9. $ 4.25
   × 6

10. $ 7.30
    × 5

11. $ 2.07
    × 8

12. $ 4.76
    × 9

13. $ 5.35
    × 3

14. $ 8.95
    × 2

15. $ 9.57
    × 5

Estimate the products. (Round to the nearest dollar and multiply.)

Example:
6 × $3.20
6 × $3 = $18

16. 3 × $4.85

17. 7 × $2.19

18. 5 × $4.33

19. 4 × $2.98

20. 5 × $7.89

21. 6 × $8.05

22. 9 × $3.27

23. 2 × $9.19

24. 8 × $4.95

25. 3 × $7.75

26. 6 × $8.98

27. 8 × $7.15

28. 4 × $6.35

29. Erin bought 4 swordtail fish for $1.75 each. How much for all 4?

☆ 30. Find the price of something you would like to buy. How much would you have to pay for 3 of them?

Find each product. How are they all alike?

A   1089
     ×   9

B   10 989
     ×   9

C   109 989
     ×   9

D   1 099 989
     ×   9

Can you find another product like these?

Answers for Self-check 1. 69 2. 86 3. 224 4. 228 5. 370 6. 1848 7. 7047 8. 7120 9. 3630
10. 2268 11. $13.60 12. $14.10 13. $10.45 14. $11.36 15. $23.70 16. 1152 17. 3132 18. 1242

More practice, page 361

Multiply.

1. 23 × 3	2. 43 × 2	3. 56 × 4	4. 38 × 6	5. 74 × 5
6. 264 × 7	7. 783 × 9	8. 890 × 8	9. 605 × 6	10. 567 × 4
11. $ 3.40 × 4	12. $ 4.70 × 3	13. $ 2.09 × 5	14. $ 5.68 × 2	15. $ 3.95 × 6

Find the products. Multiply the shaded numbers first.

16. $9 \times 32 \times 4$ 17. $6 \times 87 \times 6$ 18. $46 \times 3 \times 9$

Answers for Self-check—page 149

Multiply.

1. 34 × 2	2. 52 × 3	3. 73 × 5	4. 68 × 6	5. 86 × 3
6. 972 × 9	7. 640 × 7	8. 396 × 8	9. 403 × 6	10. 429 × 5
11. $ 4.20 × 5	12. $ 5.60 × 3	13. $ 3.08 × 4	14. $ 4.75 × 3	15. $ 6.98 × 7

Find the products. Multiply the shaded numbers first.

16. $8 \times 47 \times 4$ 17. $7 \times 63 \times 8$ 18. $59 \times 4 \times 9$

Geometric Designs

Make and color some geometric designs.

Design 1 Draw a circle.

Draw 6 arcs as in the pictures below.

 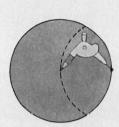  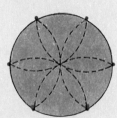

Design 2 Draw a square.

Draw 4 arcs as shown below.

 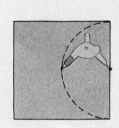 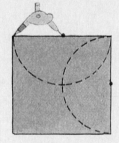 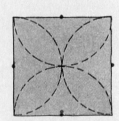

Design 3 Draw a circle.

Make 6 marks on your circle, as in Design 1.

Connect the points.

 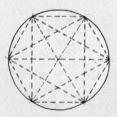

Design 4 Make up some interesting designs of your own.

Multiplying by 2-Digit Factors

Choose any 2 cards.
To find your score, first
place the cards like this:

20	3
70	4

Then cover pairs of numbers as shown. Multiply
the pairs of numbers that are not covered.

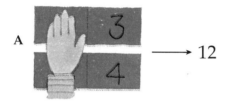 A $\longrightarrow$ 12

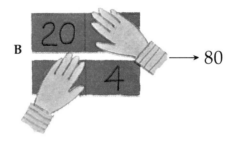 B $\longrightarrow$ 80

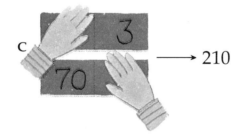 C $\longrightarrow$ 210

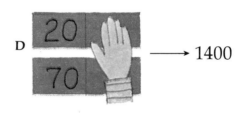 D $\longrightarrow$ 1400

Now add.

$$
\begin{array}{r}
12 \\
80 \\
210 \\
+\ 1400 \\
\hline
\end{array}
$$

Score: 1702

What would be your
score for these cards?

20	7
60	8

Copy the problem.
Give the missing numbers.

Example: Answer:

```
        43                          43          1.        57
      × 26                        × 26                  × 32
   ▦▦   6 × 3                      18              ▦▦    2 × 7
  ▦▦▦   6 × 40                    240            ▦▦▦    2 × 50
   ▦▦   20 × 3                     60             ▦▦    30 × 7
  ▦▦▦   20 × 40                   800           ▦▦▦    30 × 50
 ▦▦▦▦   Total                    1118          ▦▦▦▦    Total
```

```
2.      48                3.      35          4.      76
      × 26                      × 47                 × 63
   ▦▦   6 × 8                 ▦▦                   ▦▦
  ▦▦▦   6 × 40               ▦▦▦                  ▦▦▦
  ▦▦▦   20 × 8               ▦▦▦                  ▦▦▦
  ▦▦▦   20 × 40             ▦▦▦▦                 ▦▦▦▦
 ▦▦▦▦   Total              ▦▦▦▦                 ▦▦▦▦
```

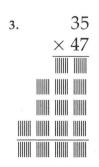 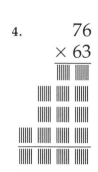

Multiplying by a multiple of ten

Ron takes 23 breaths in 1 minute.
How many breaths is that in an
hour (60 minutes)?

Finding the answer

Write zero in the ones' place	→	Multiply by the tens' digit

$$\begin{array}{r} 23 \\ \times\ 60 \\ \hline 0 \end{array}$$

$$\begin{array}{r} {\scriptstyle 1} \\ 23 \\ \times\ 60 \\ \hline 1380 \end{array}$$

That is 1380 breaths in an hour.

Other examples

$$\begin{array}{r} 23 \\ \times\ 30 \\ \hline 690 \end{array} \qquad \begin{array}{r} {\scriptstyle 4} \\ 48 \\ \times\ 50 \\ \hline 2400 \end{array} \qquad \begin{array}{r} {\scriptstyle 1} \\ 243 \\ \times\ \ 30 \\ \hline 7290 \end{array}$$

Find the products.

1.	24 × 30	2.	32 × 40	3.	49 × 50	4.	63 × 20	5.	81 × 70	6.	74 × 60
7.	37 × 50	8.	54 × 30	9.	79 × 20	10.	94 × 60	11.	85 × 40	12.	54 × 80
13.	26 × 70	14.	38 × 60	15.	43 × 50	16.	256 × 70	17.	164 × 80	18.	279 × 90

Multiply.

1. $\begin{array}{r} 17 \\ \times\ 20 \\ \hline \end{array}$	2. $\begin{array}{r} 24 \\ \times\ 30 \\ \hline \end{array}$	3. $\begin{array}{r} 56 \\ \times\ 40 \\ \hline \end{array}$	4. $\begin{array}{r} 57 \\ \times\ 20 \\ \hline \end{array}$	5. $\begin{array}{r} 64 \\ \times\ 50 \\ \hline \end{array}$
6. $\begin{array}{r} 137 \\ \times\ \ 60 \\ \hline \end{array}$	7. $\begin{array}{r} 827 \\ \times\ \ 40 \\ \hline \end{array}$	8. $\begin{array}{r} 146 \\ \times\ \ 60 \\ \hline \end{array}$	9. $\begin{array}{r} 275 \\ \times\ \ 30 \\ \hline \end{array}$	10. $\begin{array}{r} 342 \\ \times\ \ 30 \\ \hline \end{array}$
11. $\begin{array}{r} 232 \\ \times\ \ 40 \\ \hline \end{array}$	12. $\begin{array}{r} 163 \\ \times\ \ 50 \\ \hline \end{array}$	13. $\begin{array}{r} 274 \\ \times\ \ 30 \\ \hline \end{array}$	14. $\begin{array}{r} 196 \\ \times\ \ 40 \\ \hline \end{array}$	15. $\begin{array}{r} 241 \\ \times\ \ 40 \\ \hline \end{array}$
16. $\begin{array}{r} 177 \\ \times\ \ 60 \\ \hline \end{array}$	17. $\begin{array}{r} 158 \\ \times\ \ 50 \\ \hline \end{array}$	18. $\begin{array}{r} 319 \\ \times\ \ 30 \\ \hline \end{array}$	19. $\begin{array}{r} 46 \\ \times\ 50 \\ \hline \end{array}$	20. $\begin{array}{r} 29 \\ \times\ 70 \\ \hline \end{array}$
21. $\begin{array}{r} 19 \\ \times\ 40 \\ \hline \end{array}$	22. $\begin{array}{r} 363 \\ \times\ \ 20 \\ \hline \end{array}$	23. $\begin{array}{r} 195 \\ \times\ \ 80 \\ \hline \end{array}$	24. $\begin{array}{r} 99 \\ \times\ 50 \\ \hline \end{array}$	25. $\begin{array}{r} 307 \\ \times\ \ 30 \\ \hline \end{array}$
☆ 26. $\begin{array}{r} 68 \\ \times\ 200 \\ \hline \end{array}$	☆ 27. $\begin{array}{r} 25 \\ \times\ 400 \\ \hline \end{array}$	☆ 28. $\begin{array}{r} 97 \\ \times\ 200 \\ \hline \end{array}$	☆ 29. $\begin{array}{r} 84 \\ \times\ 300 \\ \hline \end{array}$	☆ 30. $\begin{array}{r} 76 \\ \times\ 400 \\ \hline \end{array}$

☆ 31. Do you take more breaths per minute after certain activities? Make and finish a chart like this.

Activity	Breaths per minute	Breaths per hour
After sitting still	▥	▥
After walking 100 steps	▥	▥
After running in place 1 minute	▥	▥
After doing 5 pushups	▥	▥

Find the product 9 × 374 without using multiplication!

More practice, page 362, Set A

Multiplying: 2-digit factors

There are 24 hours in a day. Columbus's first voyage across the Atlantic Ocean took 36 days. How many hours was this?

Finding the answer

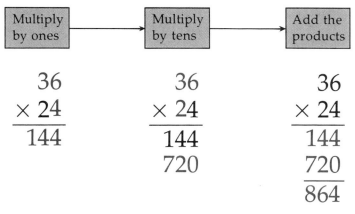

Multiply by ones	Multiply by tens	Add the products

$$\begin{array}{r} 36 \\ \times\ 24 \\ \hline 144 \end{array}$$

$$\begin{array}{r} 36 \\ \times\ 24 \\ \hline 144 \\ 720 \end{array}$$

$$\begin{array}{r} 36 \\ \times\ 24 \\ \hline 144 \\ 720 \\ \hline 864 \end{array}$$

Columbus's first voyage took 864 hours.

Other examples

$$\begin{array}{r} 34 \\ \times\ 47 \\ \hline 238 \\ 1360 \\ \hline 1598 \end{array} \qquad \begin{array}{r} 26 \\ \times\ 45 \\ \hline 130 \\ 1040 \\ \hline 1170 \end{array} \qquad \begin{array}{r} 32 \\ \times\ 23 \\ \hline 96 \\ 640 \\ \hline 736 \end{array}$$

Find the products.

1. $\begin{array}{r} 24 \\ \times\ 21 \\ \hline \end{array}$
2. $\begin{array}{r} 43 \\ \times\ 12 \\ \hline \end{array}$
3. $\begin{array}{r} 36 \\ \times\ 21 \\ \hline \end{array}$
4. $\begin{array}{r} 37 \\ \times\ 23 \\ \hline \end{array}$
5. $\begin{array}{r} 48 \\ \times\ 32 \\ \hline \end{array}$
6. $\begin{array}{r} 72 \\ \times\ 13 \\ \hline \end{array}$

7. $\begin{array}{r} 83 \\ \times\ 42 \\ \hline \end{array}$
8. $\begin{array}{r} 93 \\ \times\ 26 \\ \hline \end{array}$
9. $\begin{array}{r} 43 \\ \times\ 29 \\ \hline \end{array}$
10. $\begin{array}{r} 38 \\ \times\ 56 \\ \hline \end{array}$
11. $\begin{array}{r} 27 \\ \times\ 13 \\ \hline \end{array}$
12. $\begin{array}{r} 46 \\ \times\ 35 \\ \hline \end{array}$

Multiply.

1. 36 × 42	2. 45 × 22	3. 55 × 16	4. 71 × 24	5. 64 × 25	6. 57 × 58
7. 27 × 74	8. 57 × 61	9. 39 × 93	10. 46 × 46	11. 34 × 95	12. 55 × 26
13. 42 × 36	14. 22 × 99	15. 45 × 38	16. 58 × 19	17. 68 × 86	18. 68 × 25
19. 37 × 29	20. 46 × 38	21. 54 × 26	22. 97 × 84	23. 76 × 29	24. 47 × 98

Find the products. Then add.

☆ 25. 46 × 20 + 46 × 3

☆ 26. 39 × 50 + 39 × 4

☆ 27. 67 × 30 + 67 × 8

Add. Then find the products.

46 × 20 + 3

39 × 50 + 4

67 × 30 + 8

28. Almost a hundred years ago a newspaper writer named Nellie Bly made a record trip around the world. Her trip took 72 days. How many hours was this?

29. One crew of astronauts spent 84 days in space. How many hours was this?

What number times itself gives 1024?

▦ × ▦ = 1024

↑   ↑

same number

Guess! Check your guess by multiplying. Keep on guessing and checking until you find the number.

More practice, page 362, Set B

A glacier may move as fast as 18 m a day. At this rate, how many meters would it move in a year? (Use 365 days in a year.)

Finding the answer

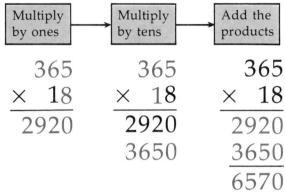

Multiply by ones	→	Multiply by tens	→	Add the products

$$\begin{array}{r} 365 \\ \times\ 18 \\ \hline 2920 \end{array} \qquad \begin{array}{r} 365 \\ \times\ 18 \\ \hline 2920 \\ 3650 \end{array} \qquad \begin{array}{r} 365 \\ \times\ 18 \\ \hline 2920 \\ 3650 \\ \hline 6570 \end{array}$$

It would move 6570 m in a year.

Other examples

$$\begin{array}{r} 387 \\ \times\ 23 \\ \hline 1161 \\ 7740 \\ \hline 8901 \end{array} \qquad \begin{array}{r} 506 \\ \times\ 19 \\ \hline 4554 \\ 5060 \\ \hline 9614 \end{array} \qquad \begin{array}{r} 230 \\ \times\ 43 \\ \hline 690 \\ 9200 \\ \hline 9890 \end{array}$$

Find the products.

1. $\begin{array}{r} 594 \\ \times\ 15 \\ \hline \end{array}$
2. $\begin{array}{r} 198 \\ \times\ 47 \\ \hline \end{array}$
3. $\begin{array}{r} 276 \\ \times\ 31 \\ \hline \end{array}$
4. $\begin{array}{r} 416 \\ \times\ 23 \\ \hline \end{array}$
5. $\begin{array}{r} 175 \\ \times\ 26 \\ \hline \end{array}$

6. $\begin{array}{r} 430 \\ \times\ 18 \\ \hline \end{array}$
7. $\begin{array}{r} 309 \\ \times\ 27 \\ \hline \end{array}$
8. $\begin{array}{r} 597 \\ \times\ 13 \\ \hline \end{array}$
9. $\begin{array}{r} 168 \\ \times\ 57 \\ \hline \end{array}$
10. $\begin{array}{r} 296 \\ \times\ 29 \\ \hline \end{array}$

Multiply.

1. 398
    × 23

2. 456
    × 21

3. 534
    × 12

4. 86
    × 52

5. 97
    × 84

6. 250
    × 29

7. 618
    × 14

8. 408
    × 22

9. 132
    × 56

10. 303
    × 28

Find the products.

11. 43 × 3 × 54

12. 56 × 7 × 24

13. 29 × 3 × 25

14. 4 × 37 × 23

15. 6 × 72 × 19

16. 8 × 36 × 23

Estimate each product. Then find the product.
Find the difference between the product and your estimate.

☆ 17. 286 × 47   ☆ 18. 313 × 18   ☆ 19. 198 × 31   ☆ 20. 306 × 28

21. There are 12 months in a year.
    If a person lives for 113 years,
    how many months is that?

☆ 22. On your last birthday, how
    many months had you lived?
    How many weeks?
    (Use 52 weeks in a year.)
    How many days?
    (Use 365 days in a year.)

Can you draw 3 straight lines
which cut a pie into

A 4 pieces?   B 5 pieces?
C 6 pieces?   D 7 pieces?

Pieces may be of different
sizes. Draw pictures to show
your answers.

Answers for Self-check   1. 141   2. 1680   3. 6750   4. 1720   5. 1696   6. 2226   7. 2100   8. 2714
9. 9880   10. 9108   11. 8112   12. 8400   13. 6808   14. 8060

Find the products.

1. $\begin{array}{r} 47 \\ \times\ 3 \\ \hline \end{array}$

2. $\begin{array}{r} 56 \\ \times\ 30 \\ \hline \end{array}$

3. $\begin{array}{r} 75 \\ \times\ 90 \\ \hline \end{array}$

4. $\begin{array}{r} 86 \\ \times\ 20 \\ \hline \end{array}$

5. $\begin{array}{r} 53 \\ \times\ 32 \\ \hline \end{array}$

6. $\begin{array}{r} 42 \\ \times\ 53 \\ \hline \end{array}$

7. $\begin{array}{r} 75 \\ \times\ 28 \\ \hline \end{array}$

8. $\begin{array}{r} 59 \\ \times\ 46 \\ \hline \end{array}$

9. $\begin{array}{r} 247 \\ \times\ 40 \\ \hline \end{array}$

10. $\begin{array}{r} 396 \\ \times\ 23 \\ \hline \end{array}$

11. $\begin{array}{r} 507 \\ \times\ 16 \\ \hline \end{array}$

12. $\begin{array}{r} 350 \\ \times\ 24 \\ \hline \end{array}$

13. $8 \times 23 \times 37$

14. $4 \times 65 \times 31$

Answers for Self-check—page 159

Find the products.

1. $\begin{array}{r} 58 \\ \times\ 4 \\ \hline \end{array}$

2. $\begin{array}{r} 74 \\ \times\ 20 \\ \hline \end{array}$

3. $\begin{array}{r} 68 \\ \times\ 80 \\ \hline \end{array}$

4. $\begin{array}{r} 97 \\ \times\ 40 \\ \hline \end{array}$

5. $\begin{array}{r} 61 \\ \times\ 23 \\ \hline \end{array}$

6. $\begin{array}{r} 33 \\ \times\ 43 \\ \hline \end{array}$

7. $\begin{array}{r} 58 \\ \times\ 26 \\ \hline \end{array}$

8. $\begin{array}{r} 74 \\ \times\ 38 \\ \hline \end{array}$

9. $\begin{array}{r} 168 \\ \times\ 50 \\ \hline \end{array}$

10. $\begin{array}{r} 324 \\ \times\ 30 \\ \hline \end{array}$

11. $\begin{array}{r} 699 \\ \times\ 12 \\ \hline \end{array}$

12. $\begin{array}{r} 209 \\ \times\ 43 \\ \hline \end{array}$

13. $8 \times 36 \times 23$

14. $6 \times 72 \times 14$

Making a Magic Strip

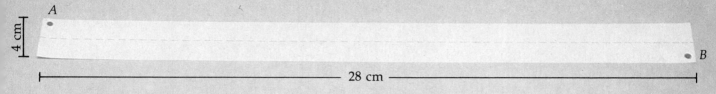

Cut out a strip of paper like this.

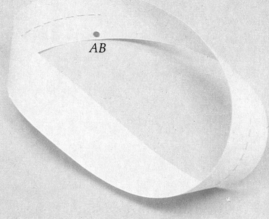

Give the strip a half-twist and tape the ends together so that points A and B meet.

Guess what will happen if you cut all the way around the middle of the strip. Then do it. The result may surprise you!

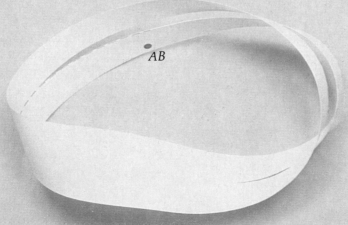

The strip you made is called a Moebius strip.

Using Your Skills

Getting started

1. Bought a special stamp pack for 75¢.
   Bought a paperback book for 95¢.
   How much for both?

2. Bought 2 coin books for 75¢ each.
   How much for both?

3. What other problems about the items
   in the store can you solve?

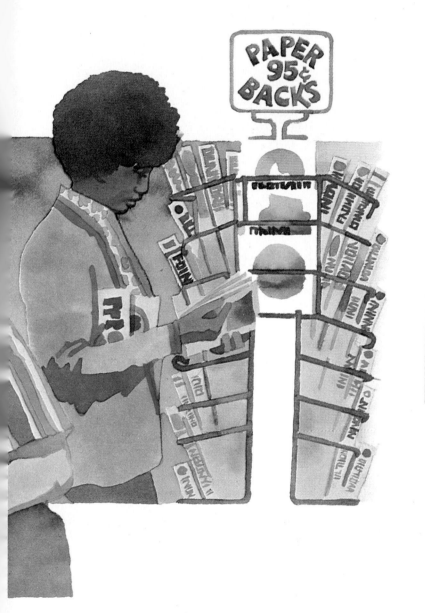

PAPER
95¢
BACKS

Solving Problems

1. Read carefully to find the facts.

2. Look for the question.

3. Decide what to do. (+,−,×,÷).

4. Find the answer.

5. Read again.
   Does your answer make sense?

You may need to use
two steps $(+, -, \times, \div)$
to solve some problems.

Try these.

1. Charles bought 8 packs
   of baseball cards. They
   cost 35¢ a pack. He also
   bought some candy for 25¢.
   How much did Charles spend
   altogether?

2. Aimee worked in the garden
   3 hours a day. She worked
   5 days each week. How many
   hours did she work in 4
   weeks?

1. The average lifetime of a dollar bill is 18 months. How many days is this? (Use 30 days in a month.)

2. A baseball pitch might go as fast as 158 km/h. A well-hit golf ball might go as fast as 224 km/h. How much faster might the golf ball go?

4. A lost cat once had to go 640 km to reach its home. If it traveled 10 km a day for 60 days, how many more kilometers would it still have to go?

3. There is enough lead in 1 pencil to draw a line 56 km long. How long a line could you draw if you had 3 boxes of pencils with 5 in each box?

5. Your hair grows at a rate of about 2 cm each month. How many centimeters would it grow in 3 years?

6. A hen's egg was once thrown 91 m without being broken. A paper airplane was once flown 11 times that far. How many meters did the paper airplane fly?

9. A person sat at the top of a pole for 253 days. How many hours less than a year was this? (Use 24 hours in a day, 365 days in a year.)

7. A person once rode on a ferris wheel for 14 days and 21 hours. How many hours was this in all?

10. Someone once threw a rolling pin 42 m. If you double this and add 1 m, you get the distance for a record Frisbee throw. How many meters was the Frisbee throw?

8. The record for playing a drum is 215 hours. The record for playing a piano is 1091 hours. How many hours longer is the record for a piano?

Here is another way
to find this product:

$$\begin{array}{r} 234 \\ \times\ \ \ 6 \\ \hline 1404 \end{array}$$

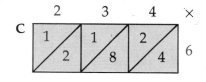

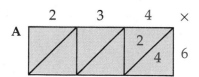

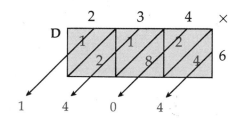

Now copy and try these problems.

1.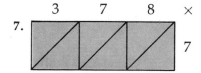

2.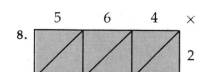

3.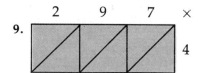

4.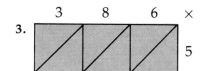

5.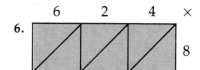

6.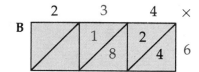

7.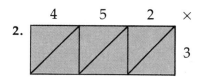

8.

9.

Here is a way to do
problems like this:

$$
\begin{array}{r}
34 \\
\times\, 26 \\
\hline
204 \\
680 \\
\hline
884
\end{array}
$$

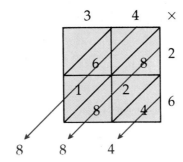

Study the example.
Then copy these and try them.

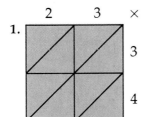

1.

2.

3.

4.

5.

6.

Practicing your skills

Add or subtract.

1. $\begin{array}{r} 35 \\ +\,56 \\ \hline \end{array}$	2. $\begin{array}{r} 17 \\ +\,92 \\ \hline \end{array}$	3. $\begin{array}{r} 206 \\ +\,349 \\ \hline \end{array}$	4. $\begin{array}{r} 472 \\ +\,488 \\ \hline \end{array}$	5. $\begin{array}{r} 724 \\ +\,579 \\ \hline \end{array}$
6. $\begin{array}{r} 79 \\ -\,46 \\ \hline \end{array}$	7. $\begin{array}{r} 55 \\ -\,38 \\ \hline \end{array}$	8. $\begin{array}{r} 467 \\ -\,249 \\ \hline \end{array}$	9. $\begin{array}{r} 605 \\ -\,391 \\ \hline \end{array}$	10. $\begin{array}{r} 840 \\ -\,748 \\ \hline \end{array}$

Grocery store problems

Grocery store managers must be able to do many things. They must hire and train other workers. They must order the food that their stores sell. Many managers also must decide what prices to charge and what ads they should put in newspapers. Above all, they must know how to please the shoppers who come to their stores.

1. Canned juice order: 30 cases
    24 cans in each case
    How many cans in all?

2. Cost of a newspaper ad:
    $3 for each line
    How much for a 90-line ad?

3. Number of customers:
    597 on Thursday
    786 on Friday
    974 on Saturday
    How many in all?

4. Checker's work record:
    8 hours each day
    5 days each week
    How many hours of work
    in 8 weeks?

☆ 5. Customer's order:
    5 cans of soup—34¢ a can
    2 pies—98¢ each
    3 bars of soap—35¢ a bar
    Total cost?

Choose the best estimate. Then find the exact amount.
Was your estimate correct?

1. Fruit punch costs 18¢ a can.
   About how much for 32 cans?

   A $3.00   B $6.00   C $9.00

2. A one-liter carton of milk
   costs 59¢. A two-liter
   carton costs 98¢. Jan
   bought 2 small cartons.
   Fran bought 1 large carton.
   About how much more
   did Jan pay?

   A 20¢   B 40¢   C 10¢

3. Soup is 38¢ a can.
   About how much will 24 cans cost?

   A $12.00   B $6.00   C $8.00

4. A box of 24 cans of dog
   food is on sale for $7.20.
   The regular price is 36¢
   a can. About how much less
   is the cost of 24 cans at
   the sale price?

   A $1.00   B $2.00   C $3.00

★ 5. 6 cans of juice cost $2.94.
   About how much is this
   a can?

   A 60¢   B 40¢   C 50¢

Estimation problems

Choose the best estimate.

1. Bought these items:
   Bike horn: $3.99
   Reflectors: $2.99
   Speedometer: $8.29
   About how much did
   they cost altogether?

   A $12   B $15   C $20

2. Bike flags cost $1.89 each.
   Need 3 for your family.
   About how much will
   they cost?

   A $4   B $8   C $6

3. Need 9 square meters of
   new carpet.
   Each square meter costs $7.95.
   About how much will the
   new carpet cost?

   A $63   B $80   C $72

4. Need 4 cans of paint.
   Costs $2.98 a can.
   About how much will
   they cost?

   A $12   B $8   C $10

5. Had $40.45.
   Spent $29.95 to build
   a new dog house.
   About how much was left?

   A $15   B $20   C $10

☆ 6. Travel 88 km each hour. Travel about how many kilometers in 7 hours?

A 560   B 630   C 700

☆ 7. Want to make a model train track 179 cm long. Need about how many 19-cm pieces of track?

A 8   B 9   C 10

☆ 9. Bought these items:
Camera—$9.95
Flashbulbs—$1.69
Film—$3.29
Paid about how much?

A $15   B $20   C $13

☆ 8. Want to make a side track long enough for 7 cars. Each car is 18 cm long. Need about how many centimeters of track?

A 70   B 100   C 140

☆ 10. Had 20 pictures made at 29¢ per picture. About how much did they cost?

A $4.00   B $5.00   C $6.00

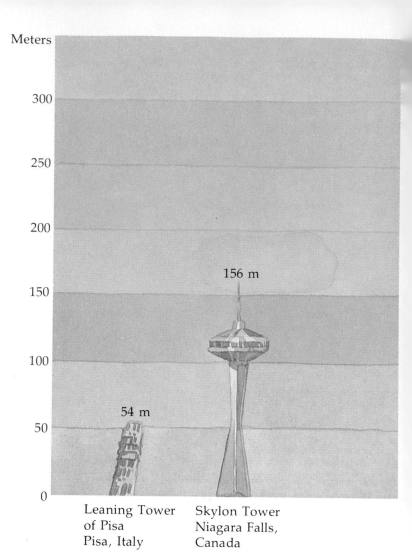

Meters

1. How much taller is the tallest tower in the picture than the shortest?

2. How much taller is the Eiffel Tower than the Skylon Tower?

3. How much shorter is the Cairo Tower than the sum of the heights of the Stuttgart Tower and the Space Needle?

4. The Polish National TV Service Tower is 4 times as tall as the Skylon Tower. How tall is the TV tower?

5. The Statue of Liberty in New York harbor is 93 m tall. London's Museum Tower is 2 times that tall. How tall is the Museum Tower?

300

250

200

156 m

150

100

54 m

50

0

Leaning Tower
of Pisa
Pisa, Italy

Skylon Tower
Niagara Falls,
Canada

6. Multiply the height of the Stuttgart Tower by 3. Then subtract 116. Your answer is the height of the Moscow Tower. How high is it?

7. The world's highest mountain, Mt. Everest, is about 48 times as high as the Space Needle. About how high is Mt. Everest?

180 m

211 m

225 m

295 m

Space Needle	Stuttgart Tower	Cairo Tower	Eiffel Tower
Seattle, U.S.A.	Stuttgart,	Cairo, Egypt	Paris, France
	W. Germany		

☆ 8. The Washington Monument is 9 m taller than 3 times as high as the Leaning Tower of Pisa. How tall is the Washington Monument?

9. An airplane flew 45 times as high as the Cairo Tower. How high did it fly?

☆ 10. Add the heights of the 3 tallest towers in the chart. Add the heights of the 3 shortest towers. What is the difference?

☆ 11. Which tower is 101 m less than twice the height of the Skylon Tower?

Answers for Self-check   1. $2.52   2. 800   3. 8760   4. $1.99   5. Estimate: $3.60; exact: $3.54; difference: 6¢ or $0.06

Self-check

1. Bought 6 pads of paper.
   Paid 42¢ for each pad.
   Spent how much?

2. 32 rows of seats
   25 seats in each row
   How many seats in all?

3. 24 hours in a day
   How many hours in a year?
   (Use 365 days in a year.)

4. Phil bought 3 books that
   cost $1.99 each.
   Betty bought 1 record
   for $3.98.
   How much more did Phil spend?

5. Estimate the cost of 6 boxes
   of cereal at 59¢ a box. Then
   find the exact cost. What is
   the difference?

Answers for Self-check—page 173

Test

1. Traveled at a speed of
   72 km/h for 6 hours.
   Went how far?

2. 60 minutes in 1 hour
   24 hours in 1 day
   How many minutes in 1 day?

3. 12 eggs in a carton
   How many eggs in 385
   cartons?

4. Armando worked 7 hours
   each day for 6 days.
   Keith worked 8 hours a
   day for 5 days.
   Who worked more hours?
   How many more?

5. Estimate the cost of 5 cans
   of juice at 62¢ a can. Then
   find the exact cost. What
   is the difference?

Greatest-Product Game

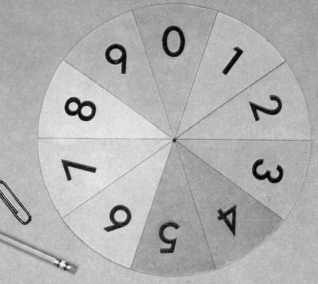

1. Use stiff paper, a pencil, and a paper clip to make a spinner like this.

2. Draw a multiplication grid for each player.

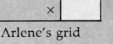
Arlene's grid

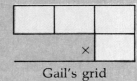
Gail's grid

3. Players take turns spinning the spinner. After each spin, the players write the number spun in one of the boxes of their grids.

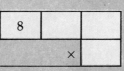
Arlene's grid

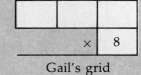
Gail's grid

4. After 4 spins, players find the products of the numbers on their grids. The winner is the player who has the greatest product. Who won this game?

Arlene's grid

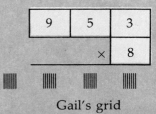
Gail's grid

Graphs

Getting started

Outline an 11-by-10 area on graph paper. Make it look like this:

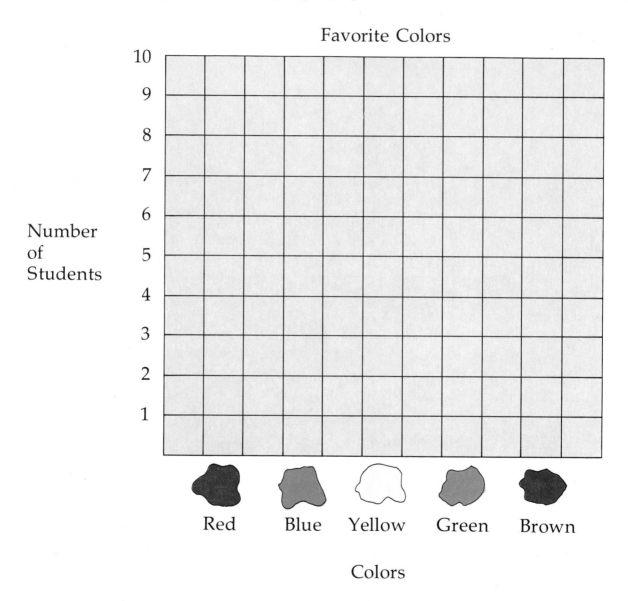

In Terry's class, 9 students chose red as their favorite color,
5 chose blue, 6 chose yellow, 4 chose green,
and 2 chose brown. Color your graph to show this.

Here is a bar graph that Kelly's class made.

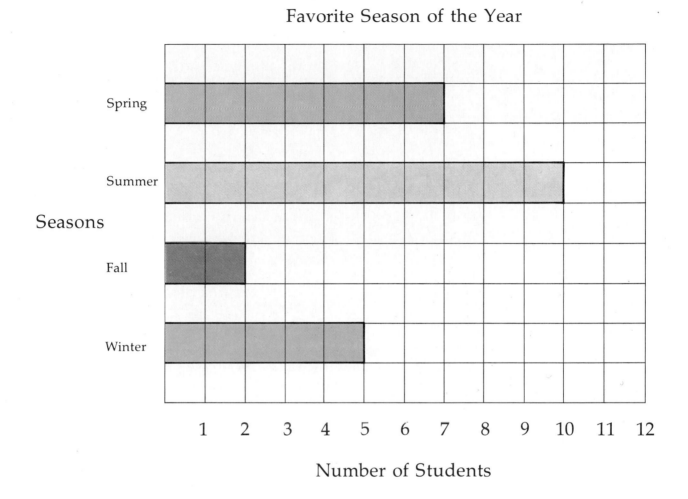

Favorite Season of the Year

1. How many students think spring is the best season?
2. How many students chose summer?
3. How many more students chose summer than chose winter?
4. How many students are in the class?
5. What season was chosen by the fewest students?
6. Find out what a favorite-season graph for your class would look like.

Making bar graphs

Outline a 12-by-10 area on graph paper. Make it look like this:

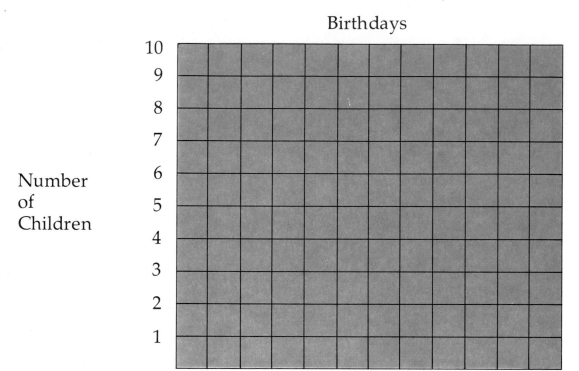

Birthdays

Number of Children

Jan. Feb. Mar. Apr. May June July Aug. Sept. Oct. Nov. Dec.

Months

This is what two fourth grade classes found out about their birthdays:

3 are in January	4 in April	5 in July	6 in October
6 in February	2 in May	3 in August	1 in November
9 in March	1 in June	8 in September	4 in December

Color your graph to show this.

1. Which month has the most birthdays? Which has the fewest?

2. How many more birthdays are in March than in December?

3. August, September, and October have 17 birthdays altogether. Is this more or less than the total for February, March, and April?

☆ 4. Make a birthday graph for your class.

Outline a 15-by-9 area on graph paper.
Make it look like this.

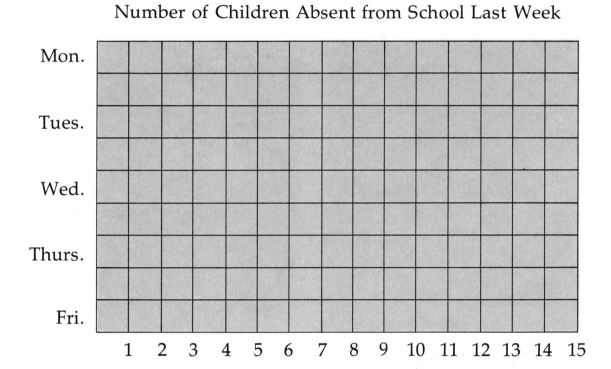

Number of Children Absent from School Last Week

Number of Children

In Jon's school 14 children were absent on Monday; 10 on Tuesday; 6 on Wednesday; 7 on Thursday; 12 on Friday.

Color your graph to show this.

1. What day were the most children absent?
   What day were the fewest absent?

2. How many more children were absent Monday than Wednesday?

3. How many absences were there altogether during the week?

☆ 4. Find out how many students in your class or school were absent each day last week. Make a graph to show this.

1. Find out how people feel about things.
   Use these questions or make up some of your own.

   A Which of these TV shows do you like best?
   B Which subject in school do you like best?
   C Which of these hamburger drive-in restaurants do you like best?

2. Ask each student in your class to answer the questions.
   Write down their answers.

3. Make bar graphs like these to show what you find.

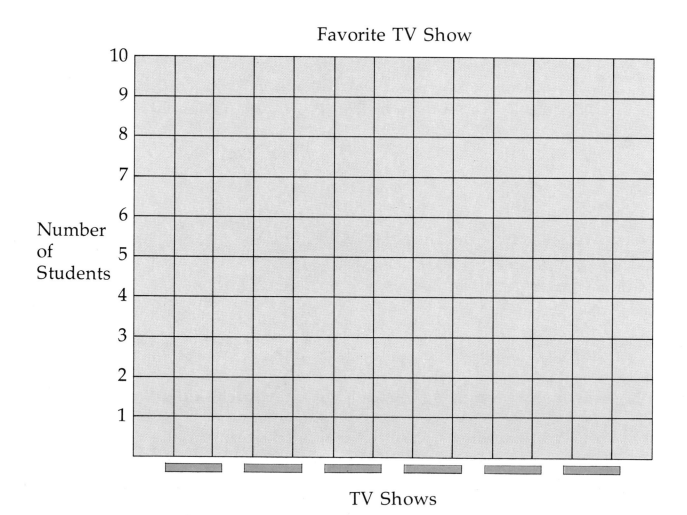

Favorite TV Show

Number
of
Students

TV Shows

Favorite Class

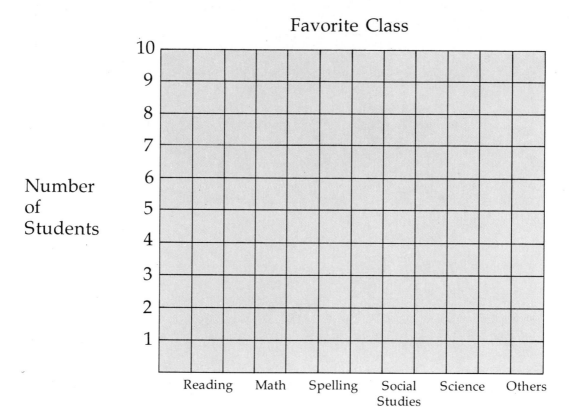

Number of Students

Reading	Math	Spelling	Social Studies	Science	Others

Favorite Drive-in Restaurant

Number of Students

Drive-in

⊛ Reading picture graphs

Sales at the Ice Cream Store

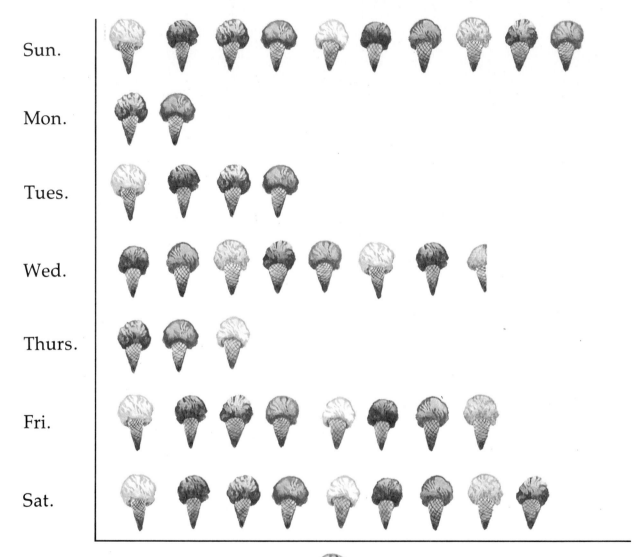

Each 🍦 stands for 20 ice cream cones.

1. On what day were the fewest cones sold? How many were sold?

2. On what day were the most cones sold? How many were sold?

3. How many ice cream cones does half a cone 🍦 stand for?

4. How many cones were sold on Wednesday?

Cars Entering the Amusement Park

Spring

Summer

Fall

Winter

Each 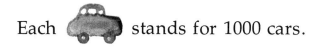 stands for 1000 cars.

1. How many cars does half a car 🚗 stand for?

2. In which season did the most cars enter? How many?

3. In which season did the fewest cars enter? How many?

4. How many cars entered in the fall?

5. How many cars entered during the whole year?

Answers for Self-check 1. 132 and 138 2. 7 3. 25 4. Wednesday 5. 60

Self-check

1. The height of most children in the class is between what two numbers?

2. How many children are more than 138 cm tall?

3. How many records were sold on Thursday?

4. On what day were the fewest records sold?

5. What was the record sales total for Friday and Saturday?

Answers for Self-check—page 183

Test

1. How many children are less than 133 cm tall?

2. How many children are between 132 and 138 cm tall?

3. How many records were sold on Friday?

4. On what day were the most records sold?

5. What was the total record sale for Thursday and Saturday?

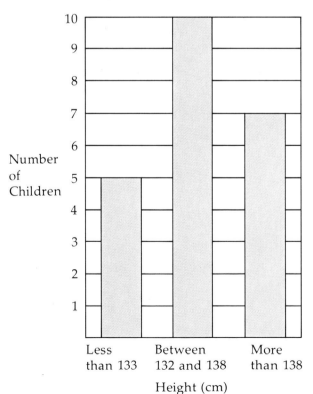

Heights of Children in Our Class

Number of Children

Height (cm)

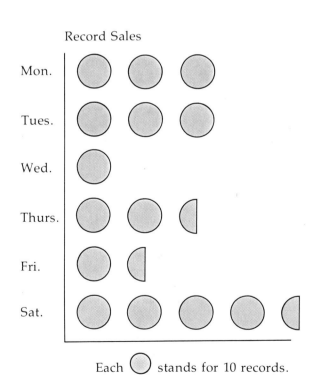

Record Sales

Each ◯ stands for 10 records.

Number–Pair Pictures

1. To graph the point for the numbers $(3, 2)$

THINK

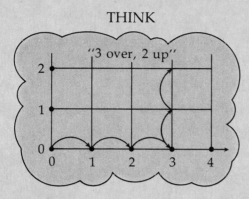

"3 over, 2 up"

DRAW

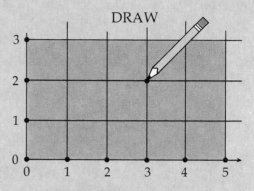

2. This picture was made by graphing and connecting these points in order:

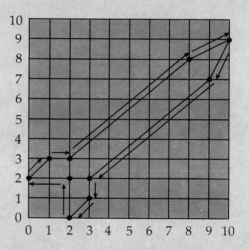

START
$(2, 2) \rightarrow (0, 2) \rightarrow (1, 3)$
$\rightarrow (2, 3) \rightarrow (8, 8) \rightarrow (10, 9)$
$\rightarrow (9, 7) \rightarrow (3, 2) \rightarrow (3, 1)$
$\rightarrow (2, 0) \rightarrow (2, 2)$
END

Can you make a picture on graph paper by connecting these points in order?

$(4, 0) \rightarrow (5, 3) \rightarrow (7, 1) \rightarrow (8, 1) \rightarrow (8, 2)$
$\rightarrow (9, 1) \rightarrow (10, 2) \rightarrow (9, 4) \rightarrow (5, 8) \rightarrow (5, 10) \rightarrow (4, 8)$
$\rightarrow (3, 10) \rightarrow (0, 4) \rightarrow (4, 0)$

3. Now try this.

$(1, 4) \rightarrow (3, 7) \rightarrow (3, 9) \rightarrow (2, 7) \rightarrow (3, 4) \rightarrow (4, 5) \rightarrow (3, 6)$
$\rightarrow (5, 6) \rightarrow (6, 4) \rightarrow (7, 6) \rightarrow (7, 2) \rightarrow (6, 1) \rightarrow (6, 2) \rightarrow (9, 5)$
$\rightarrow (8, 6) \rightarrow (8, 5) \rightarrow (9, 4) \rightarrow (10, 4)$

Level 19 review

Multiply.

1. $\begin{array}{r} 10 \\ \times\ 8 \\ \hline \end{array}$
2. $\begin{array}{r} 50 \\ \times\ 10 \\ \hline \end{array}$
3. $\begin{array}{r} 97 \\ \times\ 10 \\ \hline \end{array}$
4. $\begin{array}{r} 10 \\ \times\ 10 \\ \hline \end{array}$
5. $\begin{array}{r} 5 \\ \times\ 100 \\ \hline \end{array}$

6. $\begin{array}{r} 100 \\ \times\ 6 \\ \hline \end{array}$
7. $\begin{array}{r} 346 \\ \times\ 10 \\ \hline \end{array}$
8. $\begin{array}{r} 28 \\ \times\ 100 \\ \hline \end{array}$
9. $\begin{array}{r} 60 \\ \times\ 9 \\ \hline \end{array}$
10. $\begin{array}{r} 700 \\ \times\ 4 \\ \hline \end{array}$

11. 20×30
12. 40×80
13. 90×20
14. 3×800

Divide.

15. $240 \div 8$
16. $420 \div 7$
17. $3600 \div 9$
18. $560 \div 70$

19. $320 \div 4$
20. $2800 \div 70$
21. $360 \div 60$
22. $810 \div 9$

Find the products.

23. $\begin{array}{r} 32 \\ \times\ 3 \\ \hline \end{array}$
24. $\begin{array}{r} 58 \\ \times\ 1 \\ \hline \end{array}$
25. $\begin{array}{r} 24 \\ \times\ 4 \\ \hline \end{array}$
26. $\begin{array}{r} 41 \\ \times\ 9 \\ \hline \end{array}$
27. $\begin{array}{r} 36 \\ \times\ 5 \\ \hline \end{array}$

28. $\begin{array}{r} 67 \\ \times\ 8 \\ \hline \end{array}$
29. $\begin{array}{r} 431 \\ \times\ 2 \\ \hline \end{array}$
30. $\begin{array}{r} 527 \\ \times\ 3 \\ \hline \end{array}$
31. $\begin{array}{r} 386 \\ \times\ 7 \\ \hline \end{array}$
32. $\begin{array}{r} 806 \\ \times\ 4 \\ \hline \end{array}$

33. $\begin{array}{r} \$\ 2.20 \\ \times\ 3 \\ \hline \end{array}$
34. $\begin{array}{r} \$\ 3.15 \\ \times\ 6 \\ \hline \end{array}$
35. $\begin{array}{r} \$\ 6.08 \\ \times\ 5 \\ \hline \end{array}$
36. $\begin{array}{r} \$\ 4.98 \\ \times\ 2 \\ \hline \end{array}$
37. $\begin{array}{r} \$\ 3.59 \\ \times\ 7 \\ \hline \end{array}$

38. $\begin{array}{r} 45 \\ \times\ 20 \\ \hline \end{array}$
39. $\begin{array}{r} 227 \\ \times\ 40 \\ \hline \end{array}$
40. $\begin{array}{r} 36 \\ \times\ 24 \\ \hline \end{array}$
41. $\begin{array}{r} 68 \\ \times\ 53 \\ \hline \end{array}$
42. $\begin{array}{r} 123 \\ \times\ 36 \\ \hline \end{array}$

Level 20

Dividing: 1-Digit Divisors with Remainders
Dividing: 2-Digit Divisors with Remainders
Using Your Skills
Geometry (Relationships)

Dividing: 1-Digit Divisors with Remainders

Getting started

How many 6-button bracelets can you make with 75 buttons?
(Use any way you want to find the answer.)

Will there be any extra buttons left over?

How many fives in 189?
These papers show how four students answered the question.

Ginger
```
  189
-  50  (10)
 ─────
  139
-  50  (10)
 ─────
   89
-  50  (10)
 ─────
   39
-  35  (7)
 ─────
    4   37
```
Remainder 4

Bill
```
        37
    5)189
      100  ←20×5
     ─────
       89
       50  ←10×5
      ────
       39
       35  ←7×5
      ────
        4
```
37, remainder 4

Cathy
```
      37
  5)189
    150
   ────
    39
    35
   ───
     4
```
37, R4

Dan
```
      36
  5)189
    150
   ────
    39
    30
   ───
     9
```
36, Remainder 9

1. How many fives did Ginger subtract the first time?

2. How many fives did Bill subtract the first time?

3. How many fives did Cathy subtract the first time?

4. Which paper is not correct? Why?

5. Study this example.

$$\begin{array}{r} 8 \leftarrow \text{quotient} \\ \text{divisor} \rightarrow 6)\overline{50} \leftarrow \text{dividend} \\ -48 \\ \hline 2 \leftarrow \text{remainder} \end{array}$$

Read: 50 divided by 6 is 8, remainder 2.

Give the **divisor, dividend, quotient,** and **remainder** for the problem the children worked.

Finding quotients and remainders

44 fire fighters
5 fire fighters on each truck crew
How many truck crews?
How many extra fire fighters?

Finding the answer

How many can be subtracted?	→	Multiply		Subtract		Show the remainder with the quotient

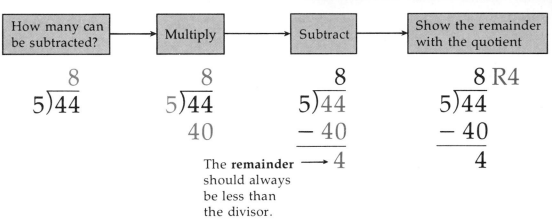

$$\begin{array}{r} 8 \\ 5\overline{)44} \end{array}$$

$$\begin{array}{r} 8 \\ 5\overline{)44} \\ 40 \end{array}$$

$$\begin{array}{r} 8 \\ 5\overline{)44} \\ -40 \\ \hline 4 \end{array}$$

The **remainder** ⟶ 4
should always
be less than
the divisor.

$$\begin{array}{r} 8\ \text{R4} \\ 5\overline{)44} \\ -40 \\ \hline 4 \end{array}$$

There are 8 truck crews and 4 extra fire fighters.

Other examples

$$\begin{array}{r} 8 \\ 7\overline{)56} \\ 56 \\ \hline 0 \end{array} \qquad \begin{array}{r} 7\ \text{R1} \\ 9\overline{)64} \\ 63 \\ \hline 1 \end{array} \qquad \begin{array}{r} 7\ \text{R2} \\ 4\overline{)30} \\ 28 \\ \hline 2 \end{array}$$

Find the quotients and remainders.

1. $6\overline{)39}$ 2. $4\overline{)33}$ 3. $5\overline{)28}$ 4. $4\overline{)18}$ 5. $3\overline{)25}$

6. $6\overline{)50}$ 7. $8\overline{)62}$ 8. $7\overline{)41}$ 9. $9\overline{)58}$ 10. $4\overline{)38}$

11. $8\overline{)54}$ 12. $9\overline{)65}$ 13. $2\overline{)13}$ 14. $4\overline{)26}$ 15. $6\overline{)43}$

16. $8\overline{)33}$ 17. $5\overline{)44}$ 18. $9\overline{)62}$ 19. $7\overline{)30}$ 20. $6\overline{)58}$

Divide.

1. $4\overline{)29}$ 2. $6\overline{)27}$ 3. $7\overline{)38}$ 4. $8\overline{)67}$

5. $2\overline{)11}$ 6. $3\overline{)26}$ 7. $5\overline{)39}$ 8. $9\overline{)66}$

9. $8\overline{)43}$ 10. $6\overline{)20}$ 11. $3\overline{)28}$ 12. $4\overline{)14}$

Two of the problems below are not correct. Find them and correct them.

13.
$$\begin{array}{r} 5\,\text{R}5 \\ 8\overline{)45} \\ -40 \\ \hline 5 \end{array}$$

14.
$$\begin{array}{r} 6\,\text{R}7 \\ 6\overline{)43} \\ -36 \\ \hline 7 \end{array}$$

15.
$$\begin{array}{r} 5\,\text{R}4 \\ 9\overline{)49} \\ -45 \\ \hline 4 \end{array}$$

16.
$$\begin{array}{r} 6\,\text{R}2 \\ 8\overline{)51} \\ -48 \\ \hline 2 \end{array}$$

☆ 17. Divide these numbers by 3 and list the remainders. 12, 13, 14, 15, 16, 17, 18, 19, 20, 21, 22, 23, 24, 25, 26, 27, 28, 29, 30

☆ 18. List the possible remainders when any number is divided by 4.

19. Need 6 fire fighters to answer each alarm. 21 fire fighters are on duty. How many alarms can they answer at one time? How many fire fighters left over?

20. Have 31 fire engine tires. Need 4 tires for each engine. Enough tires for how many engines? How many extra tires?

Blocks:
2 layers
2 × 2 in
each layer
↓

Blocks:
3 layers
3 × 3 in
each layer
↓

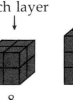
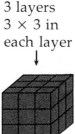

1   8   27

These numbers are "cubes." Do you see why? Can you find the next two numbers that are cubes?

Estimating 2-digit quotients

252 tennis balls
About how many cans of 3?

Finding the answer

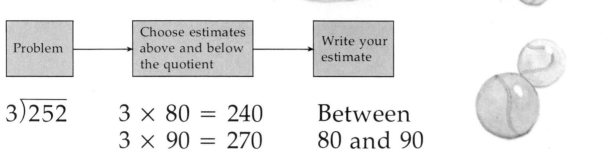

| Problem | → | Choose estimates above and below the quotient | → | Write your estimate |

$3)\overline{252}$ $3 \times 80 = 240$ **Between**
$3 \times 90 = 270$ **80 and 90**

There would be between 80 and 90 cans.

Use the product table to help you estimate the quotients.

1. $6)\overline{318}$ 2. $6)\overline{276}$ 3. $6)\overline{210}$

4. $6)\overline{402}$ 5. $6)\overline{174}$ 6. $6)\overline{498}$

7. $6)\overline{513}$ 8. $6)\overline{145}$ 9. $6)\overline{347}$

10. $8)\overline{424}$ 11. $8)\overline{272}$ 12. $8)\overline{360}$

13. $8)\overline{216}$ 14. $8)\overline{656}$ 15. $8)\overline{544}$

16. $8)\overline{300}$ 17. $8)\overline{399}$ 18. $8)\overline{587}$

10	20	30
$\times\ 6$	$\times\ 6$	$\times\ 6$
60	120	180
40	50	60
$\times\ 6$	$\times\ 6$	$\times\ 6$
240	300	360
70	80	90
$\times\ 6$	$\times\ 6$	$\times\ 6$
420	480	540
10	20	30
$\times\ 8$	$\times\ 8$	$\times\ 8$
80	160	240
40	50	60
$\times\ 8$	$\times\ 8$	$\times\ 8$
320	400	480
70	80	90
$\times\ 8$	$\times\ 8$	$\times\ 8$
560	640	720

Estimate the quotients.

1. $7\overline{)162}$ 2. $7\overline{)375}$ 3. $7\overline{)450}$

4. $7\overline{)515}$ 5. $7\overline{)304}$ 6. $7\overline{)612}$

7. $7\overline{)97}$ 8. $7\overline{)573}$ 9. $7\overline{)215}$

10. $9\overline{)210}$ 11. $9\overline{)300}$ 12. $9\overline{)556}$

13. $9\overline{)702}$ 14. $9\overline{)805}$ 15. $9\overline{)495}$

16. $9\overline{)425}$ 17. $9\overline{)537}$ 18. $9\overline{)135}$

10	20	30
× 7	× 7	× 7
70	140	210
40	50	60
× 7	× 7	× 7
280	350	420
70	80	90
× 7	× 7	× 7
490	560	630
10	20	30
× 9	× 9	× 9
90	180	270
40	50	60
× 9	× 9	× 9
360	450	540
70	80	90
× 9	× 9	× 9
630	720	810

19. 438 baseballs
How many boxes of 6?

   A between 70 and 80
   B between 60 and 70
   C between 50 and 60

Use the sign +, −, ×, or ÷ in each .
Copy and complete these equations.

(4 ▦ 4) + (4 ▦ 4) = 1
(4 ▦ 4) + (4 ▦ 4) = 2
(4 ▦ 4 ▦ 4) ▦ 4 = 3
4 ▦ 4 ▦ 4 ▦ 4 = 8
4 ▦ 4 ▦ 4 ▦ 4 = 16

20. 362 table tennis balls
How many boxes of 5?

   A between 60 and 70
   B between 80 and 90
   C between 70 and 80

Finding 2-digit quotients

Summer camp:
8 cabins for 112 children
Same number of children in each cabin
How many children in each cabin?

Finding the answer

Divide the tens	→	Multiply and subtract	→	Divide the ones, multiply and subtract

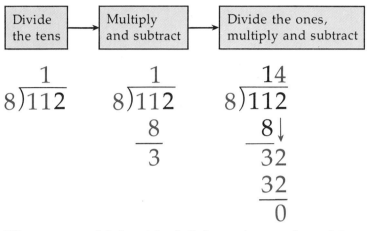

$$
\begin{array}{r}
1 \\
8\overline{)112}
\end{array}
\qquad
\begin{array}{r}
1 \\
8\overline{)112} \\
8 \\
\hline
3
\end{array}
\qquad
\begin{array}{r}
14 \\
8\overline{)112} \\
8\downarrow \\
\hline
32 \\
32 \\
\hline
0
\end{array}
$$

There would be 14 children in each cabin.

Other examples

$$
\begin{array}{r}
23 \\
2\overline{)46} \\
4 \\
\hline
6 \\
6 \\
\hline
0
\end{array}
\qquad
\begin{array}{r}
27\,R2 \\
3\overline{)83} \\
6 \\
\hline
23 \\
21 \\
\hline
2
\end{array}
\qquad
\begin{array}{r}
15 \\
6\overline{)90} \\
6 \\
\hline
30 \\
30 \\
\hline
0
\end{array}
\qquad
\begin{array}{r}
20\,R4 \\
5\overline{)104} \\
10 \\
\hline
4 \\
0 \\
\hline
4
\end{array}
$$

Find the quotients and remainders.

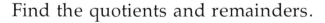

1. $3\overline{)96}$
2. $4\overline{)84}$
3. $2\overline{)48}$
4. $3\overline{)63}$
5. $4\overline{)88}$

6. $2\overline{)36}$
7. $3\overline{)84}$
8. $4\overline{)92}$
9. $3\overline{)75}$
10. $2\overline{)72}$

11. $5\overline{)96}$
12. $4\overline{)87}$
13. $3\overline{)76}$
14. $6\overline{)85}$
15. $7\overline{)98}$

Divide.

1. $2\overline{)128}$ 2. $4\overline{)224}$ 3. $5\overline{)185}$ 4. $3\overline{)276}$

5. $7\overline{)511}$ 6. $8\overline{)272}$ 7. $6\overline{)278}$ 8. $9\overline{)225}$

9. $4\overline{)113}$ 10. $3\overline{)185}$ 11. $2\overline{)193}$ 12. $9\overline{)432}$

13. $7\overline{)170}$ 14. $8\overline{)360}$ 15. $6\overline{)174}$ 16. $5\overline{)230}$

17. $3\overline{)124}$ 18. $7\overline{)289}$ 19. $6\overline{)328}$ 20. $4\overline{)209}$

21. $2\overline{)130}$ 22. $3\overline{)192}$ 23. $9\overline{)149}$

24. $8\overline{)500}$ 25. $4\overline{)268}$ 26. $3\overline{)263}$

27. 96 canoe paddles
    6 paddles for each canoe
    How many canoes?

28. Crafts class:
    Had 131 beads.
    Made 5 bracelets.
    Put same number of beads
    on each bracelet.
    How many beads on each?
    How many beads left over?

Start with	252
Subtract 9	− 9
	243
Subtract 9	− 9
	234
⋮	⋮

Keep on subtracting nines.
Guess how many times you must
subtract 9 to reach 0.

Try it! Was your guess too large,
too small, or just right?

More practice, page 364, Set B

Checking quotients and remainders

How can you check Pat's paper to see if she found the correct quotient and remainder?

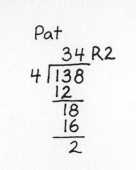

Pat

$$\begin{array}{r} 34\ R2 \\ 4\overline{)138} \\ 12 \\ \hline 18 \\ 16 \\ \hline 2 \end{array}$$

Finding the answer

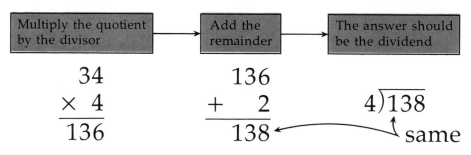

| Multiply the quotient by the divisor | → | Add the remainder | → | The answer should be the dividend |

$$\begin{array}{r} 34 \\ \times\ 4 \\ \hline 136 \end{array} \qquad \begin{array}{r} 136 \\ +\ \ 2 \\ \hline 138 \end{array} \qquad 4\overline{)138} \ \text{same}$$

The quotient is correct.

Other examples

$$\begin{array}{r} 37\,R3 \\ 6\overline{)225}\ \checkmark \\ 18 \\ \hline 45 \\ 42 \\ \hline 3 \end{array} \qquad \begin{array}{r} \text{Check} \\ 37 \\ \times\ 6 \\ \hline 222 \\ +\ \ 3 \\ \hline 225\ \checkmark \end{array}$$

(correct)

$$\begin{array}{r} 58\,R2 \\ 3\overline{)178} \\ 15 \\ \hline 28 \\ 26 \\ \hline 2 \end{array} \qquad \begin{array}{r} \text{Check} \\ 58 \\ \times\ 3 \\ \hline 174 \\ +\ \ 2 \\ \hline 176 \end{array}$$

(not correct)

A quotient and remainder are given in each problem.
Show the check and tell whether or not they are correct.

1. $3\overline{)127}$ 42 R1

2. $5\overline{)184}$ 36 R4

3. $4\overline{)224}$ 54 R3

4. $6\overline{)299}$ 49 R5

5. $7\overline{)167}$ 23 R6

6. $9\overline{)424}$ 43 R1

7. $8\overline{)412}$ 51 R4

8. $2\overline{)119}$ 59 R1

9. $4\overline{)259}$ 64 R3

10. $5\overline{)412}$ 82 R2

Divide.
Check each exercise.

1. 3)276
2. 6)438
3. 4)268
4. 5)397
5. 8)99

6. 7)532
7. 4)314
8. 9)654
9. 6)94
10. 2)135

11. 6)278
12. 8)635
13. 3)64
14. 4)92
15. 9)764

16. 2)83
17. 5)327
18. 4)189
19. 7)602
20. 6)400

21. 5)374
22. 9)548
23. 8)213
24. 3)56
25. 7)299

Copy the problem.
Fill in the digits so that the remainder will be 0.

☆26. 6)34▮▮▮ ☆27. 4)26▮▮▮ ☆28. 5)39▮▮▮ ☆29. 7)3▮▮▮▮▮ ☆30. 8)▮▮▮▮▮▮

Some ink was spilled on these papers.
Can you give the missing numbers?

☆31.

Pam

    54 R3
6)▮▮▮▮
   30
   27
   24
    3

☆32.

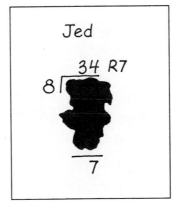

Jed

    34 R7
8)▮▮▮

    7

Here is an unusual
number:

    4 1 0 2 5 6

Divide this number
by 4. What do you
notice?

Finding 3-digit quotients

Satellite speed: 8 km a second
Distance from San Francisco to New York: 4112 km
How many seconds would the satellite take?

Finding the answer

Divide the hundreds, multiply, and subtract	Divide the tens, multiply, and subtract	Divide the ones, multiply, and subtract

$$\begin{array}{r} 5 \\ 8\overline{)4112} \\ 40 \\ \hline 1 \end{array}$$

$$\begin{array}{r} 51 \\ 8\overline{)4112} \\ 40\downarrow \\ \hline 11 \\ 8 \\ \hline 3 \end{array}$$

$$\begin{array}{r} 514 \\ 8\overline{)4112} \\ 40 \\ \hline 11 \\ 8\downarrow \\ \hline 32 \\ 32 \\ \hline 0 \end{array}$$

It would take about 514 seconds.

Other examples

$$\begin{array}{r} 287\,R1 \\ 3\overline{)862} \\ 6 \\ \hline 26 \\ 24 \\ \hline 22 \\ 21 \\ \hline 1 \end{array}$$

$$\begin{array}{r} 237\,R4 \\ 5\overline{)1189} \\ 10 \\ \hline 18 \\ 15 \\ \hline 39 \\ 35 \\ \hline 4 \end{array}$$

$$\begin{array}{r} 841 \\ 6\overline{)5046} \\ 48 \\ \hline 24 \\ 24 \\ \hline 6 \\ 6 \\ \hline 0 \end{array}$$

Find the quotients and remainders.

1. $2\overline{)735}$

2. $3\overline{)871}$

3. $4\overline{)986}$

4. $3\overline{)794}$

5. $5\overline{)966}$

6. $4\overline{)579}$

7. $6\overline{)894}$

8. $7\overline{)957}$

9. $3\overline{)698}$

10. $2\overline{)564}$

11. $4\overline{)683}$

12. $5\overline{)843}$

Divide.

1. $5\overline{)3742}$ 2. $2\overline{)1637}$ 3. $4\overline{)974}$ 4. $3\overline{)2472}$

5. $6\overline{)4856}$ 6. $7\overline{)5230}$ 7. $5\overline{)4250}$ 8. $8\overline{)6375}$

9. $9\overline{)7638}$ 10. $2\overline{)758}$ 11. $4\overline{)1896}$ 12. $6\overline{)4378}$

13. $3\overline{)1268}$ 14. $9\overline{)8470}$ 15. $7\overline{)5732}$ 16. $8\overline{)4269}$

17. $5\overline{)2340}$ 18. $4\overline{)1927}$ 19. $6\overline{)4918}$ 20. $9\overline{)7384}$

Divide. Check each exercise.

21. $6\overline{)1279}$ 22. $8\overline{)2581}$ 23. $9\overline{)3975}$ 24. $4\overline{)2653}$

25. $3\overline{)864}$ 26. $5\overline{)4267}$ 27. $2\overline{)1748}$ 28. $7\overline{)4638}$

29. $6\overline{)3930}$ 30. $4\overline{)1326}$ 31. $8\overline{)5462}$ 32. $3\overline{)1984}$

☆ 33. $3\overline{)111\ 111}$ ☆ 34. $4\overline{)49\ 380}$ ☆ 35. $6\overline{)1\ 333\ 998}$

36. Satellite speed:
8 km per second
It is about 5533 km
from New York to
London. About how
many seconds would
the satellite take?

☆ 37. Satellite speed:
8 km per second
Choose a distance
from a world atlas.
About how long would
it take the satellite
to go that distance?

Is this product

$9 \times 8 \times 7 \times 6 \times 5 \times 4 \times 3 \times 2 \times 1$

A   less than 100 000?
B   between 100 000 and 500 000?
C   more than 500 000?

Find the product.
Was your estimate correct?

More practice, page 365

Checking quotients by estimating

Ed took a plane trip from Detroit to Edmonton. The flight took 4 hours.

He wanted to find out how fast his plane was flying.

Estimate the quotient.
Does Ed's answer make sense?

Distance from Detroit to Edmonton: 3229 km

Time: 4 hours

$$
\begin{array}{r}
87\ R1 \\
4\overline{)3229} \\
\underline{32} \\
29 \\
\underline{28} \\
1
\end{array}
$$

We think

$$
\begin{array}{r}
800 \\
\times\ \ 4 \\
\hline
3200
\end{array}
\qquad
\begin{array}{r}
900 \\
\times\ \ 4 \\
\hline
3600
\end{array}
$$

3229 is between 3200 and 3600.

The quotient 4$\overline{)3229}$ is between 800 and 900.
Ed's answer does not make sense.

Estimate these quotients between 2 multiples of 100.

1. 8$\overline{)3152}$ 2. 8$\overline{)973}$ 3. 8$\overline{)7051}$

4. 8$\overline{)1794}$ 5. 8$\overline{)4537}$ 6. 8$\overline{)2825}$

7. 8$\overline{)5759}$ 8. 8$\overline{)6296}$ 9. 8$\overline{)3713}$

$$
\begin{array}{r}
100 \\
\times\ \ 8 \\
\hline
800
\end{array}
\quad
\begin{array}{r}
200 \\
\times\ \ 8 \\
\hline
1600
\end{array}
\quad
\begin{array}{r}
300 \\
\times\ \ 8 \\
\hline
2400
\end{array}
$$

$$
\begin{array}{r}
400 \\
\times\ \ 8 \\
\hline
3200
\end{array}
\quad
\begin{array}{r}
500 \\
\times\ \ 8 \\
\hline
4000
\end{array}
\quad
\begin{array}{r}
600 \\
\times\ \ 8 \\
\hline
4800
\end{array}
$$

$$
\begin{array}{r}
700 \\
\times\ \ 8 \\
\hline
5600
\end{array}
\quad
\begin{array}{r}
800 \\
\times\ \ 8 \\
\hline
6400
\end{array}
\quad
\begin{array}{r}
900 \\
\times\ \ 8 \\
\hline
7200
\end{array}
$$

Estimate each quotient between two multiples of 10 or two multiples of 100. Does the given quotient make sense?

Example: $4\overline{)256}$ → 64   Answer: between 60 and 70.
The given quotient makes sense.

1. $6\overline{)4440}$ → 74

2. $3\overline{)975}$ → 325

3. $5\overline{)1040}$ → 28

4. $7\overline{)672}$ → 96

5. $8\overline{)5040}$ → 63

6. $4\overline{)3608}$ → 92

7. $9\overline{)7947}$ → 883

8. $5\overline{)4900}$ → 98

Divide. Use estimation to see if your answer makes sense.

9. $6\overline{)89}$

10. $4\overline{)267}$

11. $5\overline{)2436}$

12. $3\overline{)1965}$

13. $2\overline{)1563}$

14. $8\overline{)678}$

15. $7\overline{)439}$

16. $9\overline{)7863}$

17. Drove 491 km.
Trip took 6 hours.
Drove how many
kilometers each hour?

Trace and cut out 4 of these.

How many different shapes
can you make by placing
"like" edges together?
Here are a few.

☆ 18. Find the distance from
your home (or a nearby city)
to Mexico City. Find out
how long a plane would take
to fly there. About how fast
must the plane travel?

Draw your findings on
graph paper.

Answers for Self-check   1. 8 R5   2. 14   3. 34   4. 25 R2   5. 122 R2   6. 43 R7   7. 699   8. 640 R2
9. between 50 and 60   10. between 70 and 80   11. between 80 and 90   12. between 40 and 50
13. between 800 and 900   14. between 400 and 500   15. between 800 and 900
16. between 800 and 900

Self-check

Divide. Check your work.

1. $8\overline{)69}$ 2. $6\overline{)84}$ 3. $4\overline{)136}$ 4. $5\overline{)127}$

5. $7\overline{)856}$ 6. $9\overline{)394}$ 7. $4\overline{)2796}$ 8. $6\overline{)3842}$

Estimate the quotients between two multiples of 10.

9. $5\overline{)278}$ 10. $6\overline{)439}$ 11. $7\overline{)568}$ 12. $8\overline{)347}$

Estimate the quotients between two multiples of 100.

13. $3\overline{)2653}$ 14. $4\overline{)1938}$ 15. $6\overline{)4975}$ 16. $9\overline{)7523}$

Answers for Self-check—page 201

Test

Divide. Check your work.

1. $9\overline{)75}$ 2. $4\overline{)76}$ 3. $5\overline{)362}$ 4. $7\overline{)597}$

5. $6\overline{)212}$ 6. $5\overline{)190}$ 7. $8\overline{)394}$ 8. $4\overline{)1344}$

Estimate the quotients between two multiples of 10.

9. $9\overline{)643}$ 10. $8\overline{)296}$ 11. $6\overline{)472}$ 12. $3\overline{)190}$

Estimate the quotients between two multiples of 100.

13. $4\overline{)3456}$ 14. $5\overline{)2134}$ 15. $7\overline{)6199}$ 16. $9\overline{)6750}$

For fun

Look Again!

First answer **yes** or **no** to each question. Then find a way to check your answer.

1. Are the circles in the center of each group the same size?

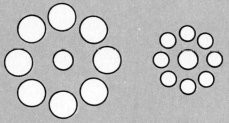

2. Are the blue line and the red line the same length?

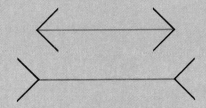

3. Is the diameter of the plate less than the height of the glass?

4. Is the middle pole taller than the pole at the left?

5. Is the blue figure a circle? Is it the size of a penny?

6. Are both red lines the same length?

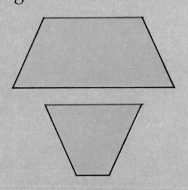

Dividing: 2-Digit Divisors with Remainders

Getting started

60 Multiplier and Divider									
1	2	3	4	5	6	7	8	9	10
60 +	60 +	60 +	60 +	60 +	60 +	60 +	60 +	60 +	60
60	120	180	240	300	360	420	480	540	600

The "60 Multiplier and Divider" was used to estimate this quotient.

$$\begin{array}{r} 7 \leftarrow \text{estimated} \\ 60\overline{)439} \quad \text{quotient} \end{array}$$

Use it to estimate these quotients.

1. $60\overline{)195}$ 2. $60\overline{)256}$ 3. $60\overline{)478}$ 4. $60\overline{)536}$

Cut out a strip of paper and make a "70 Multiplier and Divider." Use it to estimate these quotients.

5. $70\overline{)153}$ 6. $70\overline{)294}$ 7. $70\overline{)510}$ 8. $70\overline{)361}$

If you could use a Multiplier and Divider for every problem,
dividing would be easy. Study the example. Try the problems.

Example

1	2	3	4	5	6	7	8	9	10
40 +	40 +	40 +	40 +	40 +	40 +	40 +	40 +	40 +	40
40	80	120	160	200	240	280	320	360	400

$$\begin{array}{r} 6\ \text{R}16 \\ 40\overline{)256} \\ 240 \\ \hline 16 \end{array}$$

1.

1	2	3	4	5	6	7	8	9	10
30 +	30 +	30 +	30 +	30 +	30 +	30 +	30 +	30 +	30
30	60	90	120	150	180	210	240	270	300

$30\overline{)235}$

2.

1	2	3	4	5	6	7	8	9	10
50 +	50 +	50 +	50 +	50 +	50 +	50 +	50 +	50 +	50
50	100	150	200	250	300	350	400	450	500

$50\overline{)242}$

3.

1	2	3	4	5	6	7	8	9	10
80 +	80 +	80 +	80 +	80 +	80 +	80 +	80 +	80 +	80
80	160	240	320	400	480	560	640	720	800

$80\overline{)287}$

4.

1	2	3	4	5	6	7	8	9	10
90 +	90 +	90 +	90 +	90 +	90 +	90 +	90 +	90 +	90
90	180	270	360	450	540	630	720	810	900

$90\overline{)649}$

Dividing by a multiple of 10

The Dodgers and Giants once played a 9-inning baseball game that lasted 258 minutes. How many hours was this? How many extra minutes?

Finding the answer

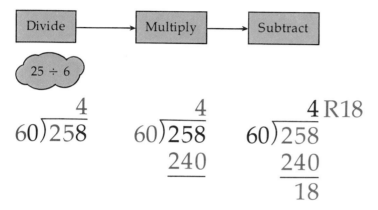

| Divide | → | Multiply | → | Subtract |

$25 \div 6$

$$\begin{array}{r} 4 \\ 60\overline{)258} \end{array} \qquad \begin{array}{r} 4 \\ 60\overline{)258} \\ 240 \end{array} \qquad \begin{array}{r} 4\,R18 \\ 60\overline{)258} \\ 240 \\ \hline 18 \end{array}$$

The game lasted 4 hours and 18 minutes.

Other examples

$$\begin{array}{r} 9\,R6 \\ 30\overline{)276} \\ 270 \\ \hline 6 \end{array} \qquad \begin{array}{r} 4\,R69 \\ 70\overline{)349} \\ 280 \\ \hline 69 \end{array} \qquad \begin{array}{r} 7\,R20 \\ 40\overline{)300} \\ 280 \\ \hline 20 \end{array}$$

Divide.

1. $40\overline{)172}$ 2. $60\overline{)503}$ 3. $50\overline{)317}$ 4. $90\overline{)486}$

5. $80\overline{)276}$ 6. $30\overline{)270}$ 7. $70\overline{)400}$ 8. $20\overline{)167}$

9. $50\overline{)483}$ 10. $20\overline{)131}$ 11. $40\overline{)299}$ 12. $30\overline{)137}$

13. $70\overline{)619}$ 14. $60\overline{)531}$ 15. $80\overline{)666}$ 16. $90\overline{)700}$

Divide. Check your work.

1. $60\overline{)170}$ 2. $80\overline{)282}$ 3. $30\overline{)285}$

4. $20\overline{)89}$ 5. $70\overline{)480}$ 6. $50\overline{)236}$

7. $40\overline{)214}$ 8. $90\overline{)486}$ 9. $80\overline{)753}$

10. $40\overline{)263}$ 11. $20\overline{)192}$ 12. $50\overline{)401}$

13. $30\overline{)215}$ 14. $90\overline{)597}$ 15. $60\overline{)365}$

16. $70\overline{)543}$ 17. $50\overline{)483}$ 18. $20\overline{)131}$

19. $40\overline{)299}$ 20. $60\overline{)531}$ 21. $80\overline{)276}$

Try these.

☆ 22. $40\overline{)3576}$ ☆ 23. $20\overline{)874}$ ☆ 24. $30\overline{)1700}$

25. A 23-inning baseball game took 443 minutes. How many hours? How many extra minutes?

26. A 25-inning game took 424 minutes. How many hours? How many extra minutes?

Place 17 toothpicks like this.

1. Take away 5 toothpicks so that exactly 4 squares are left.

2. Take away 5 toothpicks so that exactly 3 squares are left!

More practice, page 366, Set A

Dividing: 2-digit divisors

If each child had the same number of pets, how many pets would each child have?

Total number of pets owned by children in Sharon's class:	124
Number of children in Sharon's class:	31

Finding the answer

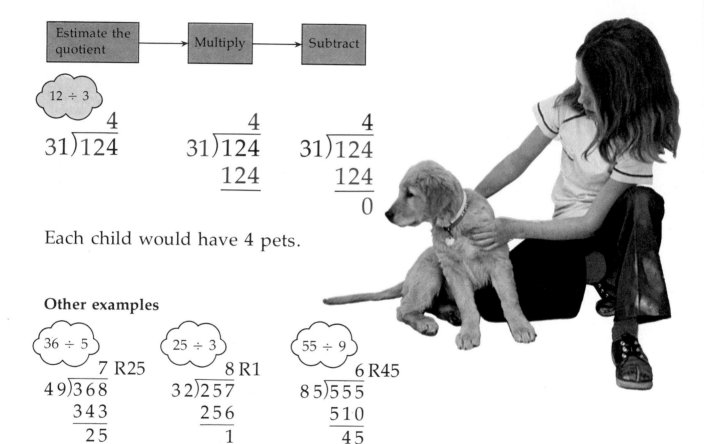

Each child would have 4 pets.

Other examples

Find the quotients and remainders.

1. $21\overline{)158}$

2. $39\overline{)173}$

3. $68\overline{)435}$

4. $52\overline{)436}$

5. $59\overline{)492}$

6. $87\overline{)652}$

7. $32\overline{)248}$

8. $48\overline{)467}$

9. $77\overline{)333}$

10. $43\overline{)375}$

11. $65\overline{)365}$

12. $91\overline{)550}$

Divide. Check your work.

1. $29\overline{)247}$ 2. $42\overline{)256}$ 3. $68\overline{)296}$ 4. $31\overline{)220}$

5. $73\overline{)582}$ 6. $38\overline{)140}$ 7. $51\overline{)415}$ 8. $42\overline{)376}$

9. $89\overline{)286}$ 10. $63\overline{)507}$ 11. $49\overline{)236}$ 12. $31\overline{)249}$

13. $57\overline{)375}$ 14. $48\overline{)463}$ 15. $71\overline{)498}$ 16. $78\overline{)423}$

17. $45\overline{)352}$ 18. $66\overline{)564}$ 19. $93\overline{)555}$ 20. $83\overline{)499}$

21. $87\overline{)286}$ 22. $92\overline{)643}$ 23. $65\overline{)142}$ 24. $78\overline{)185}$

25. Total number of pets owned in Dan's class: 96
Number of children in Dan's class: 32
How many pets per child?

★ 26. Find the total number of pets owned in your class. How many pets would that be for each child?

Trace these two hexagons. Cut along the dotted lines.

Can you put the 6 pieces together to make 3 equilateral triangles that are the same size?

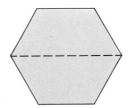 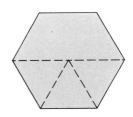

Practicing your skills

Solve.

1. 98×10 2. 56×100 3. 8×1000 4. 8×30 5. 40×9

6. 60×7 7. 20×30 8. 40×50 9. 60×70 10. 30×30

11. 567
    + 876

12. 986
    + 329

13. 657
    + 89

14. 863
    − 249

15. 803
    − 198

More practice, page 366A, Set A

✴ Dividing: 2-digit divisors and quotients

A cheetah ran 775 m in 31 seconds. How many meters each second?

Finding the answer

Estimate the tens	→	Multiply and subtract	→	Estimate the ones	→	Multiply and subtract

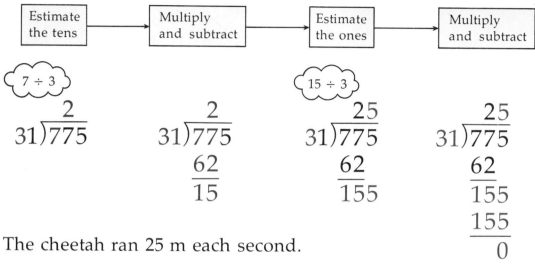

The cheetah ran 25 m each second.

Other examples

```
    41 R14          20 R9           33
23)957          32)649         54)1782
   92              64             162
   ---             ---            ---
   37               9            162
   23               0            162
   ---             ---            ---
   14               9              0
```

Find the quotients and remainders.

1. 21)657

2. 42)967

3. 32)999

4. 41)738

5. 73)3069

6. 52)2496

7. 64)2078

8. 74)1965

Find the quotients and remainders.

1. 23)746
2. 34)884
3. 42)739
4. 83)976

5. 54)2436
6. 32)3145
7. 64)3872
8. 51)4405

9. 61)2783
10. 24)736
11. 92)5340
12. 43)3189

13. 11)456
14. 53)3852
15. 41)2764
16. 72)5832

17. 64)5164
18. 24)986
19. 73)3947
20. 43)2763

21. An antelope can run 550 m in 25 seconds. How many meters each second?

☆ 22. Mark off a distance of 50 m. Find out how many seconds it takes you to run this distance. About how many meters can you run each second?

123

If you use only the digits 1, 2, and 3, how many different 3-digit numbers can you make for bike license plates?
How many different 4-digit plates could you make with the digits 1, 2, 3, and 4?

Answers for Self-check   1. 8 R5   2. 7 R34   3. 6 R18   4. 8 R32   5. 5 R12   6. 8 R11   7. 8 R17
8. 6 R28   9. 5 R1   10. 9   11. 4 R2   12. 7 R8   13. 6 R3   14. 7 R10   15. 9   16. 6 R6   17. 21   18. 13 R18
19. 42   20. 41 R4

More practice, page 366A, Set B

Self-check

Divide.

1. $30 \overline{)245}$
2. $70 \overline{)524}$
3. $40 \overline{)258}$
4. $60 \overline{)512}$

5. $20 \overline{)112}$
6. $90 \overline{)731}$
7. $80 \overline{)657}$
8. $50 \overline{)328}$

9. $51 \overline{)256}$
10. $43 \overline{)387}$
11. $24 \overline{)98}$
12. $63 \overline{)449}$

13. $72 \overline{)435}$
14. $51 \overline{)367}$
15. $83 \overline{)747}$
16. $92 \overline{)558}$

17. $31 \overline{)651}$
18. $42 \overline{)564}$
19. $34 \overline{)1428}$
20. $73 \overline{)2997}$

Answers for Self-check—page 211

Test

Divide.

1. $40 \overline{)246}$
2. $80 \overline{)729}$
3. $70 \overline{)563}$
4. $90 \overline{)804}$

5. $30 \overline{)275}$
6. $60 \overline{)373}$
7. $50 \overline{)421}$
8. $80 \overline{)730}$

9. $83 \overline{)747}$
10. $33 \overline{)298}$
11. $62 \overline{)397}$
12. $54 \overline{)329}$

13. $44 \overline{)325}$
14. $71 \overline{)497}$
15. $93 \overline{)656}$
16. $52 \overline{)425}$

17. $42 \overline{)882}$
18. $53 \overline{)904}$
19. $61 \overline{)2623}$
20. $32 \overline{)2051}$

Geoboard Activities

1. Make an interesting figure on your geoboard.

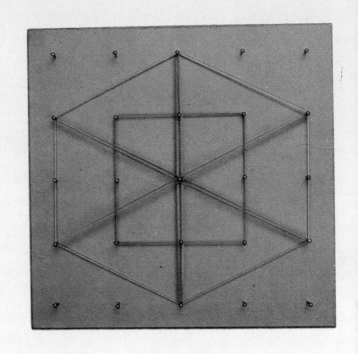

2. How many of these figures can you show on your geoboard?

 isosceles triangle

 kite

 rectangle

 right triangle

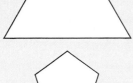 trapezoid

 parallelogram

 pentagon

 hexagon

3. The figure on the geoboard has 5 sides. It has no dents in it.

   Can you make a geoboard figure (no dents) with 6 sides? 7 sides? 8 sides? More than 8 sides?

dent

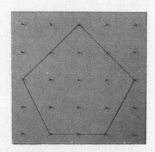

Using Your Skills

Getting started

1. About how much would 2 vases cost?

2. About how much would 1 pair of socks cost?

3. What other problems could you solve without using pencil and paper or a calculator?

Solving Problems

1. Read carefully to find the facts.

2. Look for the question.

3. Decide what to do. (+, −, ×, ÷).

4. Find the answer.

5. Read again.
   Does your answer make sense?

You can use estimation
to help you see
if your answer makes
sense.

Do these answers make sense?

1. 5 L of oil for $4.90
   How much for 1 L?
   Answer: $0.98

2. Drove 488 km.
   Used 61 L of gas.
   How many kilometers
   for each liter?
   Answer: 80

Stocking the store

Solve each problem. Use estimation to see if your answer makes sense.

1. Had 49 cases of soup.
   Put 8 cases on each shelf.
   How many shelves?
   How many cases left over?

4. Had 86 chicken legs.
   Put 6 legs in each package.
   How many packages?
   How many legs left over?

2. Had 156 bags of nuts.
   Put 8 bags on each rack.
   How many racks?
   How many bags left over?

5. Had 397 oranges.
   Put 10 oranges in each bag.
   How many bags?
   How many extra oranges?

3. Had 210 lamb chops.
   Put 3 chops in each package.
   How many packages?
   How many extra chops?

6. Had 2278 tomatoes.
   Put 4 tomatoes in each box.
   How many boxes?
   How many extra tomatoes?

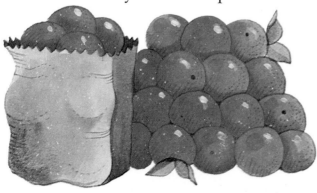

7. Had 6698 carrots.
   Put 8 carrots in each bunch.
   How many bunches?
   How many extra carrots?

8. Had 160 boxes of cereal.
   Put 20 boxes on each shelf.
   How many shelves?
   How many boxes left over?

9. Had 380 eggs.
   Put 12 eggs in each carton.
   How many cartons?
   How many eggs left over?

10. Had 1046 wieners.
    Put 12 in each package.
    How many packages?
    How many extra wieners?

☆ 11. 226 cases of juice
      6 bottles of juice in a case
      Each shelf holds 60 bottles.
      How many shelves can be filled?
      How many bottles left over?

Finding averages

First drop: caught on 36   Third drop: caught on 38
Second drop: caught on 23   Fourth drop: caught on 19

What is the **average** catch number?

Finding the answer

Add the numbers	→	Divide the sum by the number of addends	→	Check your work

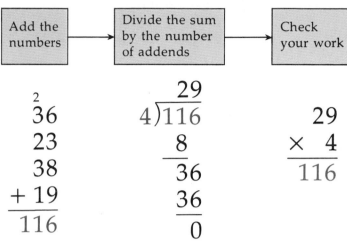

$$
\begin{array}{r}
\overset{2}{3}6 \\
23 \\
38 \\
+\,19 \\
\hline
116
\end{array}
$$

$$
\begin{array}{r}
29 \\
4\overline{)116} \\
8 \\
\hline
36 \\
36 \\
\hline
0
\end{array}
$$

$$
\begin{array}{r}
29 \\
\times\ 4 \\
\hline
116
\end{array}
$$

The average catch number is 29.

Another example

Numbers: 95, 83, 99

$$
\begin{array}{r}
\overset{1}{9}5 \\
83 \\
+\,99 \\
\hline
277
\end{array}
$$

$$
\begin{array}{r}
92\ \text{R1} \\
3\overline{)277} \\
27 \\
\hline
7 \\
6 \\
\hline
1
\end{array}
$$

Check:
$$
\begin{array}{r}
92 \\
\times\ 3 \\
\hline
276 \\
+\ \ \ 1 \\
\hline
277
\end{array}
$$

The average is about 92.

Find the average of the numbers in each group.

1. 4, 5, 9   2. 5, 6, 10   3. 5, 7, 12, 8   4. 2, 3, 10, 9, 11

5. 7, 12, 14   6. 3, 7, 6, 4   7. 21, 34, 44   8. 62, 79, 87

9. 81, 82, 91, 78   10. 23, 35, 38   11. 52, 56, 51   12. 98, 86

Find the averages.

1. Find the average daily wind speed.

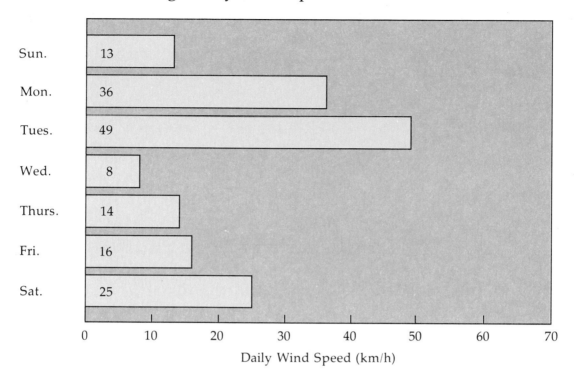

	Daily Wind Speed (km/h)
Sun.	13
Mon.	36
Tues.	49
Wed.	8
Thurs.	14
Fri.	16
Sat.	25

Daily Wind Speed (km/h)

2. Find the average morning temperature.

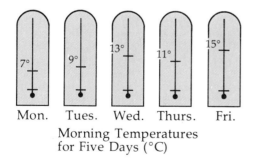

7° 9° 13° 11° 15°
Mon. Tues. Wed. Thurs. Fri.
Morning Temperatures
for Five Days (°C)

3. Find the average catch number for these meter-stick drops.

First drop: 39
Second drop: 32
Third drop: 43
Fourth drop: 30

☆ 4. Make a chart of temperatures (or other weather measures) for one week. Find the average.

☆ 5. Do meter-stick drops with a friend. Find your average catch number.
Can you lower your average catch number by practicing?

Space facts and problems

Facts

A spaceship to the moon travels 11 km each second.

A satellite travels 8 km each second.

398 auto trips of 100 km each would equal the distance around the earth.

A fast jet can travel a distance equal to the earth's diameter in 16 hours.

Problems

1. How far does it travel in one minute?

2. How many seconds would it take to go 5560 km? About how many minutes?

3. About half as many trips would equal the distance around Mars. How many trips?

4. Jupiter's diameter is 11 times as great as the earth's. How long for the jet to travel that distance?

Facts

A spring scale reading
on the moon is the earth
scale reading divided
by 6.

A scale reading on Mars is
the earth scale reading
divided by 3.

Mercury travels around the sun
at a speed of 48 km per second.
Pluto travels at 5 km per second.

The earth has 1 moon; Mercury, 0;
Venus, 0; Pluto, 0; Jupiter, 12;
Saturn, 9; Uranus, 5; Neptune, 2;
Mars, 2.

Problems

5. The scales read 72 for a person
on the earth. What is the moon
scale reading?

6. The scales read 69 for a person
on the earth. What is the Mars
scale reading?

7. About how many times as fast
does Mercury travel?

8. How many moons in all?

Answers for Self-check   1. 4 hours, 20 minutes   2. 67 packages, 1 extra   3. 88   4. 141   5. 27   6. 12

Self-check

Solve.

1. 260 minutes
   How many hours?
   How many extra minutes?

2. 269 light bulbs
   Put 4 in each package.
   How many packages?
   How many extra bulbs?

Find the averages.

3. Test scores: 83, 96, 75, 88, 98

4. Bowling scores:
   138, 129, 156

5. Temperatures: 26, 34, 19, 29

Solve.

6. It is 4 times as far around the earth as around the moon. It takes about 48 hours to fly around the earth. How many hours would it take to fly around the moon at the same speed?

Answers for Self-check—page 221

Test

Solve.

1. 215 days
   How many months?
   How many extra days?
   (Use 30 days in a month.)

2. 770 crayons
   8 in each box
   How many boxes?
   How many extra crayons?

Find the averages.

3. Basketball scores: 58, 64, 78, 47, 83

4. Rainfall each year (cm):
   43, 48, 52, 49

5. Heights (cm): 129, 138, 141

Solve.

6. A satellite travels around the earth in about 90 minutes. How many times would it go around in 720 minutes?

Greatest-Quotient Game

1. Make a spinner.

2. Draw a division grid
   for each player.

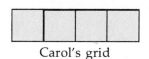

Carol's grid   Ted's grid

3. Spin the spinner.
   Each player writes the
   spinner number in one
   of the four spaces of
   the grid.

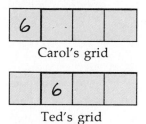

Carol's grid

Ted's grid

4. Do this four times. The
   greatest quotient wins.

   Who won this game?

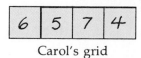

Carol's grid

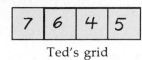

Ted's grid

Geometry (Relationships)

Getting started

Tangram puzzle pieces

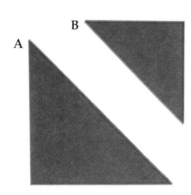

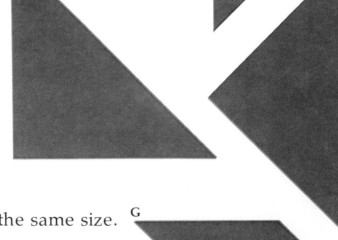

Find two pieces that have
   the same shape, but not the same size.
   the same size and shape.
   a different size and shape.

Write

D if the two objects have **different** shapes.

SS if they have the **same size** and **shape.**

S if they have the **same shape,** but not the same size.

1.

2.

3.

4.

5.

6.

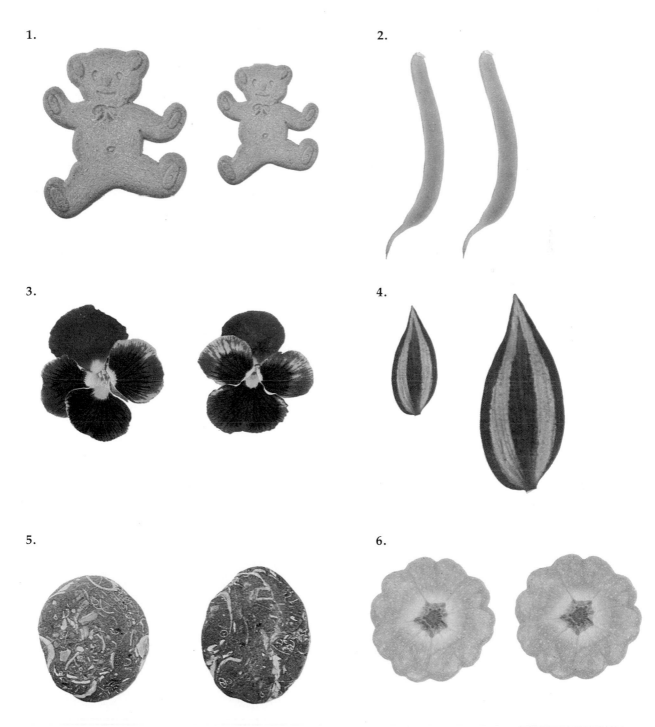

Similar figures

Two figures that have the same shape are **similar** to each other.

Which pictures below seem to be similar figures?

1.

2.

3.

4.

Which figure in each row is similar to the first?

1.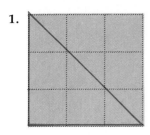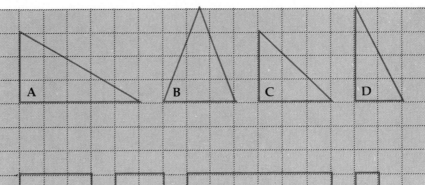

2.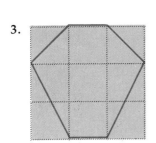

3.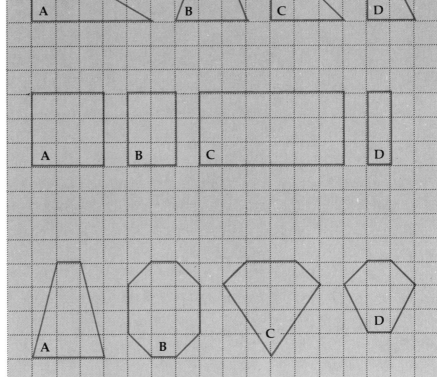

Write **similar** or **not similar** for each pair of figures.

4.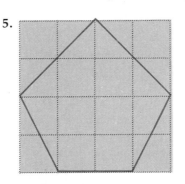

5.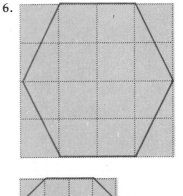

6.

 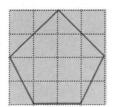 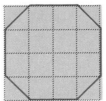

Congruent figures

Figures that have the same size and shape are **congruent** to each other. They will fit exactly on each other.

tracing   picture

The tracing and the picture are **congruent** to each other.

Which of these pairs of figures seem to be congruent?

1.

2.

3.

4.

Which figure is congruent to the first?

1.

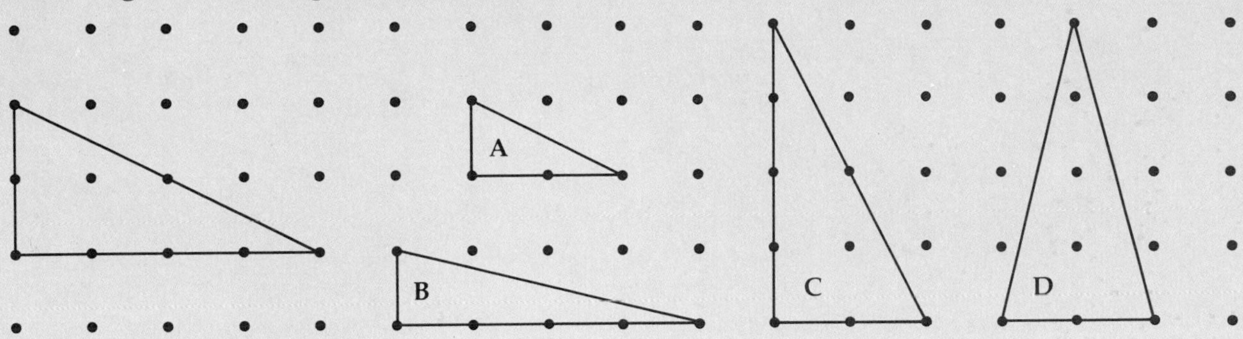

2.

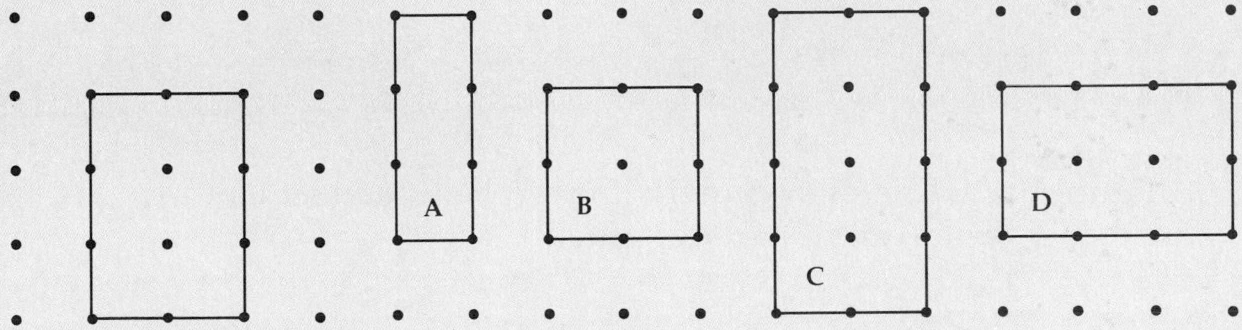

3.

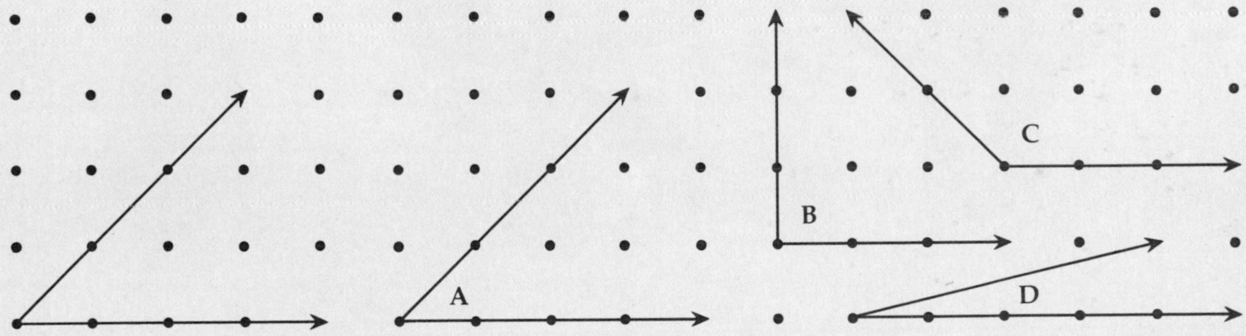

4.

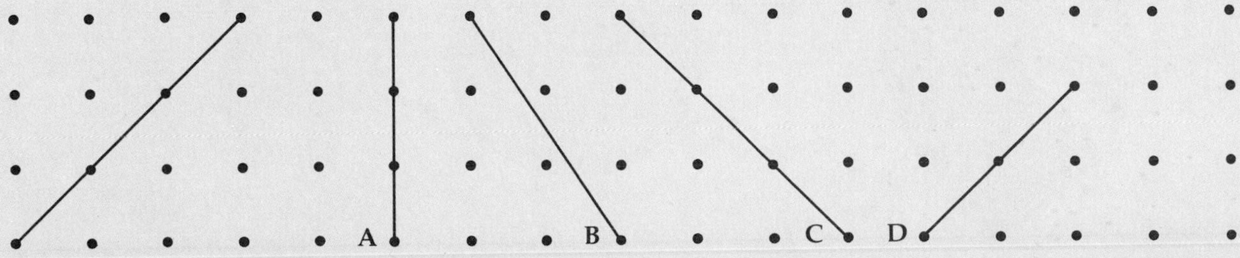

Symmetric figures

fold

A figure has a **line of symmetry** if it can be folded so that the two sides fit exactly (are congruent).

Which of these figures seem to be symmetric? Write **yes** or **no**.

1.

2.

3.

4.

5.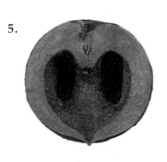

6.

Here is a way to make a figure with symmetry.

Fold a piece
of paper.

Make a cut that
starts and ends
on the fold.

Unfold the piece
you cut out.

Tell what each figure will be when cut out and unfolded.

1.

2.

3.

4.

5.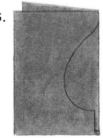

6.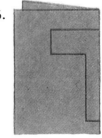

7.

8.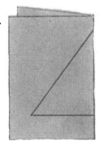

9.

Answers for Self-check   1. not similar   2. similar   3. congruent   4. not congruent   5. yes

Write **similar** or **not similar** for each pair of figures.

1.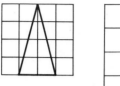

2.

Write **congruent** or **not congruent** for each pair of figures.

3.

4.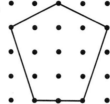

5. Is the small figure in exercise 1 symmetric?

Answers for Self-check—page 231

Test

Write **similar** or **not similar** for each pair of figures.

1.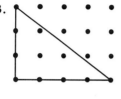

2.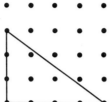

Write **congruent** or **not congruent** for each pair of figures.

3.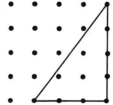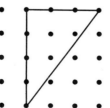

4.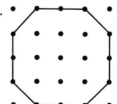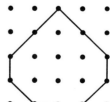

5. Is the small figure in exercise 1 symmetric?

Paper Snowflakes

Make some paper snowflakes.

1. Fold a square piece
    of paper twice.

2. Then fold along
    the diagonal.

3. Cut in and out around
    the edges.

4. Unfold your paper.

Level 20 review

Find the quotients and remainders.

1. $4\overline{)35}$ 2. $7\overline{)44}$ 3. $5\overline{)46}$ 4. $9\overline{)60}$ 5. $8\overline{)74}$

6. $3\overline{)38}$ 7. $6\overline{)66}$ 8. $4\overline{)62}$ 9. $2\overline{)39}$ 10. $8\overline{)97}$

11. $5\overline{)162}$ 12. $7\overline{)193}$ 13. $6\overline{)282}$ 14. $9\overline{)600}$ 15. $3\overline{)265}$

16. $6\overline{)728}$ 17. $4\overline{)692}$ 18. $8\overline{)975}$ 19. $5\overline{)846}$

20. $3\overline{)1895}$ 21. $7\overline{)5040}$ 22. $9\overline{)6517}$ 23. $6\overline{)3728}$

24. $50\overline{)467}$ 25. $20\overline{)148}$ 26. $60\overline{)332}$ 27. $80\overline{)417}$

28. $31\overline{)219}$ 29. $48\overline{)456}$ 30. $92\overline{)560}$ 31. $57\overline{)380}$

32. $13\overline{)274}$ 33. $42\overline{)868}$ 34. $64\overline{)2078}$ 35. $51\overline{)2348}$

Fractional Numbers
Larger Fractional Numbers
Adding and Subtracting Fractional Numbers
Ratio

Fractional Numbers

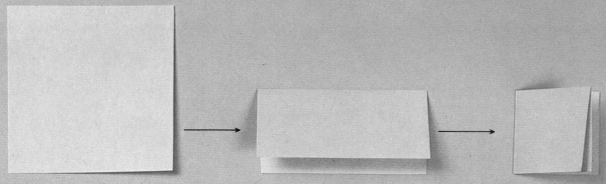

Fold a square piece of paper two times.

It should look like
this when unfolded.

Color and mark the paper so that:

1 of the 4 equal parts is red.

2 of the 4 equal parts are blue.

3 of the 4 equal parts have an "x" on them.

4 of the 4 equal parts have a check mark (√) on them.

You can use a **fractional number** to tell what part
of the paper is colored.

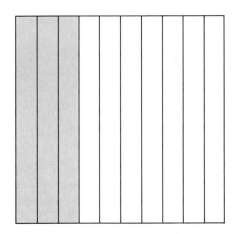

3 colored parts $\longrightarrow$ **3** $\longleftarrow$ numerator

10 equal parts in all $\longrightarrow$ **10** $\longleftarrow$ denominator

Three tenths $\left(\frac{3}{10}\right)$ of the paper is colored.

Use a fractional number to tell what part is colored.

1.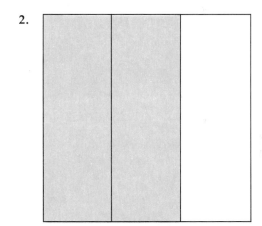

2.

3.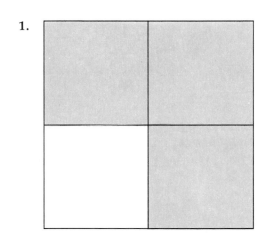

4.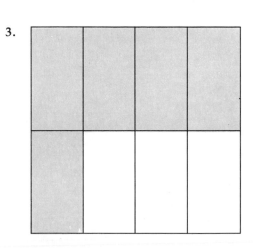

Writing and reading fractional numbers

Write and read the fractional number
for the shaded part of each figure.

Example:

Answer: $\frac{1}{4}$

1.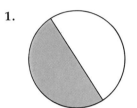

2.

3.

4.

5.

6.

7.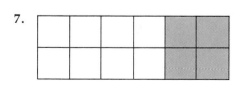

Give the fractional number for each ||||| .

Example:

||||| of the beads have been used.

Answer: $\frac{7}{10}$

1.

||||| of the chess pieces are black.

2.

||||| of the cans have been opened.

3.

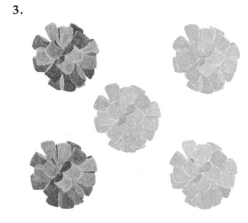

||||| of the bows are yellow.

4.

||||| of the apples are red.

5.

||||| of the crayons are missing.

6.

||||| of the marbles are blue.

7.

||||| of the stars are yellow.

Fractional numbers and the number line

The picture shows that Sue
has walked $\frac{6}{10}$ of the distance.

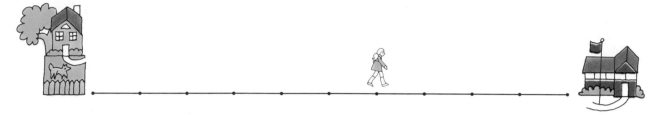

Give a fraction to tell what part
of the distance has been covered.

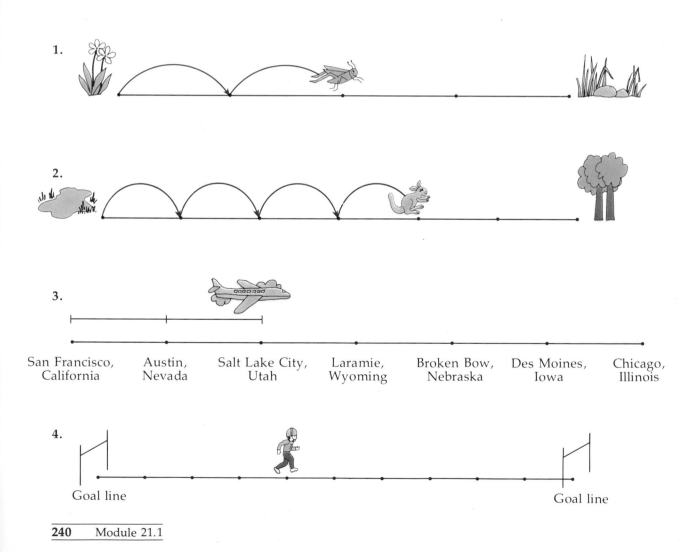

1.

2.

3.

San Francisco,   Austin,   Salt Lake City,   Laramie,   Broken Bow,   Des Moines,   Chicago,
California   Nevada   Utah   Wyoming   Nebraska   Iowa   Illinois

4.

Goal line   Goal line

Fractional numbers can be used to name points on the number line.
Give a fractional number for each ▥.

Example:

Answer: $\frac{2}{3}$

1.

2.

3.

4.

5.

6.

Fred gave Tom $\frac{1}{2}$ of his peanuts. Tom gave Ned $\frac{1}{2}$ of the peanuts he got from Fred. Ned gave Sam $\frac{1}{2}$ of the peanuts he got from Tom. Sam got only 6 peanuts. How many did Fred start with?

Estimating fractional numbers

Choose the fractional number that best answers the question.

1. About how full is the jar of red pepper?

   $\frac{1}{8}$ $\frac{1}{3}$ $\frac{5}{8}$

2. About how full is the jar of black pepper?

   $\frac{3}{10}$ $\frac{6}{10}$ $\frac{9}{10}$

3. About how full is the jar of peas?

   $\frac{1}{2}$ $\frac{7}{8}$ $\frac{1}{5}$

4. About how full is the jar of raisins?

   $\frac{1}{2}$ $\frac{1}{3}$ $\frac{7}{8}$

5. About how full is the jar of pickles?

   $\frac{5}{10}$ $\frac{2}{10}$ $\frac{8}{10}$

6. About how much of the cake is left?

   $\frac{1}{2}$ $\frac{9}{10}$ $\frac{2}{3}$

7. About how full is the glass of orange juice?

   $\frac{1}{2}$ $\frac{5}{8}$ $\frac{7}{8}$

8. About how full is the glass of grape juice?

   $\frac{5}{8}$ $\frac{1}{2}$ $\frac{1}{3}$

Choose the best estimate.

1. About what part of the whole board is the shorter piece?

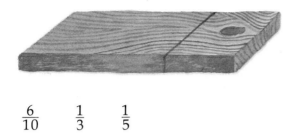

$\frac{6}{10}$ $\frac{1}{3}$ $\frac{1}{5}$

2. The nut covers about what part of the bolt?

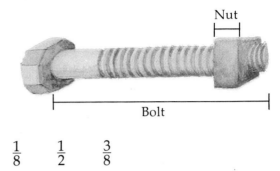

$\frac{1}{8}$ $\frac{1}{2}$ $\frac{3}{8}$

3. About what part of the garden has been plowed?

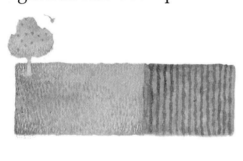

$\frac{1}{6}$ $\frac{3}{4}$ $\frac{4}{10}$

4. About what part of the floor has carpet?

$\frac{5}{10}$ $\frac{1}{4}$ $\frac{1}{8}$

5. About how full is the tank?

$\frac{1}{2}$ $\frac{7}{8}$ $\frac{8}{10}$

6. About how full is the gas tank?

$\frac{1}{6}$ $\frac{1}{4}$ $\frac{1}{10}$

Names for fractional numbers

Write two different names for the fractional number
that tells what part of the box is colored.

We see:

We think:

1 red part ⟶ $\dfrac{1}{2}$ 5 red parts ⟶ $\dfrac{5}{10}$
2 parts in all ⟶   10 parts in all ⟶

We write:

$$\dfrac{1}{2} = \dfrac{5}{10}$$

$\dfrac{1}{2}$ and $\dfrac{5}{10}$ name the same fractional number.
They are **equivalent fractions.**

Write the equivalent fractions.

1.

number of
blue fish
‾‾‾‾‾‾‾‾‾ $\dfrac{\text{||||||}}{4} = \dfrac{\text{||||||}}{2}$ number of
number of   bowls of
fish   blue fish
                         ‾‾‾‾‾‾‾‾‾
                         number of
                         bowls of
                         fish

2.

number of
gold fish
‾‾‾‾‾‾‾‾‾ $\dfrac{\text{||||||}}{6} = \dfrac{\text{||||||}}{3}$ number of
number of   bowls of
fish   gold fish
                         ‾‾‾‾‾‾‾‾‾
                         number of
                         bowls of
                         fish

Write the equivalent fractions.

1.

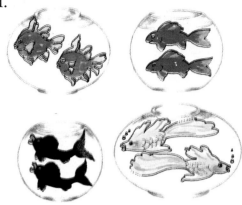

$$\frac{\text{black fish}}{\text{fish in all}} \quad \frac{\text{⫼}}{8} = \frac{\text{⫼}}{4} \quad \begin{array}{l}\text{bowls of}\\\text{black fish}\\\hline\text{bowls}\\\text{of fish}\end{array}$$

2.

$$\frac{\text{red fish}}{\text{fish in all}} \quad \frac{\text{⫼}}{6} = \frac{\text{⫼}}{2} \quad \begin{array}{l}\text{bowls of}\\\text{red fish}\\\hline\text{bowls}\\\text{of fish}\end{array}$$

3.

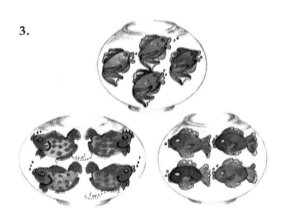

$$\frac{\text{red fish}}{\text{fish in all}} \quad \frac{\text{⫼}}{12} = \frac{\text{⫼}}{3} \quad \begin{array}{l}\text{bowls of}\\\text{red fish}\\\hline\text{bowls}\\\text{of fish}\end{array}$$

4.

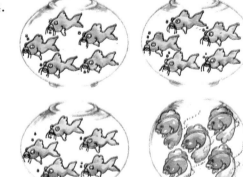

$$\frac{\text{gold fish}}{\text{fish in all}} \quad \frac{\text{⫼}}{20} = \frac{\text{⫼}}{4} \quad \begin{array}{l}\text{bowls of}\\\text{gold fish}\\\hline\text{bowls}\\\text{of fish}\end{array}$$

Which two are the same?

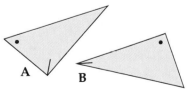

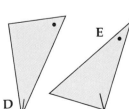
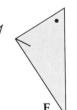

Finding equivalent fractions

This picture shows a pair of equivalent fractions. You can find equivalent fractions without drawing pictures.

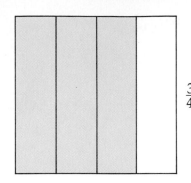
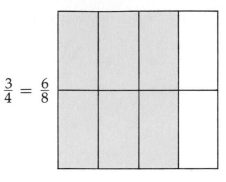

$$\frac{3}{4} = \frac{6}{8}$$

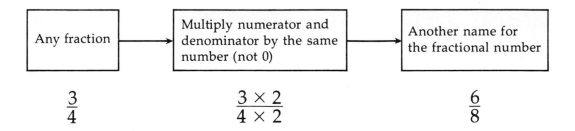

Any fraction	Multiply numerator and denominator by the same number (not 0)	Another name for the fractional number

$$\frac{3}{4} \qquad\qquad \frac{3 \times 2}{4 \times 2} \qquad\qquad \frac{6}{8}$$

Other examples

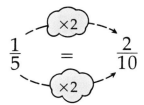

$$\frac{1}{5} = \frac{2}{10}$$

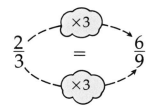

$$\frac{2}{3} = \frac{6}{9}$$

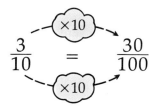

$$\frac{3}{10} = \frac{30}{100}$$

Find the equivalent fraction.

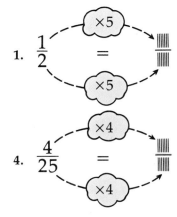

1. $\frac{1}{2} =$

4. $\frac{4}{25} =$

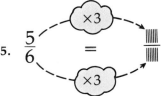
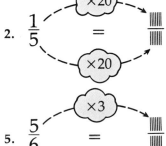

2. $\frac{1}{5} =$

5. $\frac{5}{6} =$

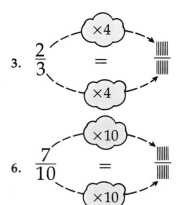

3. $\frac{2}{3} =$

6. $\frac{7}{10} =$

Find the equivalent fraction.

1. 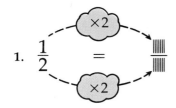 $\dfrac{1}{2} =$

2. 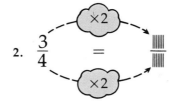 $\dfrac{3}{4} =$

3. 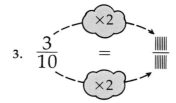 $\dfrac{3}{10} =$

4. $\dfrac{1}{2} =$

5. 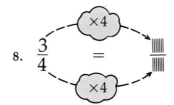 $\dfrac{3}{4} =$

6. $\dfrac{3}{10} =$

7. $\dfrac{1}{2} =$

8. $\dfrac{3}{4} =$

9. $\dfrac{3}{10} =$

Find a fraction equivalent to the one given.

10. $\dfrac{1}{3}$ 11. $\dfrac{1}{4}$ 12. $\dfrac{1}{5}$ 13. $\dfrac{1}{10}$ 14. $\dfrac{2}{3}$ 15. $\dfrac{5}{8}$

16. $\dfrac{5}{6}$ 17. $\dfrac{7}{10}$ 18. $\dfrac{4}{50}$ 19. $\dfrac{3}{25}$ 20. $\dfrac{12}{100}$ 21. $\dfrac{99}{100}$

Give three other names for each fractional number.

Example: $\dfrac{1}{2}$ Answer: $\dfrac{2}{4}, \dfrac{3}{6}, \dfrac{4}{8}$

22. $\dfrac{2}{3}$ 23. $\dfrac{2}{5}$ 24. $\dfrac{1}{8}$

25. $\dfrac{9}{10}$ 26. $\dfrac{1}{3}$ 27. $\dfrac{1}{4}$

$\dfrac{1}{2}, \dfrac{13}{?}$

Equivalent fractions you will see
When you view one half and me.
I'm thirteen above the line.
Find the name you think is mine.

Who am I?

Finding lowest-terms fractions

Baby chicks have hatched from 6 of the 8 eggs. Can you find the fraction that is equivalent to $\frac{6}{8}$ and has the smallest possible denominator?

Finding the answer

| Any fraction | → | Divide the numerator and denominator by the largest possible factor | → | Lowest-terms fraction |

$$\frac{6}{8} \qquad\qquad \frac{6 \div 2}{8 \div 2} \qquad\qquad \frac{3}{4}$$

The **lowest-terms fraction** for $\frac{6}{8}$ is $\frac{3}{4}$.

Other examples

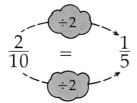 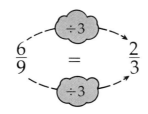 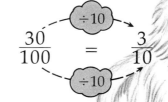

$$\frac{2}{10} \overset{\div 2}{\underset{\div 2}{=}} \frac{1}{5} \qquad \frac{6}{9} \overset{\div 3}{\underset{\div 3}{=}} \frac{2}{3} \qquad \frac{30}{100} \overset{\div 10}{\underset{\div 10}{=}} \frac{3}{10}$$

Find the lowest-terms fraction.

1. $\dfrac{8}{10} \overset{\div 2}{\underset{\div 2}{=}} \boxed{}$ 2. $\dfrac{2}{4} \overset{\div 2}{\underset{\div 2}{=}} \boxed{}$ 3. $\dfrac{12}{15} \overset{\div 3}{\underset{\div 3}{=}} \boxed{}$

4. $\dfrac{15}{50} \overset{\div 5}{\underset{\div 5}{=}} \boxed{}$ 5. $\dfrac{6}{16} \overset{\div 2}{\underset{\div 2}{=}} \boxed{}$ 6. $\dfrac{9}{12} \overset{\div 3}{\underset{\div 3}{=}} \boxed{}$

Give the lowest-terms fraction.

1. $\dfrac{6}{20} = \dfrac{3}{\text{▓}}$ ÷? ÷?

2. $\dfrac{4}{8} = \dfrac{\text{▓}}{2}$ ÷? ÷?

3. $\dfrac{6}{9} = \dfrac{\text{▓}}{3}$ ÷? ÷?

4. $\dfrac{8}{12} = \dfrac{2}{\text{▓}}$ ÷? ÷?

5. $\dfrac{4}{10} = \dfrac{\text{▓}}{5}$ ÷? ÷?

6. $\dfrac{40}{50} = \dfrac{4}{\text{▓}}$ ÷? ÷?

7. $\dfrac{2}{8} = \dfrac{\text{▓}}{4}$

8. $\dfrac{4}{8} = \dfrac{1}{\text{▓}}$

9. $\dfrac{6}{8} = \dfrac{\text{▓}}{4}$

10. $\dfrac{2}{10} = \dfrac{\text{▓}}{5}$

11. $\dfrac{4}{10} = \dfrac{2}{\text{▓}}$

12. $\dfrac{5}{10} = \dfrac{\text{▓}}{2}$

13. $\dfrac{6}{10} = \dfrac{\text{▓}}{5}$

14. $\dfrac{8}{10} = \dfrac{\text{▓}}{5}$

Find the lowest-terms fraction.

15. $\dfrac{3}{6}$

16. $\dfrac{8}{10}$

17. $\dfrac{10}{16}$

18. $\dfrac{5}{20}$

19. $\dfrac{9}{12}$

20. $\dfrac{10}{12}$

21. $\dfrac{2}{8}$

22. $\dfrac{7}{14}$

23. $\dfrac{5}{15}$

24. $\dfrac{6}{9}$

25. $\dfrac{3}{12}$

26. $\dfrac{4}{20}$

27. $\dfrac{8}{24}$

28. $\dfrac{12}{18}$

29. $\dfrac{6}{10}$

30. $\dfrac{4}{6}$

☆ 31. $\dfrac{100}{120}$

☆ 32. $\dfrac{150}{200}$

 Think!

Sometimes the two cross products of a pair of fractions are equal.

Can you find 5 pairs of fractions that have equal cross products?

The cross products are both 12.

$$1 \times 12 = 2 \times 6$$

Answers for Self-check 1. $\dfrac{7}{10}$ 2. $\dfrac{3}{5}$ 3. $\dfrac{1}{2}, \dfrac{2}{4}$ 4. $\dfrac{4}{6}, \dfrac{6}{9}, \dfrac{8}{12}, \ldots$ 5. $\dfrac{3}{4}$

Self-check

Write a fractional number to answer each question.

1. What part is colored?

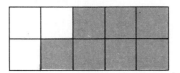

2. What fraction of the ribbons are blue?

3. Write a pair of equivalent fractions for this picture.

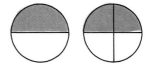

4. Give two other names for the fractional number $\frac{2}{3}$.

5. Give the lowest-terms fraction for $\frac{15}{20}$.

Answers for Self-check—page 249

Test

1. What part is white?

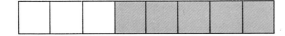

2. What fraction of the buttons are red?

3. Write a pair of equivalent fractions for this picture.

4. Give two others names for the fractional number $\frac{3}{10}$.

5. Give the lowest-terms fraction for $\frac{7}{14}$.

Jigsaw Fourths

Each piece is exactly $\frac{1}{4}$ of a square. Choose one
of the pieces. Trace it and cut out four copies.
See if you can put them together to form a square.

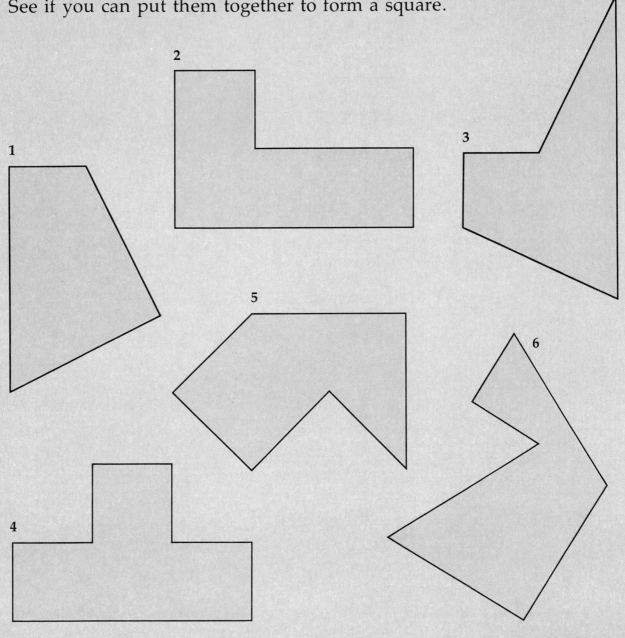

Larger Fractional Numbers

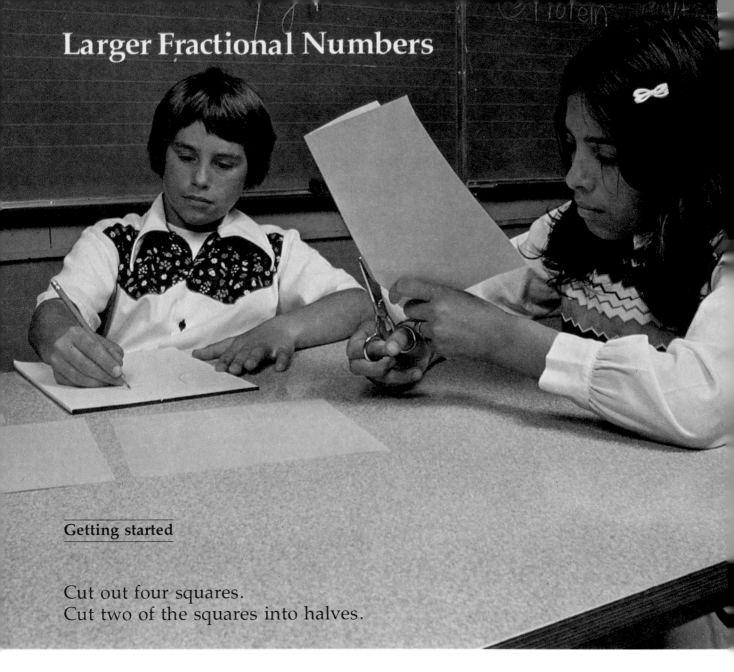

Getting started

Cut out four squares.
Cut two of the squares into halves.

Show these fractional numbers with your
squares and half squares.

$\frac{2}{2}$ (two halves) $\frac{3}{2}$ (three halves) $1\frac{1}{2}$ (one and one half)

$\frac{4}{2}$ (four halves) $2\frac{1}{2}$ (two and one half)

Mixed numerals

$$1\frac{1}{2}, \ 3\frac{3}{4}, \ 2\frac{1}{3}, \ \ldots$$

Improper fractions

$$\frac{9}{1}, \ \frac{8}{4}, \ \frac{10}{10}, \ \ldots$$

Give a mixed numeral and an improper fraction for each problem.

Example:

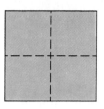  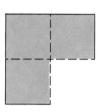

Answer: $2\frac{3}{4}, \ \frac{11}{4}$

1.

2.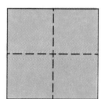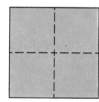

3.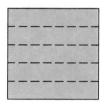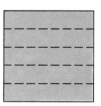

4.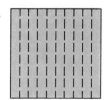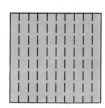

Whole numbers and fractional numbers

Joyce has 18 plants. She uses $\frac{1}{6}$ can of water for each plant, so she uses $\frac{18}{6}$ cans of water for all of them. How many full cans does she use?

Finding the answer

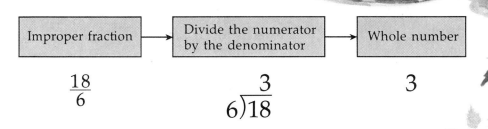

Improper fraction	Divide the numerator by the denominator	Whole number
$\frac{18}{6}$	$6\overline{)18}$ with 3 above	3

Joyce uses 3 full cans.

Other examples

$$\frac{12}{2} = 6 \qquad \frac{15}{3} = 5 \qquad \frac{40}{10} = 4$$

Give the whole number for each improper fraction.

1. $\frac{10}{5}$ 2. $\frac{8}{4}$ 3. $\frac{12}{4}$ 4. $\frac{6}{2}$ 5. $\frac{16}{4}$ 6. $\frac{24}{6}$

7. $\frac{60}{10}$ 8. $\frac{16}{8}$ 9. $\frac{5}{1}$ 10. $\frac{18}{2}$ 11. $\frac{30}{3}$ 12. $\frac{4}{4}$

13. $\frac{50}{10}$ 14. $\frac{100}{10}$ 15. $\frac{21}{1}$ 16. $\frac{32}{8}$ 17. $\frac{30}{10}$ 18. $\frac{70}{10}$

Give the whole number for each fractional number.

1. $\frac{4}{2}$ 2. $\frac{10}{10}$ 3. $\frac{8}{2}$ 4. $\frac{6}{3}$

5. $\frac{10}{1}$ 6. $\frac{30}{5}$ 7. $\frac{10}{2}$ 8. $\frac{100}{5}$

9. $\frac{100}{100}$ 10. $\frac{100}{1}$ 11. $\frac{20}{10}$ 12. $\frac{16}{4}$

Give the fraction for each whole number.

Example:

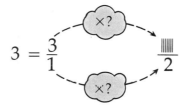

$3 = \frac{3}{1}$ Answer: $\frac{6}{2}$

13. $2 = \frac{2}{1}$ 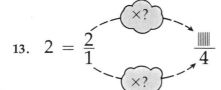   14. $3 = \frac{3}{1}$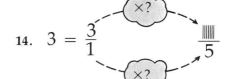

15. $1 = \frac{\text{▥}}{4}$ 16. $4 = \frac{\text{▥}}{2}$ 17. $5 = \frac{\text{▥}}{1}$

18. $6 = \frac{\text{▥}}{3}$ 19. $2 = \frac{\text{▥}}{5}$ 20. $3 = \frac{\text{▥}}{6}$

21. $4 = \frac{\text{▥}}{3}$ 22. $5 = \frac{\text{▥}}{4}$ 23. $1 = \frac{\text{▥}}{3}$

24. $25 = \frac{\text{▥}}{4}$ 25. $100 = \frac{\text{▥}}{10}$ 26. $50 = \frac{\text{▥}}{4}$

27. Jack wants to water 24 plants. He needs $\frac{1}{3}$ can of water for each plant, so he needs $\frac{24}{3}$ cans of water in all. How many full cans is this?

I'm more than two
And less than three.
Halfway between
You will find me.

$? > 2$
$? < 3$

Who am I?

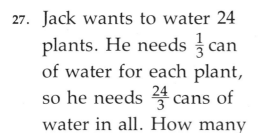

Improper fractions to mixed numerals

The picture shows that
$\frac{11}{4}$ is the same as $2\frac{3}{4}$.

How can you find the mixed numeral without pictures?

$$\frac{11}{4} = 2\frac{3}{4}$$

Finding the answer

Improper fraction	Divide the numerator by the denominator	Use the quotient, remainder, and divisor to write the mixed numeral

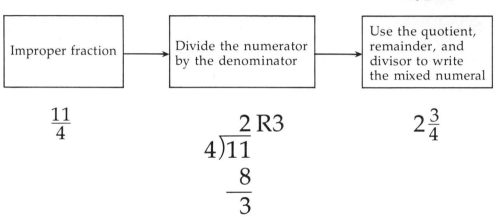

$\frac{11}{4}$

$$\begin{array}{r} 2\ \text{R}3 \\ 4\overline{)11} \\ \underline{8} \\ 3 \end{array}$$

$2\frac{3}{4}$

$\frac{11}{4}$ and $2\frac{3}{4}$ name the same fractional number.

Other examples

$\frac{7}{4} = 1\frac{3}{4}$ $\qquad$ $\frac{9}{2} = 4\frac{1}{2}$ $\qquad$ $\frac{17}{10} = 1\frac{7}{10}$

Write a mixed numeral for each improper fraction.

1. $\frac{3}{2}$ 2. $\frac{5}{2}$ 3. $\frac{7}{3}$ 4. $\frac{10}{3}$ 5. $\frac{5}{4}$ 6. $\frac{13}{4}$

7. $\frac{11}{5}$ 8. $\frac{17}{5}$ 9. $\frac{17}{6}$ 10. $\frac{7}{6}$ 11. $\frac{11}{8}$ 12. $\frac{13}{8}$

Write a mixed numeral for each improper fraction.

1. $\dfrac{15}{2}$　　2. $\dfrac{21}{2}$　　3. $\dfrac{25}{4}$　　4. $\dfrac{37}{3}$　　5. $\dfrac{65}{4}$　　6. $\dfrac{53}{2}$

7. $\dfrac{76}{5}$　　8. $\dfrac{43}{6}$　　9. $\dfrac{18}{7}$　　10. $\dfrac{26}{8}$　　11. $\dfrac{65}{8}$　　12. $\dfrac{41}{5}$

13. $\dfrac{15}{10}$　　14. $\dfrac{23}{9}$　　15. $\dfrac{47}{10}$　　16. $\dfrac{58}{9}$　　17. $\dfrac{96}{10}$　　18. $\dfrac{44}{7}$

19. $\dfrac{17}{4}$　　20. $\dfrac{23}{6}$　　21. $\dfrac{38}{7}$　　22. $\dfrac{45}{8}$　　23. $\dfrac{29}{2}$　　24. $\dfrac{70}{8}$

☆ 25. $\dfrac{137}{100}$　　☆ 26. $\dfrac{246}{100}$　　☆ 27. $\dfrac{573}{100}$　　☆ 28. $\dfrac{2896}{1000}$

29. Have $\dfrac{14}{4}$ grapefruit.
How many grapefruit?
Give the mixed numeral.

30. Have $\dfrac{17}{2}$ oranges.
How many oranges?
Give the mixed numeral.

The dime on the left is rolled around another dime
to the position shown on the right.

Which of these will it look like?

A　　B

More practice, page 368, Set A

✪ Mixed numerals to improper fractions

The picture shows that $2\frac{2}{5}$ rows are filled. Count the fifths. There are 12 fifths, so $2\frac{2}{5} = \frac{12}{5}$.

You can find the improper fraction for a mixed numeral without using a picture.

Finding the answer

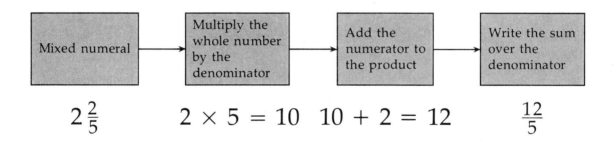

Mixed numeral	Multiply the whole number by the denominator	Add the numerator to the product	Write the sum over the denominator
$2\frac{2}{5}$	$2 \times 5 = 10$	$10 + 2 = 12$	$\frac{12}{5}$

Other examples

$$2\frac{1}{3} = \frac{7}{3} \qquad 4\frac{5}{10} = \frac{45}{10} \qquad 3\frac{7}{100} = \frac{307}{100}$$

Write an improper fraction for each mixed numeral.

1. $2\frac{3}{5}$
2. $5\frac{1}{2}$
3. $3\frac{1}{3}$
4. $6\frac{1}{4}$

5. $3\frac{3}{10}$
6. $2\frac{7}{10}$
7. $3\frac{9}{10}$
8. $1\frac{4}{10}$

9. $7\frac{1}{2}$
10. $3\frac{3}{4}$
11. $5\frac{3}{10}$
12. $7\frac{24}{100}$

Write an improper fraction for each mixed numeral.

1. $2\frac{1}{3}$ 2. $3\frac{1}{4}$ 3. $2\frac{2}{5}$ 4. $1\frac{4}{5}$

5. $2\frac{3}{10}$ 6. $3\frac{1}{2}$ 7. $5\frac{1}{6}$ 8. $1\frac{1}{5}$

9. $2\frac{7}{10}$ 10. $4\frac{3}{4}$ 11. $6\frac{3}{5}$ 12. $3\frac{2}{5}$

13. $8\frac{2}{3}$ 14. $10\frac{1}{4}$ 15. $5\frac{9}{10}$ 16. $6\frac{1}{8}$

Write both a mixed numeral and an improper fraction for the point above each arrow.

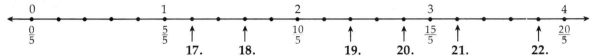

17.   18.   19.   20.   21.   22.

Practicing your skills

Add, subtract, multiply, or divide.

1. $\begin{array}{r} 964 \\ + 273 \\ \hline \end{array}$
2. $\begin{array}{r} 903 \\ - 467 \\ \hline \end{array}$
3. $\begin{array}{r} \$\ 3.59 \\ + 7.48 \\ \hline \end{array}$
4. $\begin{array}{r} \$\ 11.17 \\ - 9.68 \\ \hline \end{array}$
5. $\begin{array}{r} 38 \\ \times\ 8 \\ \hline \end{array}$

6. $\begin{array}{r} 29 \\ \times 42 \\ \hline \end{array}$
7. $8\overline{)637}$
8. $\begin{array}{r} 3278 \\ + 4596 \\ \hline \end{array}$
9. $\begin{array}{r} 364 \\ \times\ 6 \\ \hline \end{array}$
10. $30\overline{)259}$

The rubber band divides the yellow part of the geoboard into halves.

Can you find 4 other ways to place the rubber band so that it divides the yellow part into halves?

Show your ways on dot paper.

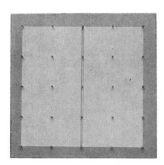

Answers for Self-check   1. 6   2. 5   3. 4   4. $\frac{8}{4}$ 5. $\frac{9}{3}$ 6. $\frac{10}{2}$ 7. $2\frac{1}{3}$ 8. $4\frac{1}{2}$ 9. $3\frac{1}{4}$ 10. $3\frac{2}{5}$ 11. $3\frac{3}{8}$
12. $4\frac{3}{10}$ 13. $\frac{10}{3}$ 14. $\frac{11}{2}$ 15. $\frac{13}{5}$ 16. $\frac{29}{8}$ 17. $\frac{47}{10}$ 18. $\frac{69}{20}$

Give the whole number
for each improper fraction.

Give the improper fraction
for each whole number.

1. $\frac{12}{2}$ 2. $\frac{15}{3}$ 3. $\frac{20}{5}$

4. $2 = \frac{\text{▥}}{4}$ 5. $3 = \frac{\text{▥}}{3}$ 6. $5 = \frac{\text{▥}}{2}$

Write a mixed numeral for each improper fraction.

7. $\frac{7}{3}$ 8. $\frac{9}{2}$ 9. $\frac{13}{4}$ 10. $\frac{17}{5}$ 11. $\frac{27}{8}$ 12. $\frac{43}{10}$

Write an improper fraction for each mixed numeral.

13. $3\frac{1}{3}$ 14. $5\frac{1}{2}$ 15. $2\frac{3}{5}$ 16. $3\frac{5}{8}$ 17. $4\frac{7}{10}$ 18. $3\frac{9}{20}$

Answers for Self-check—page 259

Give the whole number for
each improper fraction.

Give the improper fraction
for each whole number.

1. $\frac{14}{2}$ 2. $\frac{12}{4}$ 3. $\frac{27}{3}$

4. $1 = \frac{\text{▥}}{6}$ 5. $4 = \frac{\text{▥}}{2}$ 6. $3 = \frac{\text{▥}}{5}$

Write a mixed numeral for each improper fraction.

7. $\frac{10}{7}$ 8. $\frac{11}{4}$ 9. $\frac{19}{3}$ 10. $\frac{13}{6}$ 11. $\frac{15}{2}$ 12. $\frac{23}{5}$

Write an improper fraction for each mixed numeral.

13. $1\frac{4}{5}$ 14. $2\frac{1}{4}$ 15. $3\frac{3}{7}$ 16. $5\frac{3}{10}$ 17. $3\frac{2}{3}$ 18. $5\frac{7}{8}$

Mirror Activities

1. Use a mirror to read this mirror message.

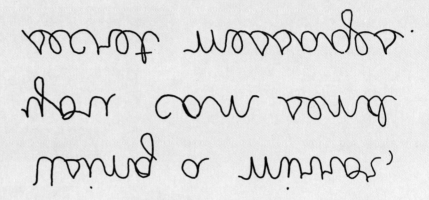

2. Use a mirror to write a mirror message to a friend.

3. When you place a mirror above a half word or a half numeral, the whole word or numeral appears.

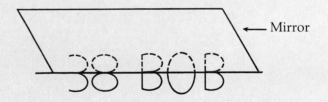

← Mirror

Try to write some more half words and half numerals.

4. Certain words make a different word when they are reflected in a mirror. Which of these do?

← Mirror

BED   WE   HEW   DID   MOOD

Adding and Subtracting Fractional Numbers

Think of the length of the orange rod as one (1). Then the lengths of the other rods are shown by the fractional numbers.

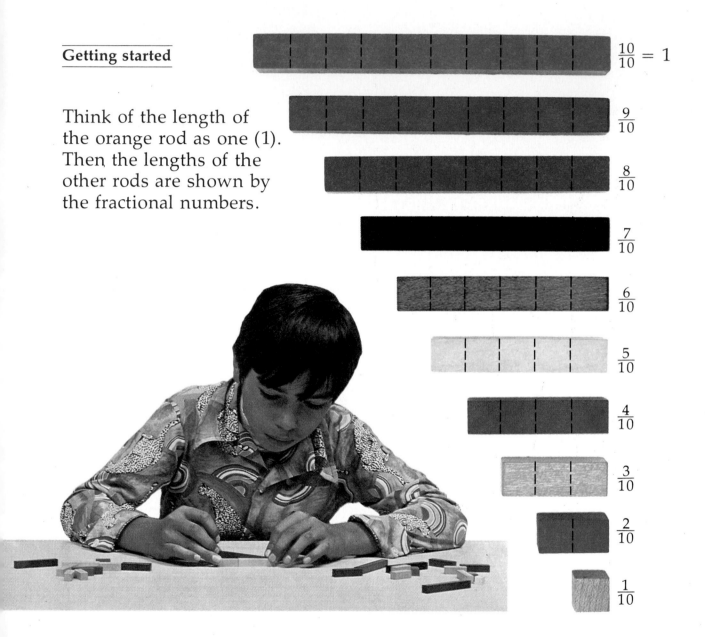

$$\frac{10}{10} = 1$$

$$\frac{9}{10}$$

$$\frac{8}{10}$$

$$\frac{7}{10}$$

$$\frac{6}{10}$$

$$\frac{5}{10}$$

$$\frac{4}{10}$$

$$\frac{3}{10}$$

$$\frac{2}{10}$$

$$\frac{1}{10}$$

The rods in the picture show:

$$\frac{3}{10} + \frac{5}{10}$$

Give the sum.

Write the complete addition equation for each picture.

Example:

$$\frac{2}{10} + \frac{3}{10} = \frac{5}{10}$$

1.

$$\frac{5}{10} + \frac{2}{10} = \frac{\text{▥}}{10}$$

2.

$$\frac{1}{10} + \frac{6}{10} = \frac{\text{▥}}{\text{▥}}$$

3.

$$\frac{4}{10} + \frac{\text{▥}}{\text{▥}} = \frac{8}{10}$$

4.

$$\frac{\text{▥}}{\text{▥}} + \frac{2}{10} = \frac{\text{▥}}{\text{▥}}$$

5.

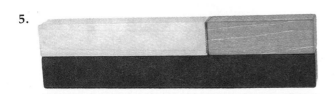

$$\frac{\text{▥}}{\text{▥}} + \frac{\text{▥}}{\text{▥}} = \frac{\text{▥}}{\text{▥}}$$

Adding fractional numbers with like denominators

Al and Gail walked $\frac{3}{10}$ km from Monkey Island to the Deer Park. Then they walked $\frac{4}{10}$ km to the Bear's Den. How far did they walk in all?

Finding the answer

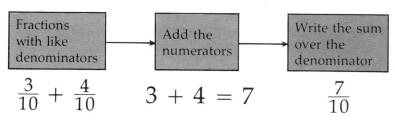

Fractions with like denominators	Add the numerators	Write the sum over the denominator
$\frac{3}{10} + \frac{4}{10}$	$3 + 4 = 7$	$\frac{7}{10}$

They walked $\frac{7}{10}$ km in all.

Other examples

$\frac{5}{10} + \frac{2}{10} = \frac{7}{10}$

$$\begin{array}{r} \frac{7}{4} \\ + \frac{3}{4} \\ \hline \frac{10}{4} \text{ or } 2\frac{1}{2} \end{array}$$

$$\begin{array}{r} 2\frac{1}{4} \\ + 3\frac{2}{4} \\ \hline 5\frac{3}{4} \end{array}$$

Find the sums.

1. $\frac{1}{2} + \frac{3}{2}$

2. $\frac{1}{4} + \frac{2}{4}$

3. $\frac{1}{3} + \frac{4}{3}$

4. $\frac{2}{5} + \frac{3}{5}$

5. $\frac{3}{10} + \frac{7}{10}$

6. $\frac{5}{2} + \frac{3}{2}$

7. $\frac{3}{4} + \frac{1}{4}$

8. $\frac{9}{10} + \frac{2}{10}$

9. $\frac{0}{5} + \frac{1}{5}$

10. $\frac{4}{10} + \frac{5}{10}$

11. $\frac{5}{3} + \frac{2}{3}$

12. $\frac{1}{10} + \frac{1}{10}$

13. $\frac{9}{2} + \frac{4}{2}$

14. $\frac{3}{8} + \frac{4}{8}$

15. $\frac{1}{6} + \frac{5}{6}$

16. $\frac{24}{100} + \frac{37}{100}$

Find the sums.

1. $\frac{2}{5}$ $+\frac{1}{5}$

2. $\frac{1}{4}$ $+\frac{2}{4}$

3. $\frac{3}{10}$ $+\frac{4}{10}$

4. $\frac{1}{5}$ $+\frac{3}{5}$

5. $\frac{6}{10}$ $+\frac{1}{10}$

6. $\frac{3}{8}$ $+\frac{2}{8}$

7. $\frac{5}{10}$ $+\frac{4}{10}$

8. $\frac{2}{5}$ $+\frac{2}{5}$

9. $\frac{5}{8}$ $+\frac{2}{8}$

10. $\frac{1}{4}$ $+\frac{1}{4}$

11. $\frac{13}{100}$ $+\frac{46}{100}$

12. $\frac{23}{100}$ $+\frac{32}{100}$

13. $4\frac{1}{4}$ $+3\frac{2}{4}$

14. $8\frac{3}{10}$ $+1\frac{4}{10}$

15. $2\frac{1}{5}$ $+3\frac{3}{5}$

16. $8\frac{6}{10}$ $+9\frac{1}{10}$

17. $7\frac{3}{8}$ $+5\frac{2}{8}$

18. $6\frac{5}{10}$ $+3\frac{3}{10}$

19. $9\frac{3}{8}$ $+3\frac{4}{8}$

20. $2\frac{8}{10}$ $+3\frac{1}{10}$

21. $5\frac{1}{5}$ $+2\frac{3}{5}$

22. $9\frac{27}{100}$ $+4\frac{36}{100}$

23. From the Zebra Pen to the Bird House: $\frac{5}{10}$ km
From the Bird House to the Hippo Pool: $\frac{2}{10}$ km
How many kilometers in all?

24. Walked $\frac{3}{10}$ km to the Ape House.
Walked $\frac{1}{10}$ km to the Rhino Pit.
Walked $\frac{5}{10}$ km to the Buffalo Range.
How many kilometers in all?

Secret Code

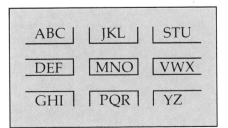

ABC	JKL	STU
DEF	MNO	VWX
GHI	PQR	YZ

Secret Message

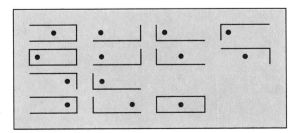

Can you find the secret message?

Subtracting fractional numbers with like denominators

Emily lives $\frac{7}{10}$ km from school.

Randy lives $\frac{4}{10}$ km from school.
How much farther from school
does Emily live?

Finding the answer

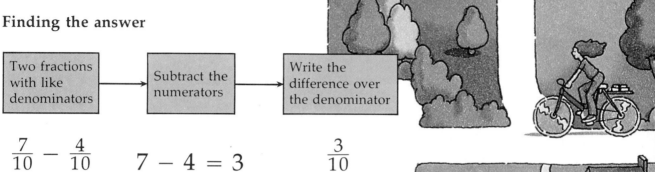

| Two fractions with like denominators | → | Subtract the numerators | → | Write the difference over the denominator |

$$\frac{7}{10} - \frac{4}{10} \qquad 7 - 4 = 3 \qquad \frac{3}{10}$$

Emily lives $\frac{3}{10}$ km farther from school.

Other examples

$$\frac{8}{10} - \frac{2}{10} = \frac{6}{10} \text{ or } \frac{3}{5} \qquad \frac{9}{4} - \frac{4}{4} = \frac{5}{4} \text{ or } 1\frac{1}{4}$$

Find the differences.

1. $\frac{3}{2} - \frac{1}{2}$ 2. $\frac{5}{4} - \frac{3}{4}$ 3. $\frac{7}{3} - \frac{2}{3}$

4. $\frac{3}{4} - \frac{1}{4}$ 5. $\frac{8}{10} - \frac{7}{10}$ 6. $\frac{4}{5} - \frac{4}{5}$

7. $\frac{9}{2} - \frac{2}{2}$ 8. $\frac{5}{6} - \frac{0}{6}$ 9. $\frac{7}{2} - \frac{3}{2}$ 10. $\frac{11}{8} - \frac{3}{8}$ 11. $\frac{15}{10} - \frac{9}{10}$

12. $\frac{6}{4} - \frac{3}{4}$ 13. $\frac{9}{10} - \frac{5}{10}$ 14. $\frac{12}{5} - \frac{9}{5}$ 15. $\frac{125}{100} - \frac{85}{100}$ 16. $\frac{75}{100} - \frac{25}{100}$

Find the differences.

Example:

$8\frac{7}{10}$
$-3\frac{4}{10}$
$\overline{5\frac{3}{10}}$

1. $5\frac{3}{4}$
    $-2\frac{1}{4}$

2. $12\frac{9}{10}$
    $-4\frac{7}{10}$

3. $8\frac{4}{5}$
    $-2\frac{1}{5}$

4. $16\frac{7}{8}$
    $-7\frac{5}{8}$

5. $10\frac{5}{3}$
    $-7\frac{2}{3}$

6. $8\frac{6}{10}$
    $-3\frac{6}{10}$

7. $13\frac{5}{6}$
    $-9\frac{3}{6}$

8. $14\frac{5}{8}$
    $-6\frac{1}{8}$

9. $24\frac{8}{10}$
    $-19\frac{5}{10}$

10. $9\frac{1}{2}$
    $-4\frac{1}{2}$

11. $42\frac{7}{10}$
    $-29\frac{4}{10}$

12. $9\frac{4}{10}$
    $-6\frac{3}{10}$

13. $12\frac{87}{100}$
    $-4\frac{32}{100}$

14. $6\frac{75}{100}$
    $-2\frac{50}{100}$

15. $\frac{8}{10}$ km from City Hall to the park

$\frac{3}{10}$ km from City Hall to the library
How much farther to the park?

16. Bicycle trips:
Rode $8\frac{7}{10}$ km on Friday. Rode $5\frac{2}{10}$ km on Saturday.
How many more kilometers on Saturday?

Open any book to page 50.
Find how thick 50 pages are.

Use this information to estimate
how many pages are in the book.

Check to see how close your
estimate was.

Adding fractional numbers with unlike denominators

Sally mowed $\frac{1}{2}$ of a lawn before lunch. She mowed $\frac{1}{4}$ of it after lunch. How much did she mow in all?

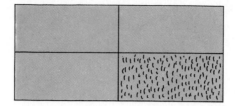

Finding the answer

Fractions with unlike denominators	→	Find equivalent fractions with the same denominator	→	Add the fractions with the same denominator

$$\frac{1}{2}$$
$$+\frac{1}{4}$$
$$\overline{?}$$

$$\frac{1}{2} = \frac{1 \times 2}{2 \times 2} = \frac{2}{4}$$
$$+\frac{1}{4}$$

$$\frac{2}{4}$$
$$\frac{1}{4}$$

$$\frac{2}{4}$$
$$+\frac{1}{4}$$
$$\overline{\frac{3}{4}}$$

Sally mowed $\frac{3}{4}$ of the lawn in all.

Other examples

$$\frac{1}{6}$$
$$+\frac{1}{3} = \frac{1 \times 2}{3 \times 2} = \frac{2}{6}$$
$$\overline{\frac{3}{6} \text{ or } \frac{1}{2}}$$

$$\frac{9}{10}$$
$$+\frac{1}{2} = \frac{1 \times 5}{2 \times 5} = \frac{5}{10}$$
$$\overline{\frac{14}{10} \text{ or } 1\frac{2}{5}}$$

Find the sums.

1. $\frac{1}{2}$
   $+\frac{1}{6}$

2. $\frac{3}{10}$
   $+\frac{1}{2}$

3. $\frac{2}{3}$
   $+\frac{5}{6}$

4. $\frac{3}{4}$
   $+\frac{1}{2}$

5. $\frac{1}{4}$
   $+\frac{3}{8}$

6. $\frac{1}{3}$
   $+\frac{2}{9}$

7. $\frac{5}{12}$
   $+\frac{1}{4}$

8. $\frac{1}{5}$
   $+\frac{3}{10}$

9. $\frac{2}{6}$
   $+\frac{3}{12}$

10. $\frac{1}{9}$
    $+\frac{2}{3}$

Sometimes two equivalent fractions are needed.
Study the example. Then find each sum.

Example:

$$\frac{1}{2} = \frac{1 \times 3}{2 \times 3} = \frac{3}{6}$$
$$+\frac{1}{3} = \frac{1 \times 2}{3 \times 2} = \frac{2}{6}$$
$$\frac{5}{6}$$

1. $\frac{1}{2}$
$+\frac{1}{5}$

2. $\frac{1}{6}$
$+\frac{1}{4}$

3. $\frac{1}{4}$
$+\frac{2}{3}$

4. $\frac{1}{4}$
$+\frac{2}{5}$

5. $\frac{1}{3}$
$+\frac{1}{4}$

6. $\frac{1}{5}$
$+\frac{2}{3}$

7. $\frac{2}{3}$
$+\frac{1}{2}$

8. $\frac{3}{4}$
$+\frac{1}{6}$

9. $\frac{3}{5}$
$+\frac{1}{3}$

10. $\frac{2}{5}$
$+\frac{1}{2}$

11. $\frac{1}{5}$
$+\frac{3}{4}$

12. $\frac{3}{6}$
$+\frac{1}{4}$

13. $\frac{2}{5}$
$+\frac{1}{4}$

14. Carpet $\frac{1}{2}$ of the floor. Then carpet $\frac{3}{10}$ of the floor. What part is now carpeted?

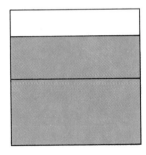

15. Paper $\frac{3}{10}$ of the wall. Then paper $\frac{1}{5}$ of it. How much is now papered?

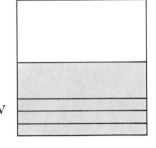

Think!

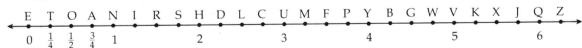

E T O A N I R S H D L C U M F P Y B G W V K X J Q Z

0 $\frac{1}{4}$ $\frac{1}{2}$ $\frac{3}{4}$ 1   2   3   4   5   6

This special number line can be used to find the "length" of a name.

Example: T   O   D
           ↓   ↓   ↓
           $\frac{1}{4}$ + $\frac{1}{2}$ + $2\frac{1}{4}$ = 3   Can you find the "length" of your name?

More practice, page 369, Set A

Making cookies:

Need $\frac{3}{4}$ cup of sugar for nut cookies.

Need $\frac{1}{2}$ cup of sugar for butter cookies.

How much more sugar for nut cookies?

Finding the answer

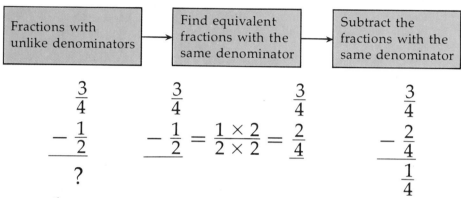

| Fractions with unlike denominators | → | Find equivalent fractions with the same denominator | → | Subtract the fractions with the same denominator |

$$\begin{array}{r} \frac{3}{4} \\ -\frac{1}{2} \\ \hline ? \end{array}$$

$$\begin{array}{r} \frac{3}{4} \\ -\frac{1}{2} = \frac{1 \times 2}{2 \times 2} = \frac{2}{4} \end{array}$$

$$\begin{array}{r} \frac{3}{4} \\ -\frac{2}{4} \\ \hline \frac{1}{4} \end{array}$$

Need $\frac{1}{4}$ cup more sugar for nut cookies.

Other examples

$$\begin{array}{r} \frac{9}{10} \\ -\frac{1}{2} = \frac{1 \times 5}{2 \times 5} = \frac{5}{10} \\ \hline \frac{4}{10} \text{ or } \frac{2}{5} \end{array}$$

$$\begin{array}{r} \frac{3}{4} = \frac{3 \times 2}{4 \times 2} = \frac{6}{8} \\ -\frac{3}{8} \qquad\qquad \frac{3}{8} \\ \hline \frac{3}{8} \end{array}$$

Find the differences.

1. $\begin{array}{r} \frac{1}{2} \\ -\frac{1}{4} \\ \hline \end{array}$

2. $\begin{array}{r} \frac{5}{6} \\ -\frac{1}{3} \\ \hline \end{array}$

3. $\begin{array}{r} \frac{3}{4} \\ -\frac{1}{8} \\ \hline \end{array}$

4. $\begin{array}{r} \frac{5}{9} \\ -\frac{1}{3} \\ \hline \end{array}$

5. $\begin{array}{r} \frac{2}{3} \\ -\frac{1}{6} \\ \hline \end{array}$

6. $\begin{array}{r} \frac{7}{8} \\ -\frac{3}{4} \\ \hline \end{array}$

7. $\begin{array}{r} \frac{2}{3} \\ -\frac{4}{9} \\ \hline \end{array}$

8. $\begin{array}{r} \frac{7}{10} \\ -\frac{2}{5} \\ \hline \end{array}$

9. $\begin{array}{r} \frac{5}{6} \\ -\frac{5}{12} \\ \hline \end{array}$

10. $\begin{array}{r} \frac{3}{5} \\ -\frac{1}{10} \\ \hline \end{array}$

Study the example. Then find the differences.

Example:

$$\frac{1}{2} = \frac{1 \times 3}{2 \times 3} = \frac{3}{6}$$
$$-\frac{1}{3} = \frac{1 \times 2}{3 \times 2} = \frac{2}{6}$$
$$\frac{1}{6}$$

1. $\frac{3}{2}$
   $-\frac{2}{5}$

2. $\frac{1}{3}$
   $-\frac{1}{4}$

3. $\frac{2}{5}$
   $-\frac{1}{4}$

4. $\frac{1}{3}$
   $-\frac{1}{5}$

5. $\frac{3}{4}$
   $-\frac{1}{6}$

6. $\frac{3}{5}$
   $-\frac{1}{2}$

7. $\frac{3}{4}$
   $-\frac{3}{5}$

8. $\frac{2}{3}$
   $-\frac{2}{4}$

9. Ginger snaps: $\frac{7}{8}$ cup of flour
   Fruit bars: $\frac{3}{4}$ cup of flour
   How much more flour for the ginger snaps?

10. Shortcake: $\frac{3}{4}$ cup of butter
    Oatmeal cookies: $\frac{1}{3}$ cup of butter
    How much more butter for the shortcake?

Copy and complete this fractional number Magic Square.

The Magic Sum is 5. (Each row, column, and diagonal should add up to 5.)

$\frac{8}{3}$	$\frac{3}{3}$	▨
$\frac{1}{3}$	▨	▨
$\frac{6}{3}$	▨	$\frac{2}{3}$

Practicing your skills

Add, subtract, multiply, or divide.

1. 596
   + 487

2.   92
   − 47

3. 346
   − 178

4. 509
   + 684

5.   86
     38
   + 59

6.   47
   × 8

7. 8)426

8.   56
   × 24

9. 30)257

10. 397
    × 13

More practice, page 369, Set B and page 369A

Self-check

Find the sums or differences.

1. $\frac{1}{4} + \frac{2}{4}$

2. $\frac{7}{5} - \frac{4}{5}$

3. $\frac{3}{10} + \frac{5}{10}$

4. $\frac{7}{8} - \frac{2}{8}$

5. $\frac{6}{7} - \frac{2}{7}$

6. $\frac{3}{6} + \frac{2}{6}$

7. $\frac{9}{10} - \frac{5}{10}$

8. $\frac{1}{5} + \frac{3}{5}$

9. $\begin{array}{r} 4\frac{1}{4} \\ + 5\frac{1}{4} \\ \hline \end{array}$

10. $\begin{array}{r} 9\frac{3}{10} \\ - 5\frac{1}{10} \\ \hline \end{array}$

11. $\begin{array}{r} 7\frac{1}{5} \\ + 2\frac{3}{5} \\ \hline \end{array}$

12. $\begin{array}{r} \frac{1}{3} \\ + \frac{3}{6} \\ \hline \end{array}$

13. $\begin{array}{r} \frac{5}{8} \\ - \frac{1}{4} \\ \hline \end{array}$

14. $\begin{array}{r} \frac{2}{3} \\ + \frac{1}{9} \\ \hline \end{array}$

15. $\begin{array}{r} \frac{1}{2} \\ + \frac{1}{3} \\ \hline \end{array}$

16. $\begin{array}{r} \frac{3}{4} \\ - \frac{1}{3} \\ \hline \end{array}$

17. $\begin{array}{r} \frac{1}{5} \\ + \frac{1}{2} \\ \hline \end{array}$

18. $\begin{array}{r} \frac{5}{6} \\ - \frac{1}{4} \\ \hline \end{array}$

Answers for Self-check—page 271

Test

Find the sums or differences.

1. $\frac{3}{8} + \frac{2}{8}$

2. $\frac{11}{10} - \frac{7}{10}$

3. $\frac{3}{7} + \frac{2}{7}$

4. $\frac{5}{6} - \frac{2}{6}$

5. $\frac{4}{5} - \frac{2}{5}$

6. $\frac{5}{12} + \frac{3}{12}$

7. $\frac{7}{8} - \frac{2}{8}$

8. $\frac{3}{10} + \frac{4}{10}$

9. $\begin{array}{r} 2\frac{1}{3} \\ + 3\frac{1}{3} \\ \hline \end{array}$

10. $\begin{array}{r} 6\frac{7}{8} \\ - 4\frac{3}{8} \\ \hline \end{array}$

11. $\begin{array}{r} 7\frac{1}{4} \\ + 2\frac{2}{4} \\ \hline \end{array}$

12. $\begin{array}{r} \frac{1}{8} \\ + \frac{1}{4} \\ \hline \end{array}$

13. $\begin{array}{r} \frac{5}{6} \\ - \frac{1}{3} \\ \hline \end{array}$

14. $\begin{array}{r} \frac{3}{4} \\ - \frac{1}{8} \\ \hline \end{array}$

15. $\begin{array}{r} \frac{1}{4} \\ + \frac{1}{3} \\ \hline \end{array}$

16. $\begin{array}{r} \frac{3}{4} \\ - \frac{1}{6} \\ \hline \end{array}$

17. $\begin{array}{r} \frac{1}{2} \\ + \frac{2}{5} \\ \hline \end{array}$

18. $\begin{array}{r} \frac{1}{5} \\ + \frac{2}{3} \\ \hline \end{array}$

Sliding Tic-Tac-Toe

Rules:

1. Each player gets 3 markers.

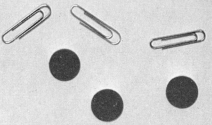

2. Players take turns putting down a marker until all markers are placed on the board.

Example: Counters win.

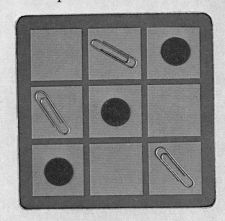

3. If neither player has 3 of his markers in a row, players take turns sliding one of their markers to an empty touching square. (No diagonal moves.)

Sliding Tic-Tac-Toe Board

Remember:

To win, get 3 of your markers in a row, either across, down, or diagonally.

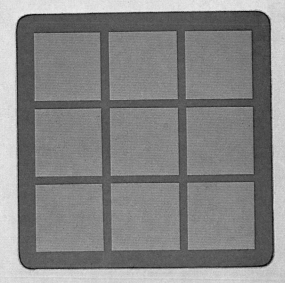

Challenge a classmate to a game of Sliding Tic-Tac-Toe.

Ratio

2 GLASSES OF LEMONADE 15¢

Getting started

Cats to dogs: 3 to 2

Boys to girls: 2 to 2

Study the pictures.

Give two more comparisons like these.

	We see:	We think:	We write:

"The **ratio** of tickets to cents is 3 to 50."

$\dfrac{3}{50}$

"The **ratio** of kilometers to hours is 20 to 1."

$\dfrac{20}{1}$

"The **ratio** of lemon juice to water is 1 to 4."

$\dfrac{1}{4}$

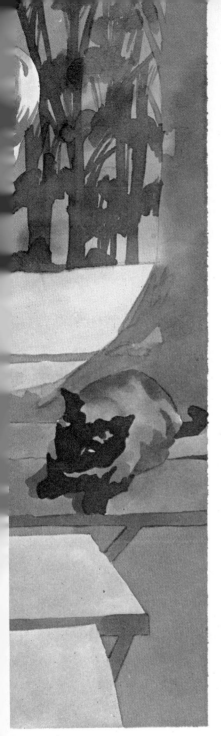

Try these. Write the ratio.

1. Jack rode 3 km in 10 minutes. What is the ratio of kilometers to minutes?

2. 4 valentine cards cost 25 cents. What is the ratio of valentines to cents?

Writing ratios

Write the ratio.

1.

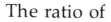

7 days in 1 week

The ratio of

$$\frac{\text{days}}{\text{weeks}} \text{ to } \text{ is } \frac{\text{|||||}}{\text{|||||}}$$

2.

20 pictures from 1 roll

The ratio of

$$\frac{\text{pictures}}{\text{rolls}} \text{ to } \text{ is } \frac{\text{|||||}}{\text{|||||}}$$

3.

5 rides for $2

The ratio of

$$\frac{\text{rides}}{\text{dollars}} \text{ to } \text{ is } \frac{\text{|||||}}{\text{|||||}}$$

4.

Rode 75 km in 2 days.

The ratio of

$$\frac{\text{kilometers}}{\text{days}} \text{ to } \text{ is } \frac{\text{|||||}}{\text{|||||}}$$

5.

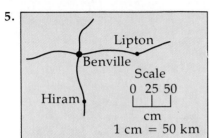

1 cm stands for 50 km.

The ratio of

centimeters on map to kilometers actual distance	is	▓▓▓▓▓ / ▓▓▓▓▓

6.

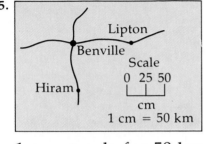

10 football cards for 25¢

The ratio of

cards to cents	is	▓▓▓▓▓ / ▓▓▓▓▓

7.

18 heartbeats in 15 seconds

The ratio of

heartbeats to seconds	is	▓▓▓▓▓ / ▓▓▓▓▓

8.

2 gifts for each person

The ratio of

gifts to persons	is	▓▓▓▓▓ / ▓▓▓▓▓

9. 3 tubes of toothpaste for $2

The ratio of tubes to dollars is ▓▓▓▓▓ .

Can you find the missing digits?

	A	653	B	794	C	▓▓▓▓27
		× ▓▓▓▓		× ▓▓▓▓		× 8
		3265		7146		4216

Ratio tables

What are some other ratios for this table?

The ratio of

		50			
pennies	to —is	50	▦	▦	▦
rolls		1	▦	▦	▦

Finding the answer

pennies ×2   pennies ×3   pennies ×4

Multiply both numbers by the same factor →	pennies	50	100	150	200
	rolls	1	2	3	4

rolls ×2   rolls ×3   rolls ×4

All the ratios tell about the rolls and pennies. They are called **equal ratios.**

Copy and finish these tables.

1.

rolls	1	2	3	4
quarters	40	▦	▦	▦

2.

erasers	3	6	9	12
cents	10	▦	▦	▦

3.

tickets	3	▦	▦	▦
dollars	2	4	6	8

4.

kilometers	40	▦	▦	▦
hours	2	4	6	8

5.

boys	2	▦	▦	▦
girls	3	▦	▦	▦

6.

cars	1	▦	▦	▦
wheels	4	▦	▦	▦

7.

children	5	▦	▦	▦
tables	1	▦	▦	▦

8.

postcards	3	▦	▦	▦
cents	25	▦	▦	▦

Use the ratio tables to solve the problems.

☆ 1. Dave can walk 5 blocks in 9 minutes. At this speed, how many minutes for 15 blocks?

blocks	5	10	15	20
minutes	9	18	27	36

☆ 2. Tina rides her bike about 20 km/h. How far will she go in 3 hours?

km	20	40	60	80
h	1	2	3	4

☆ 3. 1 can makes 8 glasses of juice. How many cans are needed for 32 glasses?

cans	1	2	3	4
glasses	8	16	24	32

☆ 4. Map scale shows 2 cm = 5 km. If map distance is 6 cm, what is the actual distance?

cm	2	4	6	8
km	5	10	15	20

☆ 5. 5 tickets to the Fun Fair cost $2. How many tickets can Jo buy for $4?

tickets	5	10	15	20
dollars	2	4	6	8

☆ 6. 3 thumbtacks have a mass of 5 g (grams). What is the mass of 12 thumbtacks?

tacks	3	6	9	12
grams	5	10	15	20

☆ 7. You need 4 cups of pancake mix for every 3 cups of milk. You have 12 cups of mix. How many cups of milk do you need?

cups of mix	4	8	12	16
cups of milk	3	6	9	12

☆ 8. The ratio of girls to boys in a class is 3 to 2. The class has 12 girls. How many boys?

girls	3	6	9	12
boys	2	4	6	8

✪ Solving ratio problems

The map scale shows 2 cm = 75 km. How many kilometers would 6 cm stand for?

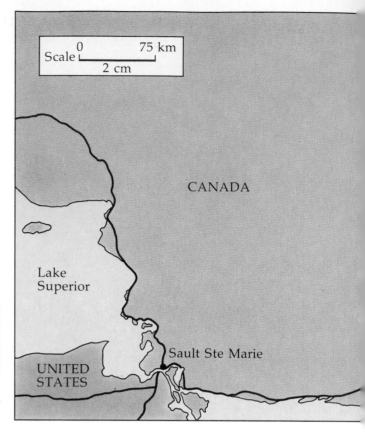

Finding the answer

Begin with the ratio given	→	Find equal ratios until you reach the one you need

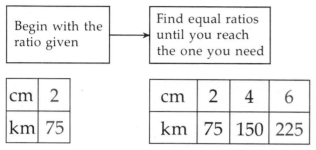

cm	2
km	75

cm	2	4	6
km	75	150	225

6 cm on the map stands for 225 km.

Make ratio tables to help you solve the problems.

1. A car goes 15 km in 10 minutes. At this rate how far will it go in 30 minutes?

kilometers	15	▥	▥	▥
minutes	10	▥	▥	▥

2. Out of every 100 light bulbs checked, 4 were broken. Checked 400 bulbs. How many were broken?

broken bulbs	4	▥	▥	▥
bulbs checked	100	▥	▥	▥

3. Three fig bars cost 25¢. What is the cost of 12 fig bars?

fig bars	3	▥	▥	▥
cents	25	▥	▥	▥

Make ratio tables to help you solve the problems.

1. 7 days is 1 week. How many weeks is 21 days?

days	7	▦	▦	▦
weeks	1	▦	▦	▦

2. 2 pencils cost 5¢. How many pencils will 20¢ buy?

pencils	2	▦	▦	▦
cents	5	▦	▦	▦

3. 3 cups of mix make 15 rolls. How many cups of mix are needed for 45 rolls?

4. 10 boxes of raisins cost 99¢. How much will 20 boxes cost?

5. A car goes 160 km in 2 hours. At this rate, how many kilometers are traveled in 6 hours?

6. Each time a bike wheel turns 2 times, the bike goes 4 m. How many turns are needed to go 12 m?

Find these products. What is unusual about them?

$$142\ 857 \times 7$$

$$12\ 345\ 679 \times 9$$

$$37\ 037 \times 3$$

Answers for Self-check   1. $\frac{30}{1}$ 2.

nickels	40	80	120	160
rolls	1	2	3	4

3.

tickets	5	10	15	20
dollars	2	4	6	8

4. $8   5. 15

Self-check

1. Write the ratio of days to months. (Use 30 days in a month.)

2. Copy and finish the table.

nickels	40	▥	▥	▥
rolls	1	2	3	4

3. A book of 5 tickets costs $2. Copy and fill in the table.

tickets	▥	▥	▥	▥
dollars	▥	▥	▥	▥

☆ 4. How much would 20 of the tickets in problem 3 cost?

☆ 5. A wheel turns 5 times in 3 seconds. How many times will it turn in 9 seconds?

Answers for Self-check—page 281

Test

1. Write the ratio of seconds to minutes.

2. Copy and finish the table.

apples	1	2	3	4
cents	10	▥	▥	▥

3. A pet shop has 3 dogs to every 2 cats. Copy and fill in the table.

dogs	▥	▥	▥	▥
cats	▥	▥	▥	▥

☆ 4. If the pet shop in problem 3 has 12 dogs, how many cats does it have?

☆ 5. A map scale reads 3 cm = 50 km. 9 cm on the map stands for how many kilometers?

Pentas and Bipeds

All of these are pentas.

   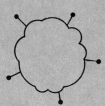

None of these are pentas.

  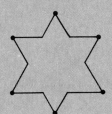 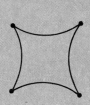

Some of these are pentas. Which ones?

A   B   C   D   E

 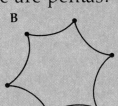 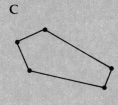 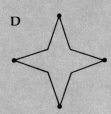 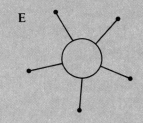

All of these are bipeds.

    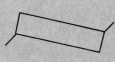

None of these are bipeds.

Some of these are bipeds. Which ones?

A   B   C   D   E

Make up some pentas and bipeds of your own.

Level 21 review

Give a fractional number to tell what part is shaded.

1.  2.  3.

Give the fractional number for each ▦ .

4.

0   ▦   1

5.

0   ▦   1

Give an equivalent fraction.

6. $\frac{1}{4}$ 7. $\frac{2}{3}$ 8. $\frac{3}{5}$

Give lowest-terms fractions.

9. $\frac{4}{8}$ 10. $\frac{3}{9}$ 11. $\frac{4}{6}$

Write as mixed numerals.

12. $\frac{4}{3}$ 13. $\frac{5}{2}$ 14. $\frac{23}{4}$

Write as improper fractions.

15. $1\frac{1}{4}$ 16. $3\frac{1}{2}$ 17. $2\frac{3}{5}$

Add or subtract.

18. $\frac{1}{5} + \frac{2}{5}$ 19. $\frac{3}{10} + \frac{4}{10}$ 20. $\frac{1}{3} + \frac{4}{3}$ 21. $\frac{3}{8} + \frac{4}{8}$

22. $\frac{3}{4} - \frac{1}{4}$ 23. $\frac{5}{6} - \frac{1}{6}$ 24. $\frac{7}{9} - \frac{2}{9}$ 25. $\frac{11}{12} - \frac{4}{12}$

26. $\begin{array}{r} 2\frac{1}{3} \\ + 1\frac{1}{3} \\ \hline \end{array}$ 27. $\begin{array}{r} 3\frac{3}{8} \\ + 4\frac{2}{8} \\ \hline \end{array}$ 28. $\begin{array}{r} \frac{1}{4} \\ + \frac{1}{2} \\ \hline \end{array}$ 29. $\begin{array}{r} \frac{1}{9} \\ + \frac{2}{3} \\ \hline \end{array}$ 30. $\begin{array}{r} \frac{1}{3} \\ + \frac{1}{4} \\ \hline \end{array}$

31. $\begin{array}{r} 3\frac{5}{8} \\ - 2\frac{1}{8} \\ \hline \end{array}$ 32. $\begin{array}{r} 7\frac{7}{12} \\ - 4\frac{5}{12} \\ \hline \end{array}$ 33. $\begin{array}{r} \frac{5}{6} \\ - \frac{2}{3} \\ \hline \end{array}$ 34. $\begin{array}{r} \frac{7}{8} \\ - \frac{1}{4} \\ \hline \end{array}$ 35. $\begin{array}{r} \frac{2}{3} \\ - \frac{1}{2} \\ \hline \end{array}$

22

Decimals
Adding and Subtracting Decimals
Using Your Skills
Area, Volume, and Mass
Using Larger Numbers

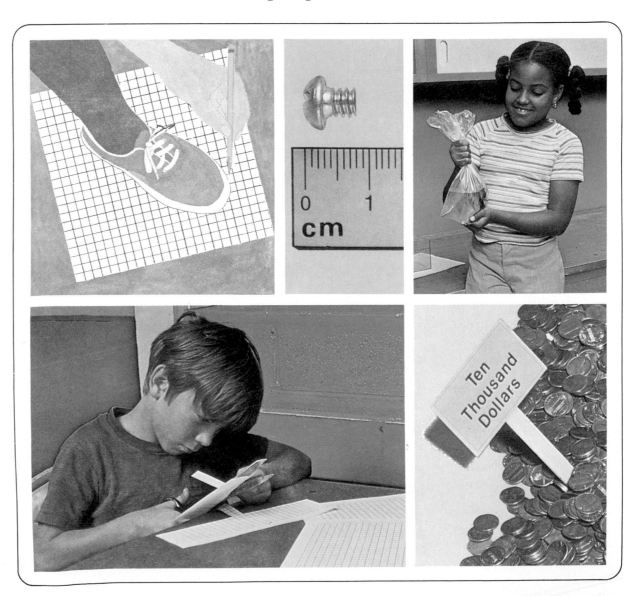

Decimals

Getting started

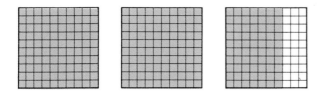

$2\frac{7}{10}$ of these squares are shaded.

Using a **decimal,** we write: 2.7
We say: two and seven tenths

$\frac{3}{10}$ of this square is shaded.

We write: 0.3
We say: three tenths

1. Cut out four 10-by-10 squares from graph paper.

2. Color your graph paper to show these decimals:

   2.4   0.5

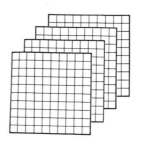

Give the missing decimals and mixed numerals or fractions.

Examples:

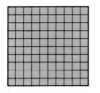

six tenths

fraction: $\frac{6}{10}$

decimal: 0.6

three and two tenths

mixed numeral: $3\frac{2}{10}$

decimal: 3.2

1.

one and nine tenths

mixed numeral: $1\frac{9}{10}$

decimal: ▓

2.

eight tenths

fraction: $\frac{8}{10}$

decimal: ▓

3.

four tenths

fraction: ▓
decimal: ▓

4.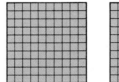

one and seven tenths

mixed numeral: ▓
decimal: ▓

Writing decimals: tenths

How much is shaded?

We think: two and three tenths

We write: $2\frac{3}{10}$ or 2.3

     mixed   decimal
     numeral

Write a decimal for each picture.

1.

2.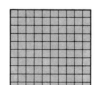

3.

4.

5.   6.

Write a decimal for each |||||.

Examples:

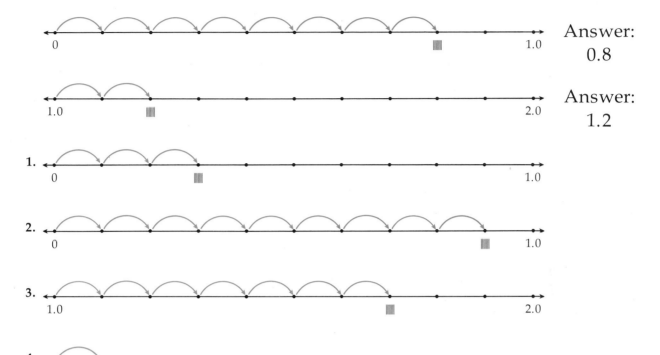

Answer:
0.8

Answer:
1.2

Read each decimal.

Example: 7.2   Answer: "seven and two tenths"

5. 0.3   6. 8.1   7. 6.4   8. 3.2   9. 0.7   10. 7.5

11. 9.5   12. 0.6   13. 5.1   14. 6.1   15. 5.4   16. 3.8

17. 1.1   18. 2.2   19. 9.8   20. 0.9   21. 9.6   22. 7.9

Find 11 different squares in the picture as quickly as you can.

Trace each different-size square that you find and tell how many of that size there are.

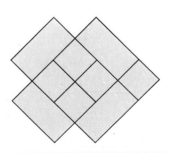

Writing decimals: hundredths

How much is shaded?

We think: two and twenty-five hundredths

We write: $2\frac{25}{100}$ or 2.25

mixed   decimal
numeral

Write a decimal for each picture.

1.

2.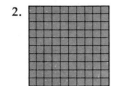

3.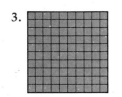

4.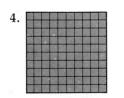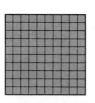

5.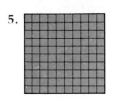

Write a decimal for each picture.

Example:

1. 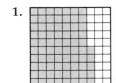   2. 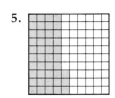   3.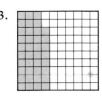

Answer: 0.25

4.   5. 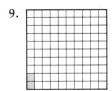   6. 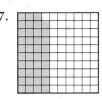   7.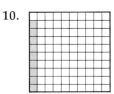

Example:

Answer: 0.08

Read each decimal.

Example: 3.15   Answer: "three and fifteen hundredths"

11. 1.24   12. 6.4   13. 3.46   14. 1.5   15. 8.6

16. 4.08   17. 0.13   18. 2.57   19. 4.5   20. 0.09

21. 6.32   22. 5.01   23. 7.69   24. 0.72   25. 9.81

Write a decimal.

26. four and six tenths   27. nine and two hundredths
28. one and thirty-one hundredths   29. six and eighteen hundredths
30. forty-three hundredths   31. seven and one hundredth

Answers for Self-check   1. 2.6   2. 0.3   3. 1.65   4. 0.37   5. 2.6   6. 0.7   7. 9.03   8. 6.45

Self-check

Write a decimal.

1.   2.

3.   4.

5. two and six tenths   6. seven tenths
7. nine and three hundredths   8. six and forty-five hundredths

Answers for Self-check—page 291

Test

Write a decimal.

1.   2.

3.   4.

5. one and eight tenths   6. four tenths
7. eight and fifty-three hundredths   8. nine and eight hundredths

Roman Numerals

The Romans used
letters to write
their numerals.

I = 1	C = 100
V = 5	D = 500
X = 10	M = 1000
L = 50	

Find the number
by adding.

II = 1 + 1 = ▥
VI = 5 + ▥ = ▥
XI = 10 + ▥ = ▥
LX = 50 + ▥ = ▥

Find the number
by subtracting.

IV = 5 − 1 = ▥
IX = 10 − ▥ = ▥
XL = 50 − ▥ = ▥
XC = 100 − ▥ = ▥

Read the Roman numerals.

1.

2.

The long hand is at ▥.
The short hand is at ▥.
What time is it?

3.

4.

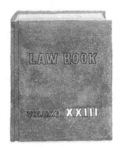

(Hint: CM = 1000 − 100 = 900
MCM = 1000 + 900)

Adding and Subtracting Decimals

	Ones	Tenths
	2	8
	1	4

Getting started

Think of this ▱▱▱▱▱▱▱▱▱▱ as 1.

Then each of these ▱ is 0.1.

Give the total number of pieces for the chart.

Whenever you can,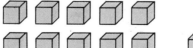
trade for a one.

10 tenths for a **one**

Give the totals. Make trades when you can.

Example:

Ones	Tenths
(rod)	(cube)
3	5
4	8
Total 7 8	13 3

{ Think: 13 tenths.
Trade 10 tenths for a one.
Have 3 tenths left, 1 more one.
Answer: 8.3

1.

Ones	Tenths
(rod)	(cube)
2	3
5	4
Total ?	?

2.

Ones	Tenths
(rod)	(cube)
5	8
1	9
Total ?	?

3.

Ones	Tenths
(rod)	(cube)
0	9
0	5
Total ?	?

4.

Ones	Tenths
(rod)	(cube)
8	7
0	6
Total ?	?

Adding decimals

Bought 15.8 L of gas for a midget racer.
Bought 3.4 L of gas for a motorbike.
Bought how much gas in all?

Finding the answer

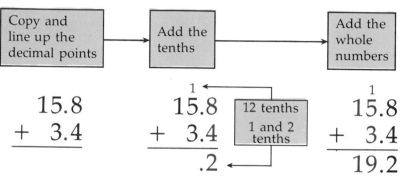

| Copy and line up the decimal points | → | Add the tenths | → | Add the whole numbers |

$$\begin{array}{r} 15.8 \\ +\ 3.4 \\ \hline \end{array}$$

$$\begin{array}{r} {}^{1}\quad \\ 15.8 \\ +\ 3.4 \\ \hline .2 \end{array}$$

12 tenths
1 and 2 tenths

$$\begin{array}{r} {}^{1}\quad \\ 15.8 \\ +\ 3.4 \\ \hline 19.2 \end{array}$$

Bought 19.2 L of gas in all.

Other examples

$$\begin{array}{r} {}^{1}\ \\ 3.7 \\ +2.8 \\ \hline 6.5 \end{array}$$

$$\begin{array}{r} {}^{1\ 1}\ \\ 24.6 \\ +37.4 \\ \hline 62.0 \end{array}$$

$$\begin{array}{r} {}^{1}\ \\ 0.9 \\ +0.7 \\ \hline 1.6 \end{array}$$

Add.

1. $\begin{array}{r} 3.7 \\ +4.5 \\ \hline \end{array}$
2. $\begin{array}{r} 2.8 \\ +5.6 \\ \hline \end{array}$
3. $\begin{array}{r} 4.2 \\ +9.3 \\ \hline \end{array}$
4. $\begin{array}{r} 8.4 \\ +7.9 \\ \hline \end{array}$

5. $\begin{array}{r} 12.7 \\ +\ 6.8 \\ \hline \end{array}$
6. $\begin{array}{r} 9.2 \\ +8.9 \\ \hline \end{array}$
7. $\begin{array}{r} 6.7 \\ +5.9 \\ \hline \end{array}$
8. $\begin{array}{r} 3.4 \\ +4.7 \\ \hline \end{array}$

9. $\begin{array}{r} 9.6 \\ +7.5 \\ \hline \end{array}$
10. $\begin{array}{r} 18.7 \\ +\ 4.9 \\ \hline \end{array}$
11. $\begin{array}{r} 0.8 \\ +7.6 \\ \hline \end{array}$
12. $\begin{array}{r} 4.6 \\ +8.6 \\ \hline \end{array}$

Add.

1. 8.7
    + 4.6

2. 9.2
    + 7.8

3. 0.7
    + 0.9

4. 0.9
    + 3.8

5. 16.7
    + 8.3

6. 18.9
    + 7.4

7. 24.6
    + 9.4

8. 43.8
    + 8.5

9. 54.7
    + 39.6

10. 47.8
    + 53.2

11. 69.4
    + 38.7

12. 37.9
    + 56.8

13. 1.4
    2.8
    + 3.6

14. 0.3
    0.5
    + 0.7

15. 15.5
    12.8
    + 18.6

16. 43.8
    56.7
    + 68.6

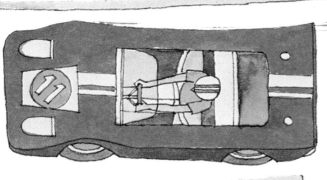

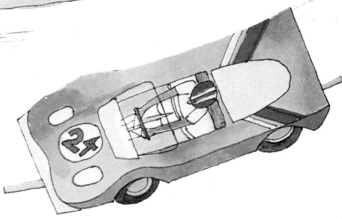

17. Bought 24.7 L of gas
    on Monday.
    Bought 16.8 L of gas
    on Tuesday.
    How many liters in all?

18. Sold 26.8 L of gas for
    one car. Then sold 23.7 L
    for another car. How many
    liters in all?

Guess this sum.

$24.9 + 25.1 + 49.8 + 50.2 + 74.7 + 75.3 + 99.6 + 100.4 = n$

Find the sum. How close was your guess?

Subtracting decimals

Paper airplane contest:
Evita's plane flew 6.5 m.
Jerry's plane flew 4.8 m.
How much farther did
Evita's plane fly?

Finding the answer

| Copy and line up the decimal points | Need more tenths Trade a one | Subtract the tenths | Subtract the whole numbers |

$$\begin{array}{r} 6.5 \\ -\ 4.8 \\ \hline \end{array}$$

$$\begin{array}{r} {}^{5}\,{}^{15} \\ \not{6}.\not{5} \\ -\ 4.8 \\ \hline \end{array}$$

$$\begin{array}{r} {}^{5}\,{}^{15} \\ \not{6}.\not{5} \\ -\ 4.8 \\ \hline .7 \end{array}$$

$$\begin{array}{r} {}^{5}\,{}^{15} \\ \not{6}.\not{5} \\ -\ 4.8 \\ \hline 1.7 \end{array}$$

Evita's plane flew 1.7 m farther.

Other examples

$$\begin{array}{r} {}^{6}\,{}^{14} \\ 1\not{7}.\not{4} \\ -\ \ 9.6 \\ \hline 7.8 \end{array}$$

$$\begin{array}{r} {}^{19}\,{}^{13} \\ 2\not{0}.\not{3} \\ -\ 13.8 \\ \hline 6.5 \end{array}$$

$$\begin{array}{r} {}^{4}\,{}^{11}\,{}^{10} \\ \not{5}\not{2}.\not{0} \\ -\ 26.7 \\ \hline 25.3 \end{array}$$

Subtract.

1. $\begin{array}{r} 9.2 \\ -\ 4.7 \\ \hline \end{array}$

2. $\begin{array}{r} 8.5 \\ -\ 3.8 \\ \hline \end{array}$

3. $\begin{array}{r} 7.6 \\ -\ 0.9 \\ \hline \end{array}$

4. $\begin{array}{r} 6.4 \\ -\ 2.6 \\ \hline \end{array}$

5. $\begin{array}{r} 15.7 \\ -\ 8.9 \\ \hline \end{array}$

6. $\begin{array}{r} 18.0 \\ -\ 9.7 \\ \hline \end{array}$

7. $\begin{array}{r} 16.4 \\ -\ 8.8 \\ \hline \end{array}$

8. $\begin{array}{r} 17.3 \\ -\ 7.7 \\ \hline \end{array}$

Subtract.

1.	12.2 − 8.6	2.	15.1 − 9.6
3.	8.7 − 0.9	4.	17.3 − 9.6
5.	43.5 − 21.7	6.	58.2 − 24.8
7.	64.5 − 36.8	8.	47.4 − 32.4
9.	60.7 − 28.8	10.	47.0 − 18.6
11.	98.4 − 59.5	12.	104.6 − 57.4
13.	80.8 − 40.9	14.	25.3 − 0.7

15. Greg's paper airplane
flew 5.9 m.
Roland's flew 11.4 m.
How much farther did
Roland's plane fly?

☆ 16. Have a paper airplane contest.
Measure the distance each plane
flies, to the nearest tenth
of a meter. Find the differences
in the distances flown.

The can contains 1000 beads. There
are red beads and black beads.

The beads are mixed up and, without
looking, Jan draws out 100 beads. She gets
90 red and 10 black. Guess how many
black beads were in the can at first.

Adding and subtracting decimals: hundredths

Very large apple: 1.38 kg
Very large pear: 1.19 kg
How many kilograms of fruit?

Finding the answer

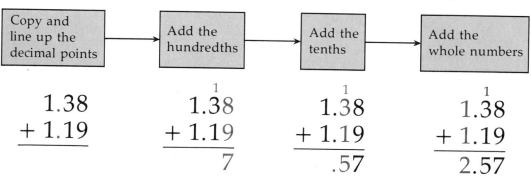

Copy and line up the decimal points	Add the hundredths	Add the tenths	Add the whole numbers

$$\begin{array}{r} 1.38 \\ + 1.19 \\ \hline \end{array}$$

$$\begin{array}{r} \overset{1}{1.38} \\ + 1.19 \\ \hline 7 \end{array}$$

$$\begin{array}{r} \overset{1}{1.38} \\ + 1.19 \\ \hline .57 \end{array}$$

$$\begin{array}{r} \overset{1}{1.38} \\ + 1.19 \\ \hline 2.57 \end{array}$$

There are 2.57 kg of fruit.

Other examples

$$\begin{array}{r} \overset{1\ 1}{3.68} \\ + 4.57 \\ \hline 8.25 \end{array} \qquad \begin{array}{r} \overset{1\quad 1}{57.09} \\ + \ \ 8.63 \\ \hline 65.72 \end{array} \qquad \begin{array}{r} \overset{3\ 13}{3.\cancel{4}\cancel{3}} \\ - 1.39 \\ \hline 2.04 \end{array} \qquad \begin{array}{r} \overset{7\ 15}{2\cancel{8}.\cancel{5}4} \\ - \ \ 7.80 \\ \hline 20.74 \end{array}$$

Add or subtract.

1. $\begin{array}{r} 5.27 \\ + 2.39 \\ \hline \end{array}$

2. $\begin{array}{r} 9.75 \\ + 6.27 \\ \hline \end{array}$

3. $\begin{array}{r} 12.68 \\ + \ \ 0.47 \\ \hline \end{array}$

4. $\begin{array}{r} 8.63 \\ + 4.97 \\ \hline \end{array}$

5. $\begin{array}{r} 24.08 \\ - \ \ 9.64 \\ \hline \end{array}$

6. $\begin{array}{r} 44.30 \\ - 17.86 \\ \hline \end{array}$

7. $\begin{array}{r} 9.98 \\ - 4.59 \\ \hline \end{array}$

8. $\begin{array}{r} 36.67 \\ - 27.38 \\ \hline \end{array}$

Add or subtract.

1. 8.62 − 4.27	2. 9.73 + 2.56	3. 12.86 − 3.79	4. 5.75 + 1.38	5. 17.27 − 8.45
6. 42.38 + 20.91	7. 65.04 − 29.76	8. 58.23 + 49.75	9. 86.17 − 38.68	10. 56.73 + 27.29
11. 38.09 − 13.67	12. 84.76 + 58.59	13. 97.33 − 48.59	14. 64.31 + 29.83	15. 29.77 − 18.99
16. 12.60 + 9.57	17. 8.67 − 0.98	18. 75.96 + 23.84	19. 99.45 − 47.69	20. 36.08 + 14.99
21. 71.43 − 62.27	22. 15.96 + 3.47	23. 11.07 − 4.89	24. 27.38 + 35.41	25. 50.27 − 38.47

26. Very large carrot: 3.29 kg
Very large cucumber: 4.57 kg
How many kilograms in all?

☆ 27. Find the mass of an apple in kilograms. How much less than 1.38 kg is its mass?

Solve the equations.

1. $1 + 2 + 3 + 4 + 5 = n$
$(5 \times 6) \div 2 = n$

2. $1 + 2 + 3 + 4 + 5 + 6 = n$
$(6 \times 7) \div 2 = n$

What did you discover?
Try to find another pair
of equations in this pattern.

Answers for Self-check   1. 9.2   2. 26.2   3. 17.86   4. 67.18   5. 3.5   6. 6.8   7. 4.14   8. 38.73   9. 20.1   10. 1.08   11. 73.17   12. 1.78

Add.

1.   3.5
     + 5.7

2.   25.4
     + 0.8

3.   9.47
     + 8.39

4.   54.36
     + 12.82

Subtract.

5.   8.2
     − 4.7

6.   15.4
     − 8.6

7.   9.32
     − 5.18

8.   54.07
     − 15.34

Add or subtract.

9.   11.7
     + 8.4

10.   4.03
     − 2.95

11.   28.50
     + 44.67

12.   31.54
     − 29.76

Answers for Self-check—page 301

Add.

1.   4.6
     + 2.8

2.   12.7
     + 1.9

3.   6.75
     + 4.98

4.   65.25
     + 18.95

Subtract.

5.   10.7
     − 2.9

6.   24.3
     − 8.5

7.   7.45
     − 5.19

8.   68.04
     − 0.98

Add or subtract.

9.   14.6
     + 16.7

10.   8.07
     − 5.49

11.   39.17
     + 6.86

12.   42.22
     − 17.35

Pentominoes

Pentominoes are figures made up of five squares.

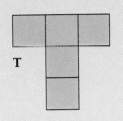 T

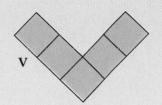 U

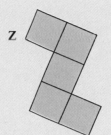 V

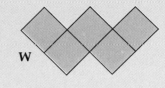 W

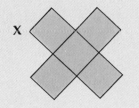 X

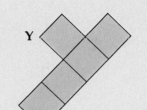 Y

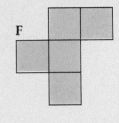 Z

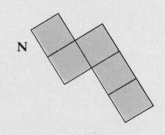 F

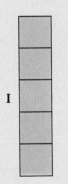 I

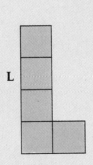 L

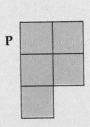 P

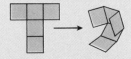 N

1. All but one of the pentominoes have a perimeter of 12 units. Which one does not? What is its perimeter?

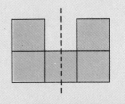

2. Some pentominoes can be folded to make a box. Find another one that can.

3. Some have a line of symmetry. They can be folded so that one half exactly fits on the other half. Find another one of these.

Using Your Skills

29.0 km Tower Junction

Mammoth Hotel

32.3 km

Norris

30.7 km

Canyon

22.6 km

West Entrance

19.4 km

Madison Junction

25.8 km

25.8 km

Lake

32.3 km

43.5 km

East Entrance

Old Faithful

27.4 km

West Thumb

Yellowstone National Park

Getting started

1. How far is Old Faithful from Norris?

2. How much farther is it from West Thumb to Old Faithful than it is from the West Entrance to Madison Junction?

3. What other problems can you solve?

Solving Problems

1. Read carefully to find the facts.

2. Look for the question.

3. Decide what to do. (+, −, ×, ÷).

4. Find the answer.

5. Read again.
   Does your answer make sense?

When you solve decimal problems, always check the position of the decimal point in your answer. Be sure your answer makes sense.

Check the answers given for these problems.
Correct them if they are wrong.

1. Kip hiked 13.5 km on Saturday.
   She hiked 14.8 km on Sunday.
   How many kilometers in all?

   Answer: 2.83 km

2. It is 4.4 km from Lake Lodge
   to Fishing Bridge.
   It is 12.2 km from Lake Lodge
   to Natural Bridge.
   How much farther to Natural
   Bridge?

   Answer: 7.8 km

3. Traveled 72.5 km before lunch
   and 91.3 km after lunch.
   How many more kilometers
   after lunch?

   Answer: 188 km

4. Horseback riding:
   24.9 km on Friday
   27.3 km on Saturday
   How many kilometers in all?

   Answer: 52.2 km

Decimals in our world

Temperatures

1. Usual body temperature: 37.0° C
   High fever temperature: 40.1° C
   How much higher is the fever temperature?

2. Room temperature: 21.6° C
   Body temperature: 37.0° C
   How much higher is the body temperature?

At the store

3. Ground beef: 1.75 kg
   Ham: 3.8 kg
   Beef roast: 4.27 kg
   How many kilograms of meat in all?

Weather

4. 10.7 cm of rain on Saturday
   9.75 cm on rain on Sunday
   How many centimeters of rain in all?

5. Average wind speed in Atlanta: 14.7 km/h
   Average wind speed in Winnipeg: 20.0 km/h
   How much greater is the average wind speed in Winnipeg?

In the shop

6. Diameter of the red rod: 2.63 cm
   Diameter of the blue rod: 0.95 cm
   How much greater is the diameter of the red rod?

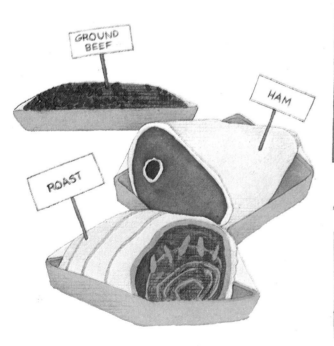

Driving

7. Monday: 137.7 km
   Tuesday: 87.3 km
   Wednesday: 44.6 km
   How many kilometers
   in all?

8. Used 15.3 L of gas on
   Monday.
   Used 9.7 L of gas on
   Tuesday.
   Used how many more
   liters on Monday?

Sewing

9. Skirt: 3.4 m of material
   Jacket: 2.8 m of material
   How many meters in all?

Speeds

10. Fast human: 43.29 km/h
    Fast horse: 69.62 km/h
    How much faster is the
    horse?

11. First place race car: 324.56 km/h
    Last place race car: 298.49 km/h
    How much faster was the
    first place car?

Space travel

12. Earth's speed around the
    sun: 29.79 km/s (kilometers
    per second)
    Apollo X spaceship's speed:
    11.08 km/s
    How much greater is the
    earth's speed?

How long are the bolts?

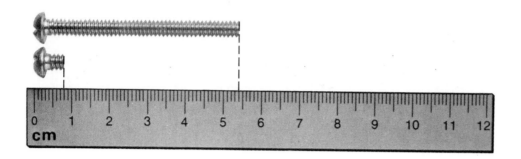

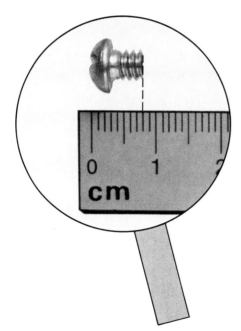

The shorter bolt is
0.8 cm long.

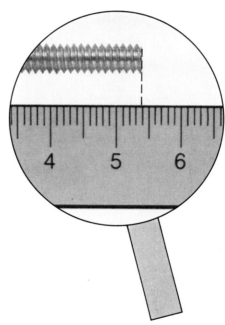

The longer bolt is
5.4 cm long.

Give the length to the nearest tenth of a centimeter.

1.

2. ▬

Use your centimeter ruler to find the lengths.

Example:

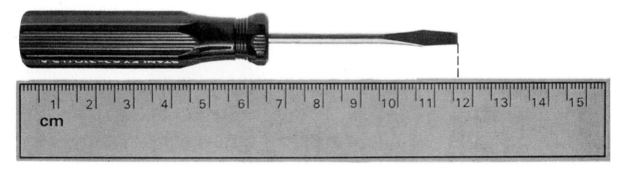

Answer: 11.6 cm

1.

2.

3.

Find the diameters.

4.

5.
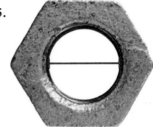

☆ 6. Use a centimeter ruler to measure things in your classroom to the nearest tenth of a centimeter. Make a table like this.

Item measured	Length
Pencil	15.8 cm

Decimals and money

Would you like to work in
a sporting goods store?

Sales clerks must be friendly
and helpful to their customers.
They must be able to find the
total costs of the things they
sell. They must also be able to
make change quickly and correctly.

Solve these problems about sales in a sporting goods store.

1. One clerk sold a baseball
   for $2.67 and a bat for
   $6.95. What was the total
   cost?

2. A boy bought a can of
   tennis balls for $2.85.
   He gave the clerk $5.00.
   How much change should
   the clerk give him?

3. A girl bought a basketball
   for $9.75 and a pair of shoes
   for $15.95. How much did
   she spend in all?

4. A man bought a tennis racket
   for $28.49. He gave the clerk
   $40.00. How much change
   should he get?

5. A woman bought two table-tennis paddles and a box of balls for $5.79. She gave the clerk $10.00. How much change should the clerk give her?

6. The regular price of a golf sweater is $24.49. The sale price is $5.54 less. What is the sale price?

7. Bowling balls cost $46.75 each. How much should the clerk charge for two bowling balls?

8. A clerk sold a softball for $3.25 and a glove for $14.69. What was the total cost?

9. Camp chairs cost $8.29 each. How much would 3 camp chairs cost?

☆ 10. A clerk sold 2 T-shirts for $2.29 each and 3 pairs of socks for $1.69 a pair. What was the total cost?

You might get sales slips like these when
you buy things at the store. Find the missing totals.

1.
	$3.69
	0.76
	4.50
	5.98
Total	▓▓▓▓▓▓

2.
	$2.80
	1.65
	0.49
	8.95
Total	▓▓▓▓▓▓

3.
	$12.75
	8.50
	3.49
	0.65
Total	▓▓▓▓▓▓

4.
	$24.95
	12.65
	8.49
Total	▓▓▓▓▓▓

5.
	$2.98
	3.49
	1.68
Total	▓▓▓▓▓▓

6.
	$0.49
	0.98
	0.56
	0.41
Total	▓▓▓▓▓▓

7.
	$ 7.59
	6.45
	10.98
	3.75
Total	▓▓▓▓▓▓

8.
	$59.50
	12.98
	6.47
Total	▓▓▓▓▓▓

Sometimes you must pay a tax on the items
you buy. Find the total amounts.

9.
Items	$12.45
Tax	0.62
Total	▓▓▓▓▓

10.
Items	$9.24
Tax	0.46
Total	▓▓▓▓▓

11.
Items	$5.49
Tax	0.27
Total	▓▓▓▓▓

12.
Items	$1.85
Tax	0.09
Total	▓▓▓▓▓

13.
Items	$24.50
Tax	1.23
Total	▓▓▓▓▓

14.
Items	$52.75
Tax	2.63
Total	▓▓▓▓▓

Some stores **subtract** some money from your bill. It is called a **discount**. Find these costs after the discount.

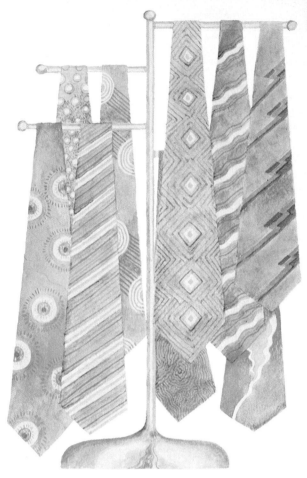

1. | Bill | $8.90 |
   |------|-------|
   | Discount | 0.89 |
   | Total | |

2. | Bill | $18.65 |
   |------|--------|
   | Discount | 1.87 |
   | Total | |

3. | Bill | $49.50 |
   |------|--------|
   | Discount | 7.62 |
   | Total | |

4. | Bill | $5.46 |
   |------|-------|
   | Discount | 1.09 |
   | Total | |

Find the correct amount of change.

5. | Amount paid | $2.00 |
   |-------------|-------|
   | Bill | 1.25 |
   | Change | |

6. | Amount paid | $1.00 |
   |-------------|-------|
   | Bill | 0.47 |
   | Change | |

7. | Amount paid | $5.00 |
   |-------------|-------|
   | Bill | 2.89 |
   | Change | |

8. | Amount paid | $10.00 |
   |-------------|--------|
   | Bill | 8.45 |
   | Change | |

9. | Amount paid | $6.00 |
   |-------------|-------|
   | Bill | 5.27 |
   | Change | |

Estimate which of these bills you can pay with $20.

	A	B	C	
	$6.00	$4.98	$5.98	Then find the sums, and
	2.95	4.98	3.98	check your estimates.
	3.98	5.98	7.98	
	7.95	5.98	1.98	
T				

Answers for Self-check   1. $10.64   2. 6.4 cm   3. $9.82   4. $16.74   5. $2.31

Self-check

Find the answer.

1. Tennis shoes: $8.95
   Socks: $1.69
   How much in all?

2. Give the length to the nearest tenth of a centimeter.

Give the missing amounts.

3.

	$2.59
	6.45
	0.78
Total	▨▨▨▨

4.

Bill	$15.95
Tax	0.79
Total	▨▨▨▨

5.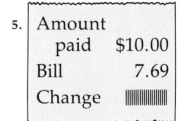

Amount paid	$10.00
Bill	7.69
Change	▨▨▨▨

Answers for Self-check—page 313

Test

Find the answer.

1. Gas used on Saturday: 19.4 L
   Gas used on Sunday: 16.9 L
   How much in all?

2. Give the length to the nearest tenth of a centimeter.

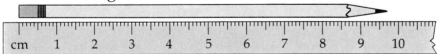

Give the missing amounts.

3.

	$3.98
	1.85
Total	▨▨▨▨

4.

Bill	$5.83
Tax	0.29
Total	▨▨▨▨

5.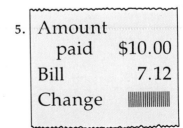

Amount paid	$10.00
Bill	7.12
Change	▨▨▨▨

Jigsaw Rectangles

Use graph paper and cut out
rectangles with these dimensions:

A   3 by 9 units

B   5 by 8 units

C   4 by 7 units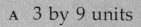

D   10 by 2 units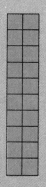

E   1 by 6 units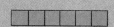

Try to arrange the rectangles
so that they form a square.

Area, Volume, and Mass

Getting started

The **area** of the figure
on the geoboard is
1 square unit.

What is the area of each
of these figures?

1. 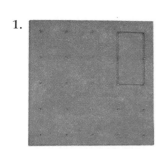 **2.** 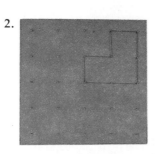 **3.** 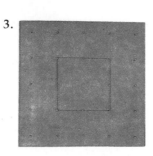 **4.**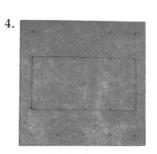

Give the areas.

1.

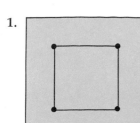

area: 1 square unit   area: ▓▓▓

2.

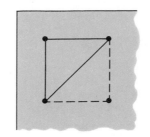

area: 2 square units   area: ▓▓▓

Give the area of each of these figures.

3.

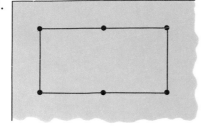

4.

5.

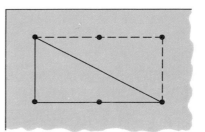

6.

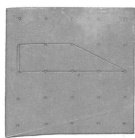

7.

8.

Betty drew a plan of the floor
of her room on graph paper.
She let each square centimeter
stand for one carpet tile.

square
centimeter

Betty's room

1. How many tiles will Betty need?
2. The tiles cost $0.37 each. What will the total cost be?

Find the number of tiles needed for each room.
Find the cost of the tile.

1. Hal's room

2. Hazel's room

☆ 3. Tim's room

Finding volume

The **volume** of this box is 6 cubic units.
It holds 6 unit cubes.

 unit
cube

3 in each row
2 rows
1 layer

Give the number of cubes for each box.

1.

8 in each row
2 rows
1 layer

2.

4 in each row
3 rows
1 layer

3.

3 in each row
2 rows
2 layers

4.

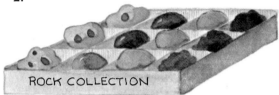

3 in each row
1 row
2 layers

5.

4 in each row
2 rows
3 layers

6.

3 in each row
3 rows
3 layers

This box is being filled with centimeter cubes.

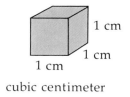

1 cm
1 cm
1 cm
cubic centimeter

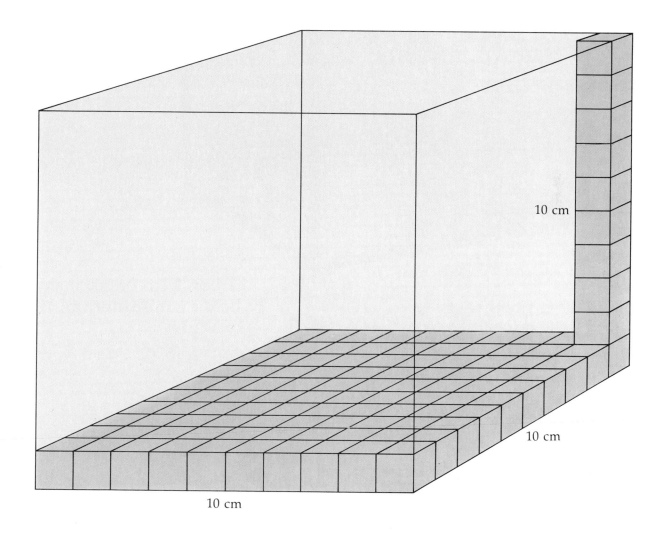

10 cm

10 cm

10 cm

The volume of the bottom layer is 100 cubic centimeters.

1. How many layers are needed to fill the box?

2. What is the volume of the box?

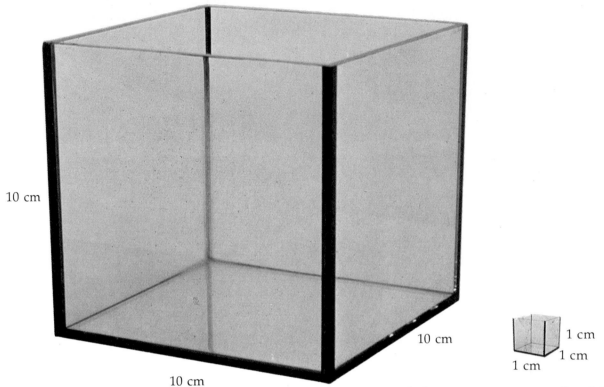

10 cm

10 cm

10 cm

1 cm
1 cm
1 cm

A box 10 cm on each side holds 1 **liter** (L) of water.

A box 1 cm on each side holds 1 **milliliter** (mL) of water.

The volume of the large box is 1000 cubic centimeters.

1 liter = 1000 milliliters
1 L = 1000 mL

1 L

1 L

1 L

Name something that holds more than 1 L.

Name something that holds less than 1 L.

Copy and finish the tables. Then answer the questions.

☆ 1.

large juice bottle	1	2
milliliters	500	|||||

How many bottles are needed to make a liter of juice?

☆ 2.

drinking glass	1	2	3	4
milliliters	250	|||||	|||||	|||||

How many glasses can you fill with a liter of water?

☆ 3.

juice glass	1	5	10
milliliters	100	|||||	|||||

A liter of juice will fill how many glasses?

☆ 4.

tablespoon	1	3	5	7
milliliters	15	|||||	|||||	|||||

About how many tablespoons does it take to fill a juice glass?

☆ 5.

teaspoon	1	2	3	4
milliliters	5	|||||	|||||	|||||

How many teaspoons are needed to fill one tablespoon?

☆ 6.

gas can	1	5	10	15
liters	4	|||||	|||||	|||||

How many cans of gas are needed to fill a tank that holds 60 L?

Kilograms and grams

1 liter (L) of water has a
mass of 1 **kilogram** (kg).

1 milliliter (mL) of water has a
mass of 1 **gram** (g).

1 kilogram = 1000 grams

  1 kg = 1000 g

Look at the scales.
Tell whether the unit is grams or kilograms.

1.

2.

3.

Tell whether each object's mass would be **more** or **less** than a kilogram.

1. a snack bar

2. a large pumpkin

3. a bowling ball

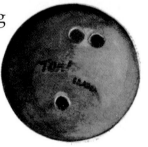

4. a box of cereal

5. a small orange

6. a portable TV set

Practicing your skills

1. 395 + 768	2. 602 + 398	3. 423 − 176	4. 907 − 318	5. 400 − 236
6. 947 × 3	7. 5826 × 8	8. 27 × 18	9. 59 × 72	10. 396 × 24
11. 6)534	12. 3)2172	13. 8)760	14. 40)376	15. 90)733

Answers for Self-check   1. 10 square units   2. 9 square units   3. 24 cubic units   4. 4   5. 1000
6. less

Self-check

Find the area
of each figure.

1. 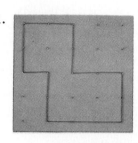 **2.**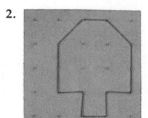

3. Find the volume
of this box.

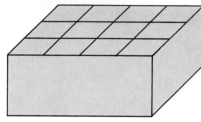

4 in each row
3 rows
2 layers

☆ **4.** A cup holds 250 ml. How many cups will a
liter of milk fill?

5. Give the number for the ▥.
1 kg = ▥ g

6. Is the mass of a baseball
more or **less** than 1 kg?

Answers for Self-check—page 325

Test

Find the area
of each figure.

1. 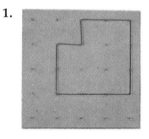 **2.**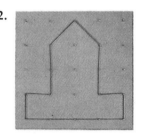

3. Find the volume
of this box.

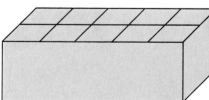

5 in each row
2 rows
2 layers

☆ **4.** How many milliliters in a liter?

5. A bag of potatoes has a mass
of 4 kg. How many grams is this?

6. Is the mass of a watermelon
more or **less** than 1 kg?

Flips and Turns

Cut out figures from a sheet of cardboard so that the
holes look like this.

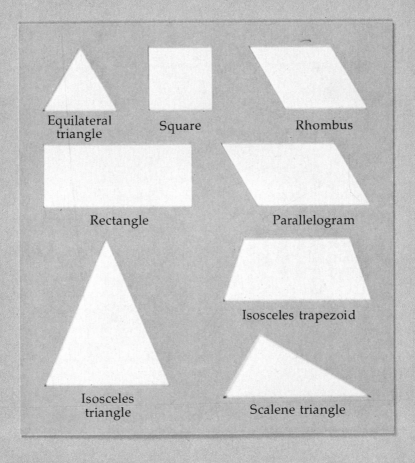

Mark an **F** on the front and a **B** on the back
of each cutout figure.

In how many different ways can you put each figure back
into its hole? Draw a picture to show each way.

Using Larger Numbers

To get to the sun, you would have to travel

 km.

"one hundred forty-nine million,
five hundred ninety-seven thousand,
eight hundred seventy"

Make a numeral reader and use it to read these numerals.

1. 3   942

2. 10   536

3. 408   212

4. 29   002

5. 2   592

6. 409   636

7. 82   746   962

8. 438   986   503

9. 971   635   887

A million is 1000 thousands.

Answer the questions.

1.

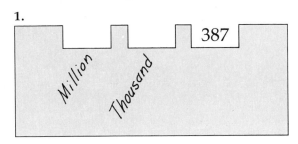

387

How many?

2.

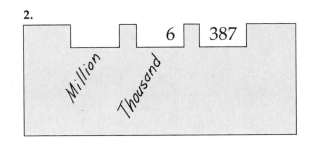

6   387

How many thousands?

3.

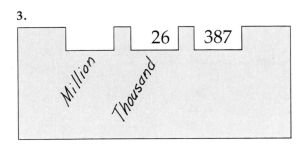

26   387

How many thousands?

4.

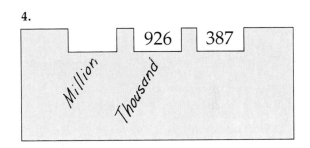

926   387

How many thousands?

5.

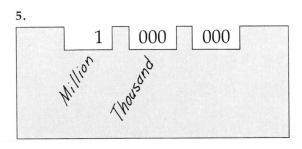

1   000   000

How many millions?

6.

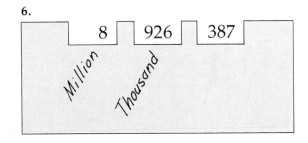

8   926   387

How many millions?

7.

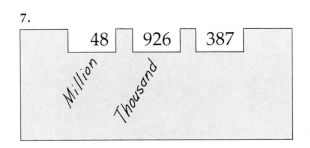

48   926   387

How many millions?

8.

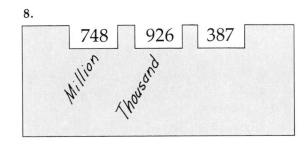

748   926   387

How many millions?

⊛Reading and writing larger numerals

Read these numerals.

Example: Answer:

Trip to the moon: "three hundred seventy-six thousand,
376 284 kilometers   two hundred eighty-four"

1. Highest mountain: 2. Deepest part   3. Earth's speed:
   8848   of the ocean: 107 240
   meters   11 033 meters   kilometers per hour

4. Mercury's speed: 5. People in the U.S.   6. People in the U.S.
   172 800   in 1870:   in 1970:
   kilometers   38 558 371   203 235 298
   per hour

7. Area of Canada: 8. Area of the U.S.:   9. Number of seconds
   9 976 139   9 363 123   in a year
   square kilometers   square kilometers   (365 days):
                                                  31 536 000

Write these numerals.

Example: Answer:

Earth's land area: 148 350 000
one hundred forty-eight
million, three hundred
fifty thousand
square kilometers

1. World's longest river: 2. Diameter of the earth:
   six thousand seven hundred   twelve thousand, seven hundred
   thirty-eight   fifty-six
   kilometers   kilometers

3. Space flight speed: 4. Area of Europe:
   twenty-eight thousand,   ten million, five hundred
   two hundred sixty   thirty-two thousand
   kilometers per hour   square kilometers

5. Area of North America: 6. Area of the earth's oceans:
   twenty-four million, three   three hundred sixty-one million,
   hundred ninety thousand   five hundred sixty-three thousand,
   square kilometers   four hundred
                                      square kilometers

☆ 7. Speed of light: ☆ 8. Circumference of the earth
   two hundred ninety-nine   at the equator:
   thousand, seven hundred   forty thousand, seventy-five
   ninety-two and five tenths   and sixteen hundredths
   kilometers per second   kilometers

I think I'm big until I spy
So many numbers larger than I.
My name has a one and zeros galore.
Seven digits in all, and not one more.

Who am I?

⊛ Thousands and millions

How large is one thousand?

$$1000 = 10 \text{ hundreds}$$

1. 1 long step is about 100 cm.

steps	1	2	3	4		
centimeters	100	200	300	400		1000

About how many steps is 1000 cm?

Ten Thousand Dollars

2. The total mass of 3 ten-year-old children might be about 100 kg.

children	3	6	9	12		
kilograms	100	200	300	400		1000

How many children would be needed for a mass of 1000 kg?

3. A ten-year-old child might drink 100 L of milk in about 4 months.

months	4	8	12	16		
liters	100	200	300	400		1000

About how many months would it take the child to drink 1000 L?

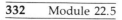

How large is one million?

$$1\,000\,000 = 1000 \text{ thousands}$$

1. There are about 100 000 hairs on the head of an average person.

persons	1	2	3	4	⦚	⦚
hairs	100 000	200 000	300 000	400 000		1 000 000

How many persons for 1 000 000 hairs?

2. It takes about 28 hours to hand out 100 000 dollar bills (one at a time).

hours	28	56	84	112	⦚	⦚
bills	100 000	200 000	300 000	400 000		1 000 000

How long would it take to hand out 1 000 000 dollars?

3. A person who has lived 11 years has lived almost 100 000 hours.

years	11	22	33	44	⦚	⦚
hours	100 000	200 000	300 000	400 000		1 000 000

About how many years old is a person who has lived 1 000 000 hours?

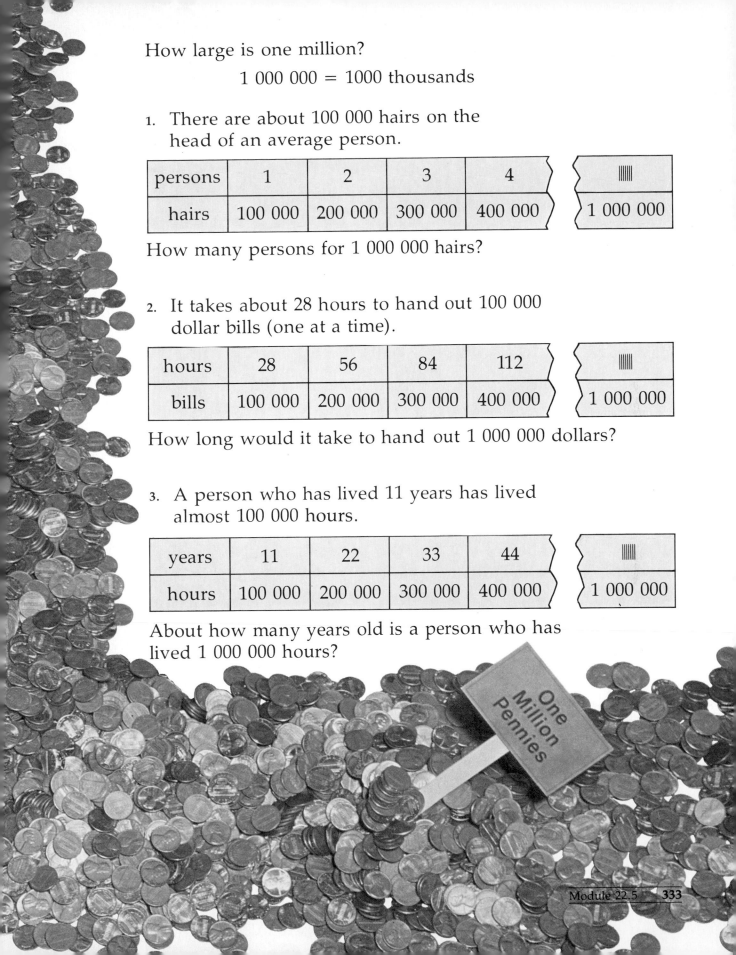

One Million Pennies

1.

More Students in City Schools This Year

Last year, our city schools had 35 375 students.
This year, our schools have 41 295 students.

How many more students this year?

2.

New Highway Almost Complete

By the end of last year, 58 585 km of the new highway had been completed. This year, work on the last 9414 km of the highway will be completed.

How many kilometers of new highway will there be in all?

3.

Thousands Visit Outdoor Art Show

An average of 3500 people a day visited this year's outdoor art show. The show lasted 5 days.

What was the total number of people who visited the show?

4.

Record Crowds at Weekend Games

Saturday night, 46 378 people watched the first game of the playoffs. The next day, 47 816 people saw the second game.

How many people in all?

5.

Voters Choose Andrews
• • • • • • •

The new leader of our city will be Mary Ann Andrews. The final count in yesterday's voting is as follows:

Mary Ann Andrews: 93 602
James E. Howard: 77 843

By how many votes did Andrews win?

6.

Scientists Say 4 out of 5 Kinds of Animals Are Insects

No one knows exactly how many different kinds of animals there are. So far, scientists have found about 1 000 000 different kinds. About 800 000 of these are insects.

About how many kinds of animals are not insects?

7.

Swimming Pool Costs Climb

The new city swimming pool will cost $250 000 more than the pool built last year. The pool built last year cost $1 375 000.

How much will the new pool cost?

8.

WHAT'S IN A NAME?

There are 1 230 500 people named Jones in this country. There are 2 238 400 people named Smith.

How many more people are named Smith than Jones?

9.

LARGE JET CARRIES A LARGE LOAD

A 747 jet has a mass of 350 100 kg when it is fully loaded. When it is empty, its mass is only 163 370 kg.

How much greater is the jet's mass when fully loaded?

10.

Beekeeper Loses Bees

A beekeeper in Newton told police that 3 beehives disappeared from her farm during the weekend. About 60 000 bees were in each hive.

About how many bees disappeared?

Answers for Self-check   1. 536 952   2. 87 902 343   3. 10   4. 10 minutes   5. $6450

Write the numerals.

1. five hundred thirty-six thousand, nine hundred fifty-two

2. eighty-seven million, nine hundred two thousand, three hundred forty-three

3. Give the missing number. 1000 = ⦀ hundreds

4. You can count to one hundred in 1 minute. About how many minutes will it take you to count to 1000?

minutes	1	2	3	4	⦀
count	100	200	300	400	1000

5. A small car might cost $3775.
   A sports car might cost $10 225.
   How much more is the sports car?

Answers for Self-check—page 335

Write the numerals.

1. four hundred twenty-three thousand, eight hundred ninety-one

2. six hundred seventy-five million, twenty-four thousand, three hundred forty-nine

3. Give the missing number. 1 000 000 = ⦀ thousands

4. 100 000 drops of water drip from a faucet in 2 days. How many days for 1 000 000 drops?

days	2	4	6	⦀
drops	100 000	200 000	300 000	1 000 000

5. Chicago to Honolulu: 6800 km
   Chicago to London: 6320 km
   How much farther to Honolulu?

Area Estimates

Use a piece of centimeter graph paper.

Draw around these objects. Count squares and parts of squares to estimate the areas.

1.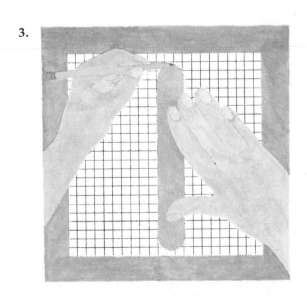

2.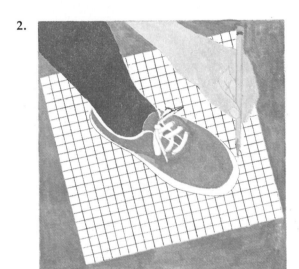

3.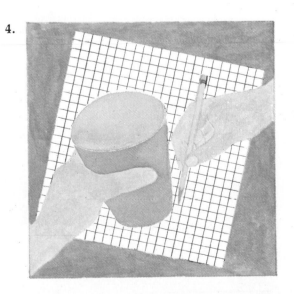

4.

Measurement: Other Units

Getting started

The length of the pen to the nearest inch is 3 inches.

| 1 | 2 | 3 | 4 | 5 |

Inches

The length of the red rod to the nearest half inch is $2\frac{1}{2}$ inches.

The length of the green rod to the nearest half inch is 5 inches.

| 0 | 1 | 2 | 3 | 4 | 5 |

Inches

Find the length to the nearest inch.

1.

2.

3.

Find the length to the nearest half inch.

4.

5.

The length of the pencil to the nearest quarter inch is $4\frac{1}{4}$ inches.

Find the length to the nearest quarter inch.

First estimate, then measure these lengths on your body.

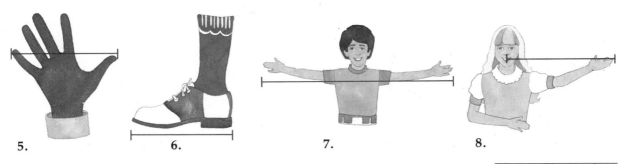

5.   6.   7.   8.

Inches, feet, and yards

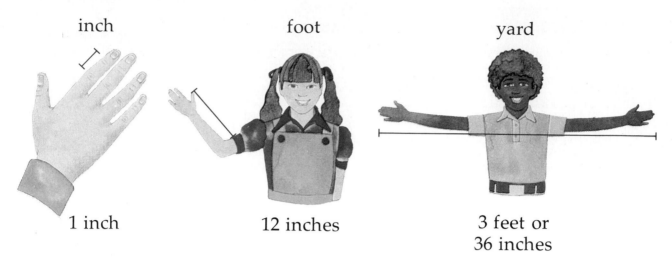

inch

1 inch

foot

12 inches

yard

3 feet or
36 inches

Give the number for each ||||| .

1. 1 foot is ||||| inches.
2. 1 yard is ||||| feet.
3. 1 yard is ||||| inches.

Write **inches, feet,** or **yards**
to complete each sentence.

4. A pencil is about 6 ___?___ long.
5. A man is about 6 ___?___ tall.
6. A basketball hoop is 10 ___?___ above the floor.
7. A football field is 100 ___?___ long.
8. A baseball bat is about 38 ___?___ long.

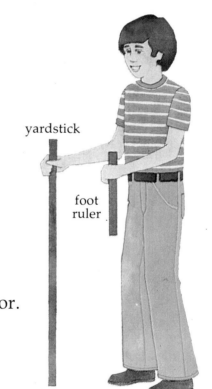

yardstick

foot
ruler

Estimate, then measure to the nearest whole unit.

9. your height, in inches
10. the width of your desk, in inches
11. the width of your classroom, in feet
12. the length of your classroom, in yards

1 mile = 1760 yards = 5280 feet

A train with 120
boxcars is about
1 mile long.

Copy and finish the tables.

1. You might walk about
    1 mile in 15 minutes.
    How many miles in 1 hour?

miles	1	2	▒	▒
minutes	15	30	45	60

2. You might ride a bike about
    3 miles in 15 minutes.
    How many miles in 1 hour?

miles	3	6	▒	▒
minutes	15	30	45	60

3. You might drive a car about
    12 miles in 15 minutes.
    How many miles in 1 hour?

miles	12	▒	▒	▒
minutes	15	30	45	60

Use the tables to answer these questions.

4. How long might it take to walk 3 miles?

5. Ride a bike for $\frac{1}{2}$ hour. About how many miles?

6. Drive for 45 minutes. About how many miles?

Finding perimeter

Marie ran around the edges
of the athletic field.
How far did she run?

120 yd

105 yd ↕ ↕ **105 yd**

120 yd

Finding the answer

Lengths of sides	→	Add	→	The distance around (perimeter)

120, 105
120, 105

$$
\begin{array}{r}
1 \\
120 \\
105 \\
120 \\
\underline{105} \\
450
\end{array}
$$

450 yd

Marie ran 450 yd.

Find the perimeter of each figure.

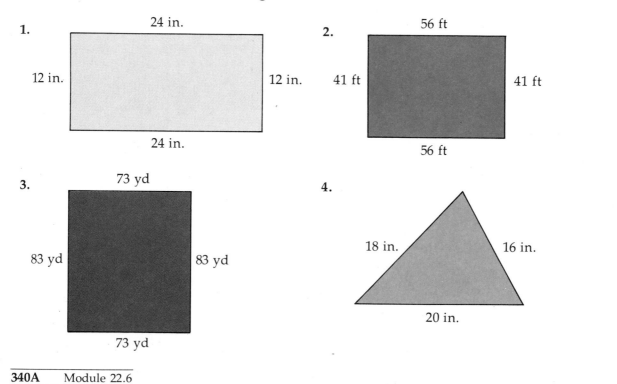

1. 24 in. / 12 in. 12 in. / 24 in.

2. 56 ft / 41 ft 41 ft / 56 ft

3. 73 yd / 83 yd 83 yd / 73 yd

4. 18 in. 16 in. 20 in.

1. How far is it around the base paths of the baseball diamond?

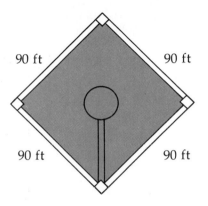

90 ft   90 ft

90 ft   90 ft

2. How much fence does it take to go all the way around the yard?

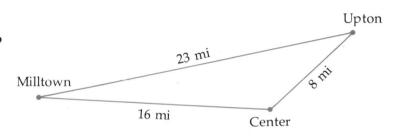

75 yds

45 yds   45 yds

75 yds

3. How many inches of yarn does it take to frame the butterfly collection?

27 in.

12 in.   12 in.

27 in.

4. How far is it from Milltown to Center, to Upton, to Milltown?

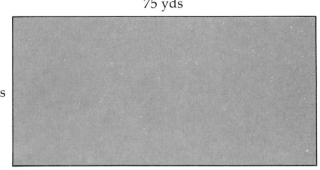

Upton

23 mi

Milltown

8 mi

16 mi   Center

Area and volume

Each square is 1 square inch. Find the area in square inches.

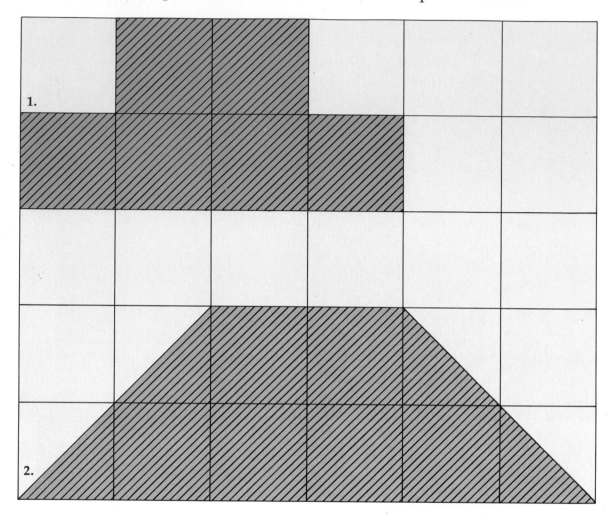

1.

2.

3. How many square inches are there in 1 square foot?

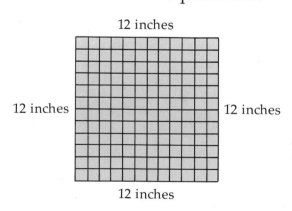

12 inches

12 inches   12 inches

12 inches

4. How many square feet are there in 1 square yard?

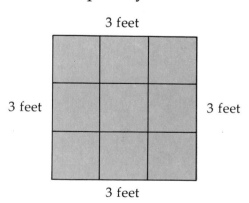

3 feet

3 feet   3 feet

3 feet

You can make a model of a
cubic inch from this pattern.

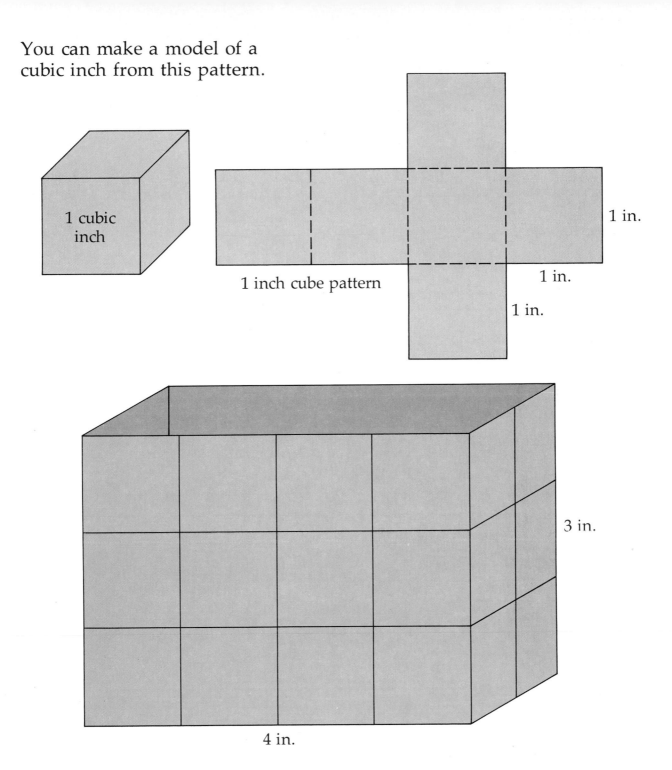

1 cubic
inch

1 inch cube pattern

1 in.

1 in.

1 in.

3 in.

4 in.

How many cubic inches are needed to fill this box?

Liquid measure

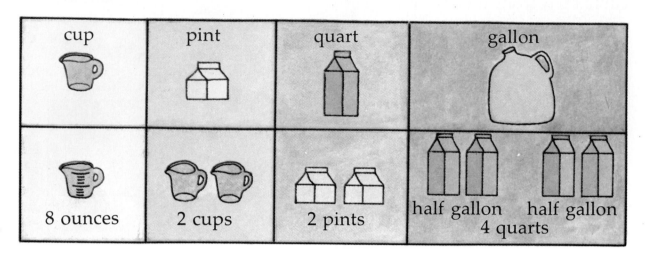

cup	pint	quart	gallon
8 ounces	2 cups	2 pints	half gallon half gallon 4 quarts

Use the chart above. Give the number for each ▥.

1. 1 cup holds ▥ ounces.

2. 1 pint will fill ▥ cups.

3. 1 quart will fill ▥ pints.

4. 1 gallon will fill ▥ quarts.

5. 2 PINT will fill ▥ CUP.

6. 1 QUART will fill ▥ CUP.

7. 4 QUART will fill ▥ CUP.

8. 1 GALLON will fill ▥ CUP.

9. 1 GALLON will fill ▥ PINT.

10. 2 GALLON will fill ▥ QUART.

Solve.

1.  $\frac{1}{2}$ pint
How many cups?

2.  1 quart (2 pints)
How many cups?

3.  How many cups
from each bottle?
How many cups
in all?

4.  $\frac{1}{2}$ gallon
How many quarts?

5. How many cups?
How many extra ounces?

6.  1 gallon (4 quarts)
How many pints?

7. How much more do you need
to fill a gallon jug after you have
poured in the amount shown?

8. How many pints?
How many cups?

Ounces and pounds

5 nickels:
about 1 ounce

pint of milk
about 1 pound

16 ounces (oz) = 1 pound (lb)

Write **ounce(s)** or **pound(s)** for each weight.

1. hand calculator

10 __?__

2. roasting chicken

$3\frac{1}{2}$ __?__

3. golf ball

2 __?__

4. small box of
paper clips

2 __?__

5. typewriter

8 __?__

6. 3 books

6 __?__

7. orange

8 __?__

8. wrist watch

$1\frac{1}{2}$ __?__

9. portable TV

20 __?__

Write **more** or **less** than a pound.

1.

carton of grape juice

2.

pair of gloves

3.

baseball

4.

gallon of milk

Give the number of ounces.

6.

5.
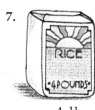

7.

5 lb   10 lb   4 lb

Estimate the following, then check.

8. your weight in pounds

9. the weight of your math book in ounces

10. the weight of a pair of your shoes in ounces

11. the weight of a basketball in ounces

Estimation problems

Choose the best estimate.

1. Hot faucet water
   - A 60°F
   - B 90°F
   - C 150°F

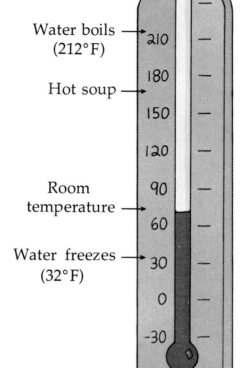

Water boils → 210
(212°F)

Hot soup → 180

150

120

2. Cool fall day
   - A 90°F
   - B 40°F
   - C 10°F

Room → 90
temperature → 60

3. Ice water
   - A 60°F
   - B 33°F
   - C 0°F

Water freezes → 30
(32°F)

0

-30

Fahrenheit

4. Temperature of your body
   - A 148°F
   - B 98°F
   - C 38°F

5. Inside a freezer
   - A 10°F
   - B 40°F
   - C 60°F

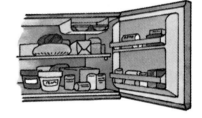

Choose the best estimate.

1. Paula wanted to make 3 quarts of fruit juice. One small can made 3 cups of juice. How many cans did she need?

   A 4   B 6   C 8

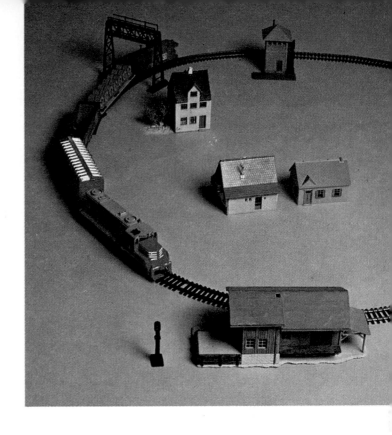

2. Carl traveled 48 miles each hour for 6 hours. About how far did he go?

   A 100 miles   B 200 miles
   C 300 miles

3. Betty had 24 sections of track for her model train. Each one was 8 inches long. What was the total length of track?

   A 200 inches   B 250 inches
   C 300 inches

4. Mr. Green paid $19.95 a square yard for carpeting. About how much did he pay for 20 square yards?

   A $300   B $400   C $500

5. It was 295 miles from Bill's house to his aunt's. About how far is it to his aunt's and back?

   A 400 mi   B 500 mi
   C 600 mi

6. Don weighed 109 pounds, Beth weighed 94 pounds, Linda weighed 97 pounds, and Fred weighed 104 pounds. How much did they weigh all together?

   A 300 lbs   B 250 lbs
   C 400 lbs

Answers for Self-check   1. $5\frac{1}{4}$ in.   2. yards   3. miles   4. 12 ft   5. 8 sq ft   6. 4 c   7. A   8. B

Self-check

1. Find the length to the nearest quarter inch.

Choose **feet**, **yards**, or **miles** to complete each sentence.

2. The soccer field was 60 __?__ wide.
3. The train went 40 __?__ in one hour.
4. Find the perimeter of the rectangle.
5. Find the area of the rectangle.
6. Two pints will fill how many cups?

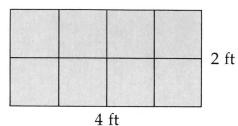

2 ft

4 ft

7. Weight of a hat is about
   A 8 ounces   B 8 pounds

8. Ice cube is about
   A 70°F   B 30°F

Answers for Self–check—page 344B

Test

1. Find the length to the nearest quarter inch.

Choose **feet**, **yards**, or **miles** to complete each sentence.

2. The table was about 8 __?__ long.
3. The cities were 50 __?__ apart.
4. Find the perimeter of the rectangle.
5. Find the area of the rectangle.
6. Two quarts will fill how many pints?

7. Weight of the dog is about
   A 20 ounces   B 20 pounds

8. Warm summer day is about
   A 90°F   B 150°F

For fun

ODD AREAS

The unit for these area problems is

The area of is $\frac{1}{2}$ unit.

1. What is the area of this shaded figure?

   Hint: half of 4

2. What is the area of this shaded figure?

   Hint: half of 2

Find the area of each shaded region.

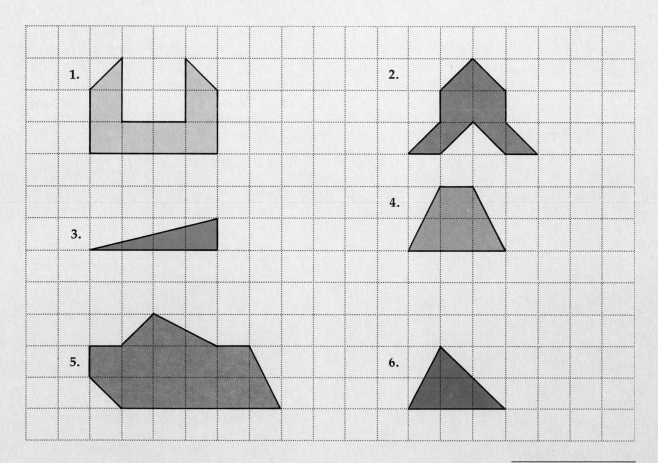

Level 22 review

Write a decimal for each picture.

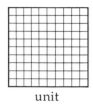 unit 1. 2.

Add.

3. 2.5
  + 6.4

4. 5.7
  + 3.6

5. 0.9
  + 0.7

6. 28.3
  + 3.9

7. 1.53
  + 4.26

8. 7.25
  + 2.38

9. 0.56
  + 0.87

10. $23.84
  + 19.79

Subtract.

11. 6.5
  − 3.4

12. 7.6
  − 5.7

13. 10.3
  − 4.9

14. 31.2
  − 17.5

15. 1.97
  − 1.43

16. 3.74
  − 2.45

17. 0.82
  − 0.65

18. $46.54
  − 26.86

Give the area of each figure.

Give the number for the ⦀.

19.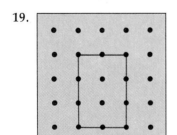

20.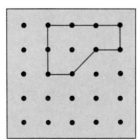

21.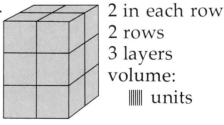
2 in each row
2 rows
3 layers
volume:
⦀ units

Write the standard numeral.

22. fifty-eight thousand, nine hundred thirty-four
23. three hundred twenty-five thousand, six hundred seventeen
24. nine million, six hundred seventy-nine thousand, five hundred forty-one

Appendix

More Practice

Table of Measures

Multiplication Facts Table

Glossary

Index

More Practice

Add.

	A	B	C	D	E	F	G	H	I	J
1.	3 +2	2 +5	1 +4	6 +0	3 +7	5 +4	2 +3	1 +5	4 +1	1 +8
2.	4 +4	0 +6	2 +0	4 +5	1 +7	3 +4	7 +2	9 +1	2 +6	0 +9
3.	0 +5	6 +3	4 +2	1 +1	0 +3	8 +1	5 +2	6 +4	1 +2	3 +5
4.	9 +0	2 +2	3 +6	4 +3	1 +0	0 +7	1 +9	8 +0	5 +5	6 +1
5.	3 +3	2 +8	5 +1	7 +3	0 +8	3 +0	2 +4	6 +2	3 +1	4 +0
6.	5 +3	4 +6	7 +1	2 +7	1 +6	1 +3	7 +0	2 +1	8 +2	5 +0
7.	6 +6	3 +8	4 +9	7 +5	0 +0	5 +8	9 +3	8 +6	0 +2	4 +7
8.	2 +9	0 +4	8 +5	4 +8	9 +6	7 +4	8 +9	9 +2	5 +6	8 +8
9.	6 +5	5 +9	6 +7	3 +9	9 +9	6 +8	8 +7	7 +7	8 +3	9 +7
10.	7 +6	9 +5	5 +7	9 +8	7 +9	9 +4	8 +4	0 +1	7 +8	6 +9

Subtract.

	A	B	C	D	E	F	G	H	I	J
1.	4 −2	6 −5	3 −0	1 −1	5 −1	3 −2	4 −0	5 −3	9 −3	8 −1
2.	2 −1	0 −0	6 −3	5 −4	7 −3	4 −1	8 −5	4 −4	9 −4	3 −1
3.	9 −6	4 −3	7 −5	8 −3	9 −2	6 −4	2 −2	5 −0	8 −6	9 −5
4.	8 −0	9 −8	5 −2	6 −6	7 −1	8 −2	3 −3	6 −1	8 −7	2 −0
5.	5 −5	8 −4	7 −2	9 −0	6 −2	1 −0	8 −8	9 −1	7 −0	9 −7
6.	7 −6	11 −7	13 −6	12 −5	14 −5	10 −4	15 −8	9 −9	10 −8	16 −9
7.	11 −4	10 −2	6 −0	14 −8	12 −6	15 −7	12 −8	10 −5	11 −5	12 −4
8.	7 −7	15 −9	13 −7	11 −2	16 −8	14 −9	11 −3	13 −8	12 −7	11 −9
9.	17 −8	13 −9	15 −6	10 −1	11 −8	13 −4	12 −3	14 −6	10 −9	14 −7
10.	18 −9	10 −3	11 −6	17 −9	13 −5	10 −6	12 −9	16 −7	7 −4	10 −7

Add.

1. 3 5 +2	2. 1 3 +6	3. 4 8 +1	4. 6 2 +3	5. 2 7 +3	6. 3 8 +3	7. 1 9 +5
8. 1 8 +1	9. 7 5 +4	10. 3 9 +4	11. 6 7 +4	12. 9 6 +3	13. 2 8 +4	14. 4 6 +1
15. 6 3 +5	16. 5 2 +4	17. 2 9 +7	18. 9 3 +5	19. 7 1 +8	20. 6 6 +2	21. 3 7 +5
22. 6 5 +8	23. 7 3 +6	24. 5 4 +4	25. 8 2 +1	26. 6 4 +5	27. 4 8 +5	28. 9 2 +1
29. 4 5 +9	30. 6 4 +3	31. 7 1 +2	32. 2 8 +6	33. 7 6 +5	34. 2 4 +6	35. 3 4 +8
36. 3 1 2 +6	37. 7 2 1 +5	38. 6 4 5 +2	39. 4 5 2 +5	40. 3 2 4 +2	41. 2 8 2 +1	42. 6 2 1 +5
43. 4 3 3 +2	44. 6 3 4 +5	45. 3 2 4 +4	46. 7 3 2 +4	47. 5 4 3 +7	48. 1 4 5 +5	49. 2 7 3 +5
50. 8 5 2 +2	51. 1 8 2 +3	52. 2 5 1 +8	53. 6 7 2 +3	54. 3 4 3 +5	55. 2 8 6 +3	56. 4 6 3 +2

Add.

1. 32
  + 48

2. 68
  + 8

3. 47
  + 36

4. 22
  + 79

5. 53
  + 47

6. 71
  + 69

7. 54
  + 67

8. 36
  + 54

9. 75
  + 46

10. 63
  + 29

11. 28
  + 85

12. 87
  + 45

13. 93
  + 38

14. 49
  + 64

15. 62
  + 79

16. 76
  + 58

17. 35
  + 64

18. 97
  + 48

19. 26
  + 35

20. 58
  + 64

21. 81
  + 39

22. 64
  + 97

23. 77
  + 37

24. 34
  + 96

25. 45
  + 97

26. 66
  + 86

27. 92
  + 18

28. 74
  + 29

29. 56
  + 57

30. 27
  + 79

31. 59
  + 85

32. 38
  + 76

33. 46
  + 99

34. 54
  + 76

35. 89
  + 28

36. 65
  + 78

37. 32
  46
  + 25

38. 52
  18
  + 39

39. 76
  44
  + 27

40. 45
  22
  + 66

41. 27
  15
  + 38

42. 21
  32
  + 49

43. 74
  33
  + 19

44. 41
  26
  + 83

45. 36
  53
  + 17

46. 24
  54
  + 35

47. 73
  47
  + 23

48. 65
  51
  + 14

49. 37
  60
  + 93

50. 55
  95
  + 20

51. 63
  31
  + 29

52. 28
  86
  + 43

53. 42
  94
  + 57

54. 67
  72
  + 13

55. 56
  30
  + 87

56. 34
  68
  + 48

57. 75
  54
  + 62

58. 91
  35
  + 28

59. 85
  58
  + 61

60. 50
  96
  + 26

Add.

1. $\begin{array}{r} 235 \\ + 326 \\ \hline \end{array}$

2. $\begin{array}{r} 462 \\ + 118 \\ \hline \end{array}$

3. $\begin{array}{r} 371 \\ + 445 \\ \hline \end{array}$

4. $\begin{array}{r} 566 \\ + 28 \\ \hline \end{array}$

5. $\begin{array}{r} 185 \\ + 452 \\ \hline \end{array}$

6. $\begin{array}{r} 841 \\ + 39 \\ \hline \end{array}$

7. $\begin{array}{r} 316 \\ + 237 \\ \hline \end{array}$

8. $\begin{array}{r} 743 \\ + 372 \\ \hline \end{array}$

9. $\begin{array}{r} 822 \\ + 191 \\ \hline \end{array}$

10. $\begin{array}{r} 246 \\ + 383 \\ \hline \end{array}$

11. $\begin{array}{r} 545 \\ + 68 \\ \hline \end{array}$

12. $\begin{array}{r} 638 \\ + 773 \\ \hline \end{array}$

13. $\begin{array}{r} 447 \\ + 674 \\ \hline \end{array}$

14. $\begin{array}{r} 376 \\ + 538 \\ \hline \end{array}$

15. $\begin{array}{r} 729 \\ + 587 \\ \hline \end{array}$

16. $\begin{array}{r} 842 \\ + 369 \\ \hline \end{array}$

17. $\begin{array}{r} 756 \\ + 467 \\ \hline \end{array}$

18. $\begin{array}{r} 328 \\ + 594 \\ \hline \end{array}$

19. $\begin{array}{r} 447 \\ + 468 \\ \hline \end{array}$

20. $\begin{array}{r} 634 \\ + 797 \\ \hline \end{array}$

21. $\begin{array}{r} 563 \\ + 669 \\ \hline \end{array}$

22. $\begin{array}{r} 849 \\ + 96 \\ \hline \end{array}$

23. $\begin{array}{r} 454 \\ + 759 \\ \hline \end{array}$

24. $\begin{array}{r} 764 \\ + 547 \\ \hline \end{array}$

25. $\begin{array}{r} 385 \\ + 936 \\ \hline \end{array}$

26. $\begin{array}{r} 736 \\ + 396 \\ \hline \end{array}$

27. $\begin{array}{r} 648 \\ + 875 \\ \hline \end{array}$

28. $\begin{array}{r} 397 \\ + 865 \\ \hline \end{array}$

29. $\begin{array}{r} 486 \\ + 647 \\ \hline \end{array}$

30. $\begin{array}{r} 874 \\ + 438 \\ \hline \end{array}$

31. $\begin{array}{r} 3465 \\ + 357 \\ \hline \end{array}$

32. $\begin{array}{r} 4627 \\ + 83 \\ \hline \end{array}$

33. $\begin{array}{r} 7648 \\ + 276 \\ \hline \end{array}$

34. $\begin{array}{r} 1755 \\ + 3806 \\ \hline \end{array}$

35. $\begin{array}{r} 5413 \\ + 2768 \\ \hline \end{array}$

36. $\begin{array}{r} 6372 \\ + 830 \\ \hline \end{array}$

37. $\begin{array}{r} 8435 \\ + 628 \\ \hline \end{array}$

38. $\begin{array}{r} 3954 \\ + 5427 \\ \hline \end{array}$

39. $\begin{array}{r} 4876 \\ + 45 \\ \hline \end{array}$

40. $\begin{array}{r} 1648 \\ + 6271 \\ \hline \end{array}$

41. $\begin{array}{r} 2821 \\ + 6739 \\ \hline \end{array}$

42. $\begin{array}{r} 4178 \\ + 3254 \\ \hline \end{array}$

43. $\begin{array}{r} 6561 \\ + 2584 \\ \hline \end{array}$

44. $\begin{array}{r} 7462 \\ + 1985 \\ \hline \end{array}$

45. $\begin{array}{r} 5186 \\ + 3399 \\ \hline \end{array}$

Set A   For use after page 37

Subtract.

1. $\begin{array}{r} 24 \\ -15 \end{array}$	2. $\begin{array}{r} 68 \\ -39 \end{array}$	3. $\begin{array}{r} 85 \\ -27 \end{array}$	4. $\begin{array}{r} 33 \\ -18 \end{array}$	5. $\begin{array}{r} 57 \\ -39 \end{array}$	6. $\begin{array}{r} 97 \\ -78 \end{array}$
7. $\begin{array}{r} 26 \\ -17 \end{array}$	8. $\begin{array}{r} 48 \\ -19 \end{array}$	9. $\begin{array}{r} 94 \\ -55 \end{array}$	10. $\begin{array}{r} 34 \\ -17 \end{array}$	11. $\begin{array}{r} 75 \\ -26 \end{array}$	12. $\begin{array}{r} 87 \\ -29 \end{array}$
13. $\begin{array}{r} 62 \\ -35 \end{array}$	14. $\begin{array}{r} 33 \\ -25 \end{array}$	15. $\begin{array}{r} 91 \\ -58 \end{array}$	16. $\begin{array}{r} 45 \\ -27 \end{array}$	17. $\begin{array}{r} 66 \\ -39 \end{array}$	18. $\begin{array}{r} 58 \\ -49 \end{array}$
19. $\begin{array}{r} 54 \\ -16 \end{array}$	20. $\begin{array}{r} 82 \\ -53 \end{array}$	21. $\begin{array}{r} 55 \\ -19 \end{array}$	22. $\begin{array}{r} 51 \\ -23 \end{array}$	23. $\begin{array}{r} 73 \\ -38 \end{array}$	24. $\begin{array}{r} 46 \\ -29 \end{array}$
25. $\begin{array}{r} 63 \\ -35 \end{array}$	26. $\begin{array}{r} 83 \\ -48 \end{array}$	27. $\begin{array}{r} 61 \\ -47 \end{array}$	28. $\begin{array}{r} 84 \\ -26 \end{array}$	29. $\begin{array}{r} 35 \\ -19 \end{array}$	30. $\begin{array}{r} 43 \\ -27 \end{array}$

Set B   For use after page 37

Subtract.

1. $\begin{array}{r} 137 \\ -29 \end{array}$	2. $\begin{array}{r} 144 \\ -18 \end{array}$	3. $\begin{array}{r} 252 \\ -66 \end{array}$	4. $\begin{array}{r} 125 \\ -18 \end{array}$	5. $\begin{array}{r} 392 \\ -95 \end{array}$	6. $\begin{array}{r} 266 \\ -38 \end{array}$
7. $\begin{array}{r} 578 \\ -89 \end{array}$	8. $\begin{array}{r} 374 \\ -26 \end{array}$	9. $\begin{array}{r} 142 \\ -26 \end{array}$	10. $\begin{array}{r} 421 \\ -17 \end{array}$	11. $\begin{array}{r} 634 \\ -97 \end{array}$	12. $\begin{array}{r} 575 \\ -37 \end{array}$
13. $\begin{array}{r} 224 \\ -59 \end{array}$	14. $\begin{array}{r} 460 \\ -42 \end{array}$	15. $\begin{array}{r} 686 \\ -38 \end{array}$	16. $\begin{array}{r} 322 \\ -66 \end{array}$	17. $\begin{array}{r} 590 \\ -57 \end{array}$	18. $\begin{array}{r} 781 \\ -25 \end{array}$
19. $\begin{array}{r} 236 \\ -59 \end{array}$	20. $\begin{array}{r} 777 \\ -39 \end{array}$	21. $\begin{array}{r} 296 \\ -47 \end{array}$	22. $\begin{array}{r} 335 \\ -86 \end{array}$	23. $\begin{array}{r} 185 \\ -38 \end{array}$	24. $\begin{array}{r} 472 \\ -96 \end{array}$
25. $\begin{array}{r} 593 \\ -95 \end{array}$	26. $\begin{array}{r} 267 \\ -88 \end{array}$	27. $\begin{array}{r} 150 \\ -33 \end{array}$	28. $\begin{array}{r} 344 \\ -76 \end{array}$	29. $\begin{array}{r} 163 \\ -58 \end{array}$	30. $\begin{array}{r} 894 \\ -39 \end{array}$

Subtract.

1. 31
    − 16

2. 45
    − 27

3. 22
    − 13

4. 50
    − 25

5. 63
    − 46

6. 74
    − 38

7. 82
    − 35

8. 54
    − 27

9. 41
    − 14

10. 36
    − 29

11. 71
    − 48

12. 93
    − 27

13. 23
    − 14

14. 70
    − 26

15. 56
    − 17

16. 84
    − 36

17. 62
    − 49

18. 47
    − 18

19. 30
    − 11

20. 21
    − 13

21. 44
    − 25

22. 72
    − 54

23. 95
    − 56

24. 64
    − 29

25. 81
    − 37

26. 73
    − 45

27. 32
    − 18

28. 91
    − 45

29. 55
    − 28

30. 42
    − 16

31. 51
    − 19

32. 65
    − 49

33. 43
    − 29

34. 80
    − 47

35. 61
    − 25

36. 53
    − 38

37. 136
    − 27

38. 217
    − 43

39. 352
    − 27

40. 781
    − 52

41. 527
    − 63

42. 683
    − 75

43. 464
    − 37

44. 365
    − 17

45. 136
    − 41

46. 215
    − 32

47. 695
    − 56

48. 820
    − 13

49. 724
    − 35

50. 462
    − 84

51. 971
    − 96

52. 523
    − 67

53. 854
    − 78

54. 651
    − 68

55. 634
    − 76

56. 312
    − 45

57. 226
    − 58

58. 843
    − 86

59. 921
    − 47

60. 472
    − 89

Subtract.

1. 569 − 283	2. 227 − 165	3. 319 − 158	4. 844 − 326	5. 742 − 215
6. 783 − 326	7. 535 − 252	8. 971 − 435	9. 636 − 217	10. 477 − 193
11. 5613 − 4472	12. 3954 − 1136	13. 9852 − 6921	14. 7948 − 3266	15. 3151 − 1601
16. 4659 − 2473	17. 2293 − 1176	18. 5548 − 3275	19. 6713 − 2507	20. 9318 − 4135
21. 6811 − 5306	22. 4942 − 3627	23. 5583 − 2921	24. 9278 − 5085	25. 8633 − 2722

Set B   For use after page 39

Subtract.

1. 685 − 297	2. 313 − 155	3. 425 − 188	4. 618 − 359	5. 576 − 299
6. 453 − 287	7. 233 − 168	8. 663 − 487	9. 911 − 734	10. 826 − 579
11. 9813 − 6455	12. 4492 − 3806	13. 5575 − 2398	14. 3362 − 1771	15. 7872 − 3688
16. 2936 − 1758	17. 4424 − 1848	18. 7213 − 5981	19. 3184 − 2699	20. 5352 − 1926
21. 7433 − 2866	22. 3643 − 1958	23. 6374 − 3897	24. 2231 − 1745	25. 9156 − 2189

Subtract.

1. 405 $-\,299$	2. 603 $-\,146$	3. 208 $-\,159$	4. 407 $-\,268$	5. 303 $-\,128$
6. 505 $-\,178$	7. 903 $-\,265$	8. 707 $-\,399$	9. 402 $-\,167$	10. 604 $-\,265$
11. 308 $-\,139$	12. 501 $-\,266$	13. 404 $-\,319$	14. 608 $-\,279$	15. 801 $-\,395$
16. 502 $-\,177$	17. 808 $-\,459$	18. 205 $-\,117$	19. 903 $-\,355$	20. 706 $-\,217$
21. 904 $-\,778$	22. 406 $-\,228$	23. 605 $-\,227$	24. 806 $-\,239$	25. 507 $-\,418$

Subtract.

1. 3018 $-\,1216$	2. 4206 $-\,1795$	3. 9031 $-\,5410$	4. 5036 $-\,2367$	5. 8003 $-\,2175$
6. 5908 $-\,1739$	7. 2009 $-\,1759$	8. 3068 $-\,2579$	9. 9001 $-\,3235$	10. 7006 $-\,2558$
11. 7603 $-\,2198$	12. 2054 $-\,1626$	13. 3007 $-\,1658$	14. 5005 $-\,1279$	15. 3082 $-\,1691$
16. 3504 $-\,1672$	17. 6033 $-\,4867$	18. 4008 $-\,1549$	19. 9008 $-\,6335$	20. 7029 $-\,5139$
21. 2001 $-\,1695$	22. 8035 $-\,7448$	23. 3607 $-\,1839$	24. 5601 $-\,4488$	25. 4009 $-\,3226$

Subtract.

1. 5034
  − 2471

2. 4500
  − 1622

3. 3100
  − 1343

4. 6300
  − 4761

5. 2001
  − 1235

6. 7100
  − 2649

7. 6005
  − 1578

8. 5100
  − 2682

9. 8003
  − 3594

10. 3700
  − 1879

11. 4200
  − 2367

12. 6502
  − 3754

13. 4004
  − 1647

14. 2600
  − 1833

15. 5006
  − 3419

16. 8300
  − 2385

17. 6002
  − 4371

18. 7600
  − 3824

19. 9100
  − 2368

20. 7005
  − 4457

21. 2033
  − 1165

22. 5600
  − 1816

23. 6200
  − 2541

24. 4003
  − 3736

25. 8200
  − 1953

26. 3007
  − 1829

27. 2300
  − 1743

28. 4062
  − 1165

29. 9008
  − 1269

30. 5001
  − 3586

31. 7301
  − 4693

32. 3000
  − 1422

33. 5200
  − 2875

34. 6004
  − 1196

35. 8400
  − 4674

36. 6400
  − 3717

37. 9002
  − 4346

38. 3504
  − 1835

39. 4006
  − 2677

40. 3005
  − 1286

41. 8004
  − 5788

42. 4600
  − 1916

43. 7400
  − 1658

44. 5300
  − 3861

45. 2002
  − 1327

46. 9500
  − 1769

47. 7007
  − 5898

48. 8100
  − 6235

49. 4100
  − 3752

50. 5003
  − 1947

Subtract.

1. 48
    $- 32$

2. 129
    $- 15$

3. 438
    $- 217$

4. 309
    $- 114$

5. 4008
    $- 3126$

6. 176
    $- 56$

7. 4818
    $- 2306$

8. 37
    $- 15$

9. 7107
    $- 3265$

10. 910
    $- 366$

11. 8018
    $- 2155$

12. 205
    $- 117$

13. 6005
    $- 1448$

14. 143
    $- 58$

15. 3702
    $- 1699$

16. 73
    $- 49$

17. 968
    $- 345$

18. 246
    $- 59$

19. 3070
    $- 1264$

20. 8001
    $- 3554$

21. 686
    $- 214$

22. 740
    $- 88$

23. 6072
    $- 3290$

24. 389
    $- 175$

25. 81
    $- 56$

26. 905
    $- 368$

27. 90
    $- 53$

28. 8715
    $- 2603$

29. 636
    $- 79$

30. 1402
    $- 1196$

31. 9530
    $- 3729$

32. 6084
    $- 5118$

33. 207
    $- 135$

34. 1792
    $- 1385$

35. 8000
    $- 3956$

36. 414
    $- 96$

37. 40
    $- 26$

38. 783
    $- 552$

39. 700
    $- 259$

40. 9004
    $- 5677$

41. 6001
    $- 3524$

42. 818
    $- 39$

43. 3260
    $- 1773$

44. 61
    $- 28$

45. 4505
    $- 3991$

46. 606
    $- 395$

47. 4942
    $- 3711$

48. 417
    $- 302$

49. 8007
    $- 3295$

50. 6112
    $- 3884$

Round to the nearest ten.

1. 34   2. 52   3. 46   4. 28   5. 71   6. 83

7. 65   8. 27   9. 38   10. 59   11. 82   12. 91

13. 43   14. 55   15. 26   16. 74   17. 67   18. 48

19. 239   20. 362   21. 185   22. 453   23. 244   24. 626

Round to the nearest hundred.

25. 231   26. 450   27. 376   28. 524   29. 761   30. 810

31. 364   32. 836   33. 963   34. 782   35. 438   36. 573

37. 1465   38. 3722   39. 2581   40. 4618   41. 5921   42. 3267

43. 4373   44. 6281   45. 7754   46. 8175   47. 9327   48. 6481

Find the sums and differences.

1. $3.46
   + 2.58

2. $4.53
   + 5.29

3. $7.15
   + 6.36

4. $5.48
   + 0.75

5. $9.25
   + 4.78

6. $0.84
   + 0.76

7. $22.15
   + 7.89

8. $18.64
   + 9.48

9. $ 5.21
     13.60
   + 4.88

10. $18.35
      7.62
   + 11.29

11. $4.23
   − 0.76

12. $5.84
   − 2.38

13. $7.14
   − 1.57

14. $13.20
   − 7.59

15. $26.42
   − 15.87

16. $41.03
   − 26.57

17. $30.01
   − 20.58

18. $15.62
   − 7.48

19. $53.11
   − 27.38

20. $64.23
   − 37.67

Multiply.

	A	B	C	D	E	F	G	H	I	J
1.	3 ×1	2 ×2	3 ×4	6 ×0	4 ×5	3 ×3	2 ×0	7 ×1	5 ×2	6 ×4
2.	5 ×1	8 ×0	3 ×2	8 ×4	3 ×5	4 ×0	1 ×2	8 ×2	2 ×3	9 ×1
3.	1 ×1	4 ×2	2 ×5	0 ×4	6 ×3	7 ×2	9 ×0	2 ×1	5 ×3	8 ×5
4.	7 ×0	8 ×3	6 ×2	4 ×1	0 ×5	2 ×4	6 ×1	1 ×3	9 ×5	0 ×0
5.	4 ×3	5 ×4	3 ×0	1 ×5	4 ×4	8 ×1	1 ×0	7 ×3	0 ×2	5 ×5
6.	0 ×1	9 ×3	1 ×4	6 ×5	5 ×0	7 ×4	9 ×2	7 ×5	9 ×4	0 ×3

Multiply.

	A	B	C	D	E	F	G	H	I	J
1.	3 ×6	0 ×8	6 ×8	2 ×6	1 ×7	3 ×9	2 ×8	7 ×7	6 ×9	4 ×6
2.	2 ×7	1 ×8	5 ×6	8 ×9	6 ×6	3 ×7	7 ×8	5 ×9	1 ×6	6 ×7
3.	5 ×8	8 ×6	4 ×7	0 ×9	9 ×6	5 ×7	1 ×9	3 ×8	9 ×7	9 ×8
4.	0 ×6	2 ×9	8 ×7	7 ×6	7 ×9	8 ×8	0 ×7	9 ×9	4 ×8	4 ×9

Set A   For use after page 95

Divide.

	A	B	C	D	E	F	G
1.	12 ÷ 3	6 ÷ 2	7 ÷ 1	4 ÷ 4	16 ÷ 4	10 ÷ 5	14 ÷ 2
2.	4 ÷ 1	3 ÷ 3	20 ÷ 5	15 ÷ 3	18 ÷ 2	32 ÷ 4	0 ÷ 3
3.	30 ÷ 5	16 ÷ 2	6 ÷ 3	9 ÷ 1	8 ÷ 4	15 ÷ 5	12 ÷ 2
4.	8 ÷ 2	6 ÷ 1	28 ÷ 4	5 ÷ 5	27 ÷ 3	2 ÷ 1	35 ÷ 5
5.	24 ÷ 4	9 ÷ 3	8 ÷ 1	0 ÷ 2	25 ÷ 5	12 ÷ 4	18 ÷ 3
6.	3 ÷ 1	45 ÷ 5	21 ÷ 3	5 ÷ 1	2 ÷ 2	0 ÷ 5	20 ÷ 4
7.	0 ÷ 4	4 ÷ 2	40 ÷ 5	36 ÷ 4	10 ÷ 2	24 ÷ 3	1 ÷ 1

Set B   For use after page 99

Divide.

	A	B	C	D	E	F
1.	56 ÷ 7	18 ÷ 6	48 ÷ 8	14 ÷ 7	0 ÷ 9	6 ÷ 6
2.	16 ÷ 8	36 ÷ 9	30 ÷ 6	21 ÷ 7	56 ÷ 8	18 ÷ 9
3.	7 ÷ 7	42 ÷ 6	27 ÷ 9	48 ÷ 6	28 ÷ 7	40 ÷ 8
4.	12 ÷ 6	64 ÷ 8	35 ÷ 7	54 ÷ 9	0 ÷ 8	9 ÷ 9
5.	0 ÷ 7	72 ÷ 9	48 ÷ 8	24 ÷ 6	72 ÷ 8	36 ÷ 6
6.	54 ÷ 6	24 ÷ 8	45 ÷ 9	8 ÷ 8	49 ÷ 7	54 ÷ 9
7.	63 ÷ 9	0 ÷ 6	32 ÷ 8	63 ÷ 7	81 ÷ 9	42 ÷ 7

Multiply.

1. 7×10 2. 3×10 3. 4×10 4. 2×10 5. 6×10

6. 32×10 7. 46×10 8. 54×10 9. 71×10 10. 82×10

11. 53×10 12. 27×10 13. 38×10 14. 41×10 15. 78×10

16. 90×10 17. 88×10 18. 76×10 19. 22×10 20. 33×10

21. 16×100 22. 31×100 23. 60×100 24. 52×100 25. 48×100

26. 93×100 27. 72×100 28. 54×100 29. 80×100 30. 62×100

31. 215×10 32. 374×10 33. 820×10 34. 633×10 35. 724×10

36. 961×10 37. 532×10 38. 652×10 39. 847×10 40. 468×10

41. 364×100 42. 714×100 43. 822×100 44. 936×100 45. 584×100

46. 639×100 47. 471×100 48. 557×100 49. 139×100 50. 853×100

Multiply.

1. 4×300 2. 3×60 3. 5×80 4. 4×400 5. 2×70

6. 6×20 7. 5×200 8. 3×40 9. 8×900 10. 9×200

11. 2×30 12. 7×80 13. 2×600 14. 2×90 15. 5×700

16. 3×600 17. 2×500 18. 3×50 19. 4×600 20. 9×50

21. 4×800 22. 8×20 23. 3×400 24. 2×300 25. 5×500

26. 5×70 27. 5×300 28. 4×700 29. 6×80 30. 3×30

31. 6×60 32. 3×500 33. 6×90 34. 7×500 35. 6×400

36. 3×700 37. 4×30 38. 2×200 39. 4×40 40. 4×90

41. 2×20 42. 2×800 43. 7×900 44. 5×60 45. 3×300

46. 4×50 47. 3×70 48. 5×40 49. 6×700 50. 4×60

Multiply.

1. 20×40	2. 60×30	3. 40×50	4. 70×20	5. 80×40
6. 30×30	7. 80×30	8. 60×70	9. 40×60	10. 30×70
11. 90×40	12. 20×60	13. 50×20	14. 30×50	15. 40×40
16. 50×70	17. 80×80	18. 90×50	19. 90×20	20. 70×80
21. 60×80	22. 20×70	23. 80×50	24. 60×90	25. 30×20
26. 40×70	27. 50×50	28. 50×60	29. 70×50	30. 90×80
31. 20×20	32. 80×20	33. 70×70	34. 30×80	35. 90×90
36. 90×70	37. 60×60	38. 50×90	39. 60×50	40. 30×90

Round the greater factor to the nearest multiple of 10 and multiply.

1. 4×36	2. 5×25	3. 6×46	4. 2×51	5. 7×83
6. 7×64	7. 3×91	8. 4×72	9. 3×27	10. 5×38
11. 6×93	12. 2×32	13. 5×43	14. 9×65	15. 8×76

Round both factors to the nearest multiple of 10 and multiply.

16. 42×73	17. 38×25	18. 84×46	19. 53×39	20. 64×58
21. 56×21	22. 76×22	23. 92×31	24. 45×56	25. 75×68
26. 38×42	27. 63×31	28. 86×52	29. 39×73	30. 26×83
31. 82×36	32. 93×48	33. 78×33	34. 51×61	35. 43×48

Round the greater factor to the nearest multiple of 100 and multiply.

36. 6×528	37. 4×371	38. 5×623	39. 3×854	40. 8×268
41. 4×746	42. 5×463	43. 3×328	44. 6×791	45. 2×563
46. 6×639	47. 5×862	48. 3×504	49. 4×928	50. 3×420
51. 5×366	52. 7×225	53. 2×752	54. 3×615	55. 4×806
56. 3×281	57. 4×571	58. 6×483	59. 5×581	60. 6×739

Divide.

1. $150 \div 3$ 2. $300 \div 6$ 3. $240 \div 4$ 4. $140 \div 2$ 5. $420 \div 7$

6. $560 \div 8$ 7. $150 \div 5$ 8. $360 \div 9$ 9. $180 \div 6$ 10. $160 \div 4$

11. $180 \div 2$ 12. $200 \div 4$ 13. $560 \div 7$ 14. $320 \div 8$ 15. $250 \div 5$

16. $210 \div 3$ 17. $160 \div 2$ 18. $420 \div 6$ 19. $450 \div 9$ 20. $490 \div 7$

21. $350 \div 5$ 22. $180 \div 3$ 23. $280 \div 7$ 24. $480 \div 8$ 25. $270 \div 9$

26. $120 \div 2$ 27. $320 \div 4$ 28. $480 \div 6$ 29. $450 \div 5$ 30. $240 \div 8$

Multiply.

1. $\begin{array}{r} 34 \\ \times\ 1 \\ \hline \end{array}$ 2. $\begin{array}{r} 56 \\ \times\ 3 \\ \hline \end{array}$ 3. $\begin{array}{r} 28 \\ \times\ 2 \\ \hline \end{array}$ 4. $\begin{array}{r} 42 \\ \times\ 5 \\ \hline \end{array}$ 5. $\begin{array}{r} 63 \\ \times\ 6 \\ \hline \end{array}$ 6. $\begin{array}{r} 75 \\ \times\ 3 \\ \hline \end{array}$

7. $\begin{array}{r} 64 \\ \times\ 5 \\ \hline \end{array}$ 8. $\begin{array}{r} 45 \\ \times\ 3 \\ \hline \end{array}$ 9. $\begin{array}{r} 72 \\ \times\ 6 \\ \hline \end{array}$ 10. $\begin{array}{r} 53 \\ \times\ 5 \\ \hline \end{array}$ 11. $\begin{array}{r} 84 \\ \times\ 4 \\ \hline \end{array}$ 12. $\begin{array}{r} 37 \\ \times\ 2 \\ \hline \end{array}$

13. $\begin{array}{r} 87 \\ \times\ 3 \\ \hline \end{array}$ 14. $\begin{array}{r} 26 \\ \times\ 4 \\ \hline \end{array}$ 15. $\begin{array}{r} 93 \\ \times\ 2 \\ \hline \end{array}$ 16. $\begin{array}{r} 48 \\ \times\ 7 \\ \hline \end{array}$ 17. $\begin{array}{r} 65 \\ \times\ 8 \\ \hline \end{array}$ 18. $\begin{array}{r} 24 \\ \times\ 9 \\ \hline \end{array}$

19. $\begin{array}{r} 52 \\ \times\ 4 \\ \hline \end{array}$ 20. $\begin{array}{r} 73 \\ \times\ 2 \\ \hline \end{array}$ 21. $\begin{array}{r} 36 \\ \times\ 6 \\ \hline \end{array}$ 22. $\begin{array}{r} 86 \\ \times\ 2 \\ \hline \end{array}$ 23. $\begin{array}{r} 93 \\ \times\ 3 \\ \hline \end{array}$ 24. $\begin{array}{r} 43 \\ \times\ 6 \\ \hline \end{array}$

25. $\begin{array}{r} 38 \\ \times\ 5 \\ \hline \end{array}$ 26. $\begin{array}{r} 62 \\ \times\ 7 \\ \hline \end{array}$ 27. $\begin{array}{r} 57 \\ \times\ 2 \\ \hline \end{array}$ 28. $\begin{array}{r} 25 \\ \times\ 6 \\ \hline \end{array}$ 29. $\begin{array}{r} 77 \\ \times\ 4 \\ \hline \end{array}$ 30. $\begin{array}{r} 85 \\ \times\ 3 \\ \hline \end{array}$

31. $\begin{array}{r} 96 \\ \times\ 4 \\ \hline \end{array}$ 32. $\begin{array}{r} 83 \\ \times\ 5 \\ \hline \end{array}$ 33. $\begin{array}{r} 44 \\ \times\ 8 \\ \hline \end{array}$ 34. $\begin{array}{r} 58 \\ \times\ 3 \\ \hline \end{array}$ 35. $\begin{array}{r} 66 \\ \times\ 4 \\ \hline \end{array}$ 36. $\begin{array}{r} 74 \\ \times\ 3 \\ \hline \end{array}$

37. $\begin{array}{r} 27 \\ \times\ 7 \\ \hline \end{array}$ 38. $\begin{array}{r} 68 \\ \times\ 3 \\ \hline \end{array}$ 39. $\begin{array}{r} 95 \\ \times\ 5 \\ \hline \end{array}$ 40. $\begin{array}{r} 35 \\ \times\ 3 \\ \hline \end{array}$ 41. $\begin{array}{r} 47 \\ \times\ 6 \\ \hline \end{array}$ 42. $\begin{array}{r} 59 \\ \times\ 7 \\ \hline \end{array}$

Multiply.

1. 233
× 3

2. 625
× 2

3. 351
× 4

4. 474
× 6

5. 542
× 3

6. 718
× 5

7. 563
× 6

8. 452
× 3

9. 734
× 4

10. 822
× 5

11. 328
× 3

12. 647
× 4

13. 418
× 5

14. 836
× 4

15. 245
× 2

16. 653
× 7

17. 572
× 5

18. 368
× 2

19. 742
× 7

20. 364
× 6

21. 528
× 4

22. 849
× 3

23. 294
× 5

24. 438
× 2

25. 268
× 4

26. 537
× 2

27. 463
× 7

28. 386
× 8

29. 672
× 3

30. 854
× 2

31. 486
× 4

32. 662
× 6

33. 338
× 5

34. 574
× 7

35. 284
× 3

36. 765
× 6

37. 644
× 5

38. 747
× 4

39. 252
× 7

40. 349
× 5

41. 637
× 4

42. 584
× 3

43. $ 2.76
× 8

44. $ 3.73
× 7

45. $ 5.97
× 5

46. $ 4.92
× 3

47. $ 7.23
× 9

48. $ 8.54
× 4

49. $ 4.86
× 3

50. $ 7.25
× 6

51. $ 5.45
× 4

52. $ 8.31
× 5

53. $ 3.82
× 6

54. $ 4.74
× 7

55. $ 9.22
× 4

56. $ 6.84
× 5

57. $ 4.76
× 6

58. $ 7.38
× 4

59. $ 5.39
× 5

60. $ 8.27
× 3

Multiply.

1. 53 × 20	2. 36 × 30	3. 62 × 30	4. 41 × 60	5. 52 × 70	6. 39 × 50
7. 75 × 30	8. 25 × 80	9. 46 × 20	10. 94 × 40	11. 38 × 60	12. 57 × 90
13. 47 × 70	14. 26 × 50	15. 38 × 30	16. 81 × 90	17. 72 × 20	18. 63 × 50
19. 35 × 40	20. 43 × 80	21. 38 × 70	22. 71 × 50	23. 26 × 30	24. 45 × 60
25. 243 × 30	26. 382 × 20	27. 461 × 30	28. 513 × 30	29. 472 × 50	30. 125 × 30

Multiply.

1. 51 × 53	2. 22 × 62	3. 54 × 75	4. 81 × 34	5. 65 × 26	6. 73 × 47
7. 71 × 64	8. 92 × 33	9. 36 × 52	10. 77 × 75	11. 44 × 48	12. 35 × 88
13. 81 × 89	14. 28 × 76	15. 83 × 64	16. 28 × 27	17. 54 × 36	18. 82 × 59
19. 65 × 35	20. 43 × 96	21. 36 × 87	22. 82 × 48	23. 54 × 64	24. 74 × 25
25. 49 × 53	26. 28 × 68	27. 53 × 95	28. 76 × 36	29. 42 × 87	30. 35 × 79

Multiply.

1.	423		
	× 32		

1. 423 × 32
2. 536 × 17
3. 742 × 49
4. 359 × 28
5. 614 × 52
6. 255 × 76

7. 542 × 58
8. 374 × 74
9. 735 × 84
10. 457 × 61
11. 841 × 29
12. 658 × 34

13. 631 × 28
14. 426 × 54
15. 337 × 66
16. 753 × 38
17. 912 × 19
18. 534 × 37

19. 356 × 51
20. 764 × 63
21. 438 × 73
22. 555 × 27
23. 642 × 46
24. 928 × 56

25. 657 × 83
26. 563 × 65
27. 728 × 52
28. 435 × 28
29. 372 × 84
30. 267 × 74

31. 234 × 25
32. 628 × 41
33. 517 × 62
34. 776 × 34
35. 843 × 55
36. 382 × 78

37. 543 × 51
38. 735 × 45
39. 856 × 27
40. 218 × 33
41. 364 × 64
42. 473 × 86

43. 639 × 32
44. 265 × 16
45. 758 × 27
46. 327 × 85
47. 482 × 43
48. 815 × 38

49. 719 × 63
50. 871 × 49
51. 529 × 38
52. 246 × 72
53. 652 × 25
54. 464 × 57

55. 832 × 74
56. 681 × 58
57. 257 × 44
58. 784 × 56
59. 593 × 63
60. 393 × 34

Divide.

1. $3\overline{)17}$ 2. $4\overline{)31}$ 3. $6\overline{)13}$ 4. $8\overline{)45}$ 5. $7\overline{)53}$ 6. $5\overline{)22}$

7. $6\overline{)38}$ 8. $7\overline{)17}$ 9. $3\overline{)23}$ 10. $4\overline{)14}$ 11. $5\overline{)33}$ 12. $8\overline{)26}$

13. $9\overline{)19}$ 14. $8\overline{)34}$ 15. $4\overline{)23}$ 16. $7\overline{)36}$ 17. $3\overline{)25}$ 18. $2\overline{)17}$

19. $4\overline{)19}$ 20. $3\overline{)28}$ 21. $5\overline{)43}$ 22. $9\overline{)56}$ 23. $6\overline{)20}$ 24. $7\overline{)44}$

25. $5\overline{)27}$ 26. $6\overline{)56}$ 27. $7\overline{)24}$ 28. $3\overline{)13}$ 29. $4\overline{)26}$ 30. $9\overline{)65}$

31. $7\overline{)30}$ 32. $5\overline{)37}$ 33. $8\overline{)18}$ 34. $6\overline{)33}$ 35. $9\overline{)75}$ 36. $3\overline{)20}$

37. $8\overline{)66}$ 38. $9\overline{)48}$ 39. $6\overline{)47}$ 40. $5\overline{)49}$ 41. $7\overline{)57}$ 42. $6\overline{)27}$

Divide.

1. $5\overline{)117}$ 2. $4\overline{)155}$ 3. $6\overline{)166}$ 4. $3\overline{)137}$ 5. $2\overline{)153}$ 6. $7\overline{)228}$

7. $6\overline{)207}$ 8. $3\overline{)169}$ 9. $5\overline{)178}$ 10. $9\overline{)257}$ 11. $7\overline{)305}$ 12. $8\overline{)229}$

13. $4\overline{)118}$ 14. $5\overline{)208}$ 15. $7\overline{)373}$ 16. $3\overline{)187}$ 17. $6\overline{)267}$ 18. $9\overline{)319}$

19. $3\overline{)157}$ 20. $7\overline{)201}$ 21. $8\overline{)275}$ 22. $4\overline{)186}$ 23. $5\overline{)321}$ 24. $6\overline{)339}$

25. $8\overline{)381}$ 26. $6\overline{)374}$ 27. $4\overline{)207}$ 28. $7\overline{)583}$ 29. $3\overline{)223}$ 30. $2\overline{)189}$

31. $7\overline{)452}$ 32. $9\overline{)392}$ 33. $8\overline{)443}$ 34. $5\overline{)382}$ 35. $4\overline{)247}$ 36. $5\overline{)291}$

37. $9\overline{)491}$ 38. $8\overline{)540}$ 39. $6\overline{)435}$ 40. $4\overline{)342}$ 41. $7\overline{)641}$ 42. $9\overline{)561}$

Divide.

1. $5\overline{)91}$ 2. $7\overline{)233}$ 3. $9\overline{)493}$ 4. $6\overline{)530}$ 5. $5\overline{)383}$

6. $4\overline{)189}$ 7. $8\overline{)749}$ 8. $7\overline{)375}$ 9. $7\overline{)553}$ 10. $9\overline{)112}$

11. $3\overline{)41}$ 12. $5\overline{)307}$ 13. $8\overline{)355}$ 14. $3\overline{)247}$ 15. $4\overline{)84}$

16. $7\overline{)315}$ 17. $6\overline{)142}$ 18. $7\overline{)255}$ 19. $2\overline{)166}$ 20. $3\overline{)206}$

21. $4\overline{)75}$ 22. $8\overline{)621}$ 23. $9\overline{)132}$ 24. $6\overline{)251}$ 25. $5\overline{)397}$

26. $6\overline{)340}$ 27. $3\overline{)59}$ 28. $9\overline{)250}$ 29. $4\overline{)267}$ 30. $8\overline{)730}$

31. $8\overline{)133}$ 32. $5\overline{)183}$ 33. $4\overline{)74}$ 34. $6\overline{)522}$ 35. $3\overline{)133}$

36. $7\overline{)188}$ 37. $9\overline{)369}$ 38. $5\overline{)167}$ 39. $4\overline{)305}$ 40. $3\overline{)176}$

41. $2\overline{)95}$ 42. $4\overline{)373}$ 43. $2\overline{)175}$ 44. $3\overline{)214}$ 45. $5\overline{)82}$

46. $9\overline{)582}$ 47. $7\overline{)208}$ 48. $9\overline{)162}$ 49. $2\overline{)177}$ 50. $7\overline{)248}$

51. $6\overline{)270}$ 52. $5\overline{)69}$ 53. $8\overline{)286}$ 54. $9\overline{)446}$ 55. $3\overline{)186}$

56. $8\overline{)115}$ 57. $3\overline{)202}$ 58. $7\overline{)92}$ 59. $4\overline{)250}$ 60. $7\overline{)381}$

61. $5\overline{)237}$ 62. $2\overline{)136}$ 63. $6\overline{)458}$ 64. $9\overline{)870}$ 65. $2\overline{)181}$

Divide.

1. $4\overline{)1045}$ 2. $2\overline{)1065}$ 3. $7\overline{)2473}$ 4. $5\overline{)2131}$ 5. $3\overline{)2053}$

6. $6\overline{)2115}$ 7. $5\overline{)3067}$ 8. $3\overline{)2230}$ 9. $4\overline{)1506}$ 10. $2\overline{)1727}$

11. $3\overline{)1643}$ 12. $7\overline{)2000}$ 13. $6\overline{)2720}$ 14. $8\overline{)2542}$ 15. $4\overline{)2091}$

16. $2\overline{)1909}$ 17. $8\overline{)3509}$ 18. $9\overline{)2359}$ 19. $7\overline{)3763}$ 20. $5\overline{)1933}$

21. $9\overline{)2858}$ 22. $3\overline{)1477}$ 23. $4\overline{)2698}$ 24. $6\overline{)1703}$ 25. $8\overline{)4553}$

26. $5\overline{)2863}$ 27. $4\overline{)2906}$ 28. $8\overline{)5451}$ 29. $3\overline{)1183}$ 30. $6\overline{)4953}$

31. $8\overline{)6106}$ 32. $6\overline{)3286}$ 33. $5\overline{)4082}$ 34. $9\overline{)3990}$ 35. $7\overline{)4447}$

36. $7\overline{)3404}$ 37. $9\overline{)5628}$ 38. $4\overline{)3746}$ 39. $6\overline{)4449}$ 40. $3\overline{)2488}$

41. $4\overline{)2247}$ 42. $5\overline{)3622}$ 43. $7\overline{)5975}$ 44. $3\overline{)2750}$ 45. $8\overline{)2841}$

46. $6\overline{)4034}$ 47. $8\overline{)6595}$ 48. $9\overline{)4837}$ 49. $4\overline{)1930}$ 50. $5\overline{)1483}$

51. $9\overline{)6413}$ 52. $3\overline{)1570}$ 53. $6\overline{)2266}$ 54. $8\overline{)7489}$ 55. $7\overline{)2980}$

56. $5\overline{)4864}$ 57. $8\overline{)3707}$ 58. $4\overline{)3501}$ 59. $3\overline{)1435}$ 60. $6\overline{)5727}$

61. $7\overline{)4638}$ 62. $6\overline{)2924}$ 63. $9\overline{)7617}$ 64. $5\overline{)3143}$ 65. $3\overline{)2962}$

Divide.

1. $50\overline{)236}$ 2. $30\overline{)202}$ 3. $70\overline{)264}$ 4. $60\overline{)343}$ 5. $20\overline{)155}$

6. $40\overline{)312}$ 7. $80\overline{)312}$ 8. $60\overline{)472}$ 9. $90\overline{)582}$ 10. $50\overline{)431}$

11. $30\overline{)165}$ 12. $60\overline{)231}$ 13. $40\overline{)341}$ 14. $70\overline{)342}$ 15. $80\overline{)466}$

16. $90\overline{)754}$ 17. $70\overline{)379}$ 18. $30\overline{)147}$ 19. $50\overline{)391}$ 20. $60\overline{)399}$

21. $80\overline{)348}$ 22. $40\overline{)267}$ 23. $50\overline{)179}$ 24. $30\overline{)229}$ 25. $70\overline{)177}$

26. $60\overline{)504}$ 27. $50\overline{)342}$ 28. $80\overline{)757}$ 29. $40\overline{)193}$ 30. $30\overline{)281}$

Divide.

1. $34\overline{)191}$ 2. $46\overline{)259}$ 3. $42\overline{)330}$ 4. $83\overline{)313}$ 5. $71\overline{)467}$

6. $92\overline{)291}$ 7. $65\overline{)547}$ 8. $38\overline{)281}$ 9. $52\overline{)329}$ 10. $46\overline{)206}$

11. $48\overline{)316}$ 12. $73\overline{)325}$ 13. $81\overline{)476}$ 14. $95\overline{)687}$ 15. $39\overline{)188}$

16. $57\overline{)219}$ 17. $36\overline{)239}$ 18. $74\overline{)564}$ 19. $28\overline{)257}$ 20. $93\overline{)589}$

21. $72\overline{)381}$ 22. $47\overline{)159}$ 23. $55\overline{)409}$ 24. $63\overline{)288}$ 25. $84\overline{)547}$

26. $64\overline{)501}$ 27. $82\overline{)221}$ 28. $43\overline{)408}$ 29. $95\overline{)268}$ 30. $59\overline{)503}$

31. $96\overline{)779}$ 32. $77\overline{)670}$ 33. $61\overline{)390}$ 34. $94\overline{)215}$ 35. $48\overline{)275}$

36. $45\overline{)381}$ 37. $54\overline{)530}$ 38. $76\overline{)219}$ 39. $87\overline{)650}$ 40. $67\overline{)243}$

Divide.

1. $32\overline{)319}$ 2. $86\overline{)747}$ 3. $26\overline{)132}$ 4. $71\overline{)508}$ 5. $68\overline{)555}$

6. $34\overline{)295}$ 7. $75\overline{)369}$ 8. $64\overline{)517}$ 9. $96\overline{)513}$ 10. $58\overline{)523}$

11. $83\overline{)340}$ 12. $22\overline{)157}$ 13. $88\overline{)809}$ 14. $35\overline{)292}$ 15. $76\overline{)506}$

16. $85\overline{)666}$ 17. $52\overline{)119}$ 18. $23\overline{)210}$ 19. $49\overline{)386}$ 20. $62\overline{)441}$

21. $78\overline{)516}$ 22. $91\overline{)555}$ 23. $12\overline{)106}$ 24. $69\overline{)606}$ 25. $24\overline{)185}$

26. $37\overline{)260}$ 27. $41\overline{)388}$ 28. $29\overline{)202}$ 29. $44\overline{)398}$ 30. $56\overline{)321}$

Divide.

1. $14\overline{)898}$ 2. $56\overline{)772}$ 3. $75\overline{)3128}$ 4. $88\overline{)7254}$ 5. $62\overline{)4963}$

6. $41\overline{)635}$ 7. $69\overline{)2724}$ 8. $24\overline{)551}$ 9. $33\overline{)484}$ 10. $87\overline{)3199}$

11. $85\overline{)939}$ 12. $55\overline{)2123}$ 13. $79\overline{)5318}$ 14. $28\overline{)872}$ 15. $81\overline{)6155}$

16. $44\overline{)956}$ 17. $72\overline{)4771}$ 18. $18\overline{)563}$ 19. $96\overline{)4625}$ 20. $49\overline{)731}$

21. $51\overline{)822}$ 22. $74\overline{)6298}$ 23. $53\overline{)644}$ 24. $78\overline{)5279}$ 25. $67\overline{)2185}$

26. $35\overline{)1116}$ 27. $42\overline{)3113}$ 28. $89\overline{)7126}$ 29. $92\overline{)3744}$ 30. $27\overline{)1895}$

31. $26\overline{)1951}$ 32. $57\overline{)2994}$ 33. $41\overline{)1868}$ 34. $73\overline{)5494}$ 35. $32\overline{)2717}$

36. $77\overline{)5080}$ 37. $25\overline{)2069}$ 38. $41\overline{)1067}$ 39. $22\overline{)598}$ 40. $68\overline{)3331}$

Give the missing numerator or denominator by using multiplication.

1. $\frac{1}{3} = \frac{}{12}$

2. $\frac{2}{4} = \frac{}{8}$

3. $\frac{1}{5} = \frac{3}{}$

4. $\frac{1}{6} = \frac{}{18}$

5. $\frac{2}{5} = \frac{8}{}$

6. $\frac{2}{3} = \frac{}{9}$

7. $\frac{1}{7} = \frac{}{35}$

8. $\frac{1}{2} = \frac{5}{}$

9. $\frac{3}{4} = \frac{}{12}$

10. $\frac{1}{10} = \frac{}{20}$

11. $\frac{5}{6} = \frac{10}{}$

12. $\frac{1}{25} = \frac{3}{}$

13. $\frac{3}{100} = \frac{}{300}$

14. $\frac{5}{50} = \frac{10}{}$

15. $\frac{3}{5} = \frac{}{25}$

16. $\frac{3}{7} = \frac{12}{}$

17. $\frac{3}{7} = \frac{9}{}$

18. $\frac{4}{9} = \frac{12}{}$

19. $\frac{4}{100} = \frac{20}{}$

20. $\frac{3}{200} = \frac{9}{}$

21. $\frac{3}{10} = \frac{9}{}$

22. $\frac{10}{50} = \frac{}{100}$

23. $\frac{5}{9} = \frac{}{45}$

24. $\frac{6}{10} = \frac{}{40}$

Find the lowest-terms fraction.

1. $\frac{2}{20}$

2. $\frac{3}{15}$

3. $\frac{6}{30}$

4. $\frac{2}{6}$

5. $\frac{4}{8}$

6. $\frac{2}{4}$

7. $\frac{12}{16}$

8. $\frac{24}{36}$

9. $\frac{8}{12}$

10. $\frac{9}{15}$

11. $\frac{15}{18}$

12. $\frac{9}{21}$

13. $\frac{6}{14}$

14. $\frac{10}{16}$

15. $\frac{15}{20}$

16. $\frac{3}{24}$

17. $\frac{4}{14}$

18. $\frac{15}{25}$

19. $\frac{21}{30}$

20. $\frac{12}{20}$

21. $\frac{24}{32}$

22. $\frac{10}{25}$

23. $\frac{12}{16}$

24. $\frac{20}{36}$

25. $\frac{15}{24}$

26. $\frac{6}{21}$

27. $\frac{12}{18}$

28. $\frac{16}{20}$

29. $\frac{28}{32}$

30. $\frac{8}{24}$

31. $\frac{12}{36}$

32. $\frac{20}{24}$

33. $\frac{15}{35}$

34. $\frac{24}{27}$

35. $\frac{25}{45}$

36. $\frac{50}{100}$

Write a mixed numeral for each improper fraction.

1. $\frac{8}{3}$ 2. $\frac{18}{5}$ 3. $\frac{23}{7}$ 4. $\frac{14}{6}$ 5. $\frac{9}{4}$ 6. $\frac{7}{2}$

7. $\frac{16}{7}$ 8. $\frac{20}{6}$ 9. $\frac{25}{9}$ 10. $\frac{11}{3}$ 11. $\frac{14}{5}$ 12. $\frac{14}{4}$

13. $\frac{47}{9}$ 14. $\frac{34}{8}$ 15. $\frac{27}{5}$ 16. $\frac{30}{4}$ 17. $\frac{57}{6}$ 18. $\frac{17}{3}$

19. $\frac{36}{7}$ 20. $\frac{28}{6}$ 21. $\frac{35}{4}$ 22. $\frac{29}{3}$ 23. $\frac{38}{9}$ 24. $\frac{49}{8}$

25. $\frac{23}{10}$ 26. $\frac{76}{10}$ 27. $\frac{38}{10}$ 28. $\frac{47}{10}$ 29. $\frac{52}{10}$ 30. $\frac{91}{10}$

31. $\frac{84}{10}$ 32. $\frac{61}{10}$ 33. $\frac{92}{10}$ 34. $\frac{29}{10}$ 35. $\frac{35}{10}$ 36. $\frac{74}{10}$

37. $\frac{342}{100}$ 38. $\frac{721}{100}$ 39. $\frac{256}{100}$ 40. $\frac{473}{100}$ 41. $\frac{829}{100}$ 42. $\frac{564}{100}$

43. $\frac{485}{100}$ 44. $\frac{365}{100}$ 45. $\frac{578}{100}$ 46. $\frac{937}{100}$ 47. $\frac{718}{100}$ 48. $\frac{653}{100}$

Write an improper fraction for each mixed numeral.

1. $3\frac{2}{4}$ 2. $5\frac{1}{5}$ 3. $2\frac{2}{3}$ 4. $3\frac{1}{6}$ 5. $4\frac{2}{5}$ 6. $5\frac{3}{4}$

7. $4\frac{2}{6}$ 8. $3\frac{1}{7}$ 9. $5\frac{1}{3}$ 10. $2\frac{3}{8}$ 11. $6\frac{5}{6}$ 12. $7\frac{2}{7}$

13. $5\frac{5}{8}$ 14. $4\frac{3}{5}$ 15. $2\frac{4}{7}$ 16. $3\frac{1}{10}$ 17. $4\frac{1}{9}$ 18. $8\frac{2}{3}$

19. $6\frac{3}{7}$ 20. $8\frac{1}{10}$ 21. $7\frac{3}{8}$ 22. $5\frac{4}{5}$ 23. $3\frac{5}{6}$ 24. $6\frac{3}{5}$

25. $3\frac{2}{9}$ 26. $2\frac{7}{8}$ 27. $5\frac{1}{10}$ 28. $7\frac{3}{10}$ 29. $6\frac{7}{10}$ 30. $4\frac{5}{7}$

31. $4\frac{12}{100}$ 32. $8\frac{21}{100}$ 33. $3\frac{52}{100}$ 34. $9\frac{4}{9}$ 35. $8\frac{7}{11}$ 36. $7\frac{4}{15}$

Add.

1. $\frac{1}{4} + \frac{1}{5}$ 2. $\frac{1}{2} + \frac{2}{3}$ 3. $\frac{1}{3} + \frac{3}{4}$ 4. $\frac{1}{6} + \frac{1}{4}$ 5. $\frac{3}{8} + \frac{1}{4}$

6. $\frac{1}{2} + \frac{3}{8}$ 7. $\frac{3}{5} + \frac{2}{4}$ 8. $\frac{1}{3} + \frac{1}{9}$ 9. $\frac{2}{3} + \frac{3}{5}$ 10. $\frac{1}{2} + \frac{2}{9}$

11. $\frac{1}{3} + \frac{2}{9}$ 12. $\frac{1}{2} + \frac{3}{5}$ 13. $\frac{1}{10} + \frac{1}{5}$ 14. $\frac{1}{9} + \frac{2}{3}$ 15. $\frac{4}{3} + \frac{3}{2}$

16. $\frac{5}{6} + \frac{2}{3}$ 17. $\frac{3}{10} + \frac{2}{5}$ 18. $\frac{1}{6} + \frac{2}{3}$ 19. $\frac{3}{2} + \frac{1}{7}$ 20. $\frac{1}{5} + \frac{3}{10}$

21. $\frac{1}{6} + \frac{1}{9}$ 22. $\frac{5}{3} + \frac{1}{2}$ 23. $\frac{7}{10} + \frac{1}{5}$ 24. $\frac{3}{4} + \frac{5}{6}$ 25. $\frac{7}{2} + \frac{9}{5}$

26. $\frac{3}{4} + \frac{5}{3}$ 27. $\frac{3}{10} + \frac{7}{5}$ 28. $\frac{8}{3} + \frac{2}{5}$ 29. $\frac{1}{10} + \frac{3}{5}$ 30. $\frac{1}{4} + \frac{5}{12}$

31. $\frac{5}{6} + \frac{1}{2}$ 32. $\frac{3}{10} + \frac{2}{5}$ 33. $\frac{5}{2} + \frac{5}{9}$ 34. $\frac{5}{12} + \frac{3}{4}$ 35. $\frac{4}{9} + \frac{1}{3}$

36. $\frac{1}{12} + \frac{7}{3}$ 37. $\frac{1}{16} + \frac{1}{12}$ 38. $\frac{5}{8} + \frac{1}{4}$ 39. $\frac{5}{6} + \frac{1}{12}$ 40. $\frac{1}{8} + \frac{5}{16}$

Subtract.

1. $\frac{2}{3} - \frac{1}{2}$ 2. $\frac{1}{4} - \frac{1}{6}$ 3. $\frac{2}{3} - \frac{2}{5}$ 4. $\frac{2}{3} - \frac{1}{9}$ 5. $\frac{3}{2} - \frac{2}{3}$

6. $\frac{2}{5} - \frac{1}{10}$ 7. $\frac{3}{5} - \frac{1}{2}$ 8. $\frac{5}{12} - \frac{1}{6}$ 9. $\frac{3}{4} - \frac{1}{5}$ 10. $\frac{3}{2} - \frac{3}{7}$

11. $\frac{3}{2} - \frac{2}{5}$ 12. $\frac{1}{2} - \frac{3}{10}$ 13. $\frac{2}{8} - \frac{3}{16}$ 14. $\frac{4}{3} - \frac{1}{4}$ 15. $\frac{3}{5} - \frac{2}{10}$

16. $\frac{4}{5} - \frac{1}{2}$ 17. $\frac{7}{2} - \frac{2}{3}$ 18. $\frac{3}{8} - \frac{1}{4}$ 19. $\frac{3}{5} - \frac{1}{3}$ 20. $\frac{7}{6} - \frac{3}{4}$

21. $\frac{6}{7} - \frac{3}{4}$ 22. $\frac{4}{3} - \frac{2}{5}$ 23. $\frac{5}{6} - \frac{5}{7}$ 24. $\frac{7}{8} - \frac{2}{3}$ 25. $\frac{5}{9} - \frac{1}{10}$

26. $\frac{7}{5} - \frac{2}{3}$ 27. $\frac{5}{2} - \frac{3}{4}$ 28. $\frac{2}{5} - \frac{3}{10}$ 29. $\frac{5}{12} - \frac{1}{6}$ 30. $\frac{7}{5} - \frac{3}{10}$

31. $\frac{7}{10} - \frac{3}{5}$ 32. $\frac{5}{4} - \frac{3}{8}$ 33. $\frac{3}{2} - \frac{2}{5}$ 34. $\frac{5}{2} - \frac{3}{10}$ 35. $\frac{7}{6} - \frac{5}{12}$

36. $\frac{3}{4} - \frac{1}{12}$ 37. $\frac{6}{7} - \frac{9}{14}$ 38. $\frac{3}{5} - \frac{2}{15}$ 39. $\frac{3}{2} - \frac{5}{7}$ 40. $\frac{9}{10} - \frac{2}{5}$

Subtract.

1. $\dfrac{1}{2}$
    $-\dfrac{1}{4}$

2. $\dfrac{2}{3}$
    $-\dfrac{1}{6}$

3. $\dfrac{3}{4}$
    $-\dfrac{1}{3}$

4. $\dfrac{1}{4}$
    $-\dfrac{1}{5}$

5. $\dfrac{5}{6}$
    $-\dfrac{1}{12}$

6. $\dfrac{4}{7}$
    $-\dfrac{1}{4}$

7. $\dfrac{5}{8}$
    $-\dfrac{1}{6}$

8. $\dfrac{9}{10}$
    $-\dfrac{1}{5}$

9. $\dfrac{7}{12}$
    $-\dfrac{1}{6}$

10. $\dfrac{4}{9}$
    $-\dfrac{3}{10}$

11. $\dfrac{1}{2}$
    $-\dfrac{3}{8}$

12. $\dfrac{7}{8}$
    $-\dfrac{1}{3}$

13. $\dfrac{5}{12}$
    $-\dfrac{1}{3}$

14. $\dfrac{8}{9}$
    $-\dfrac{1}{10}$

15. $\dfrac{5}{6}$
    $-\dfrac{1}{3}$

16. $\dfrac{3}{4}$
    $-\dfrac{2}{5}$

17. $\dfrac{8}{10}$
    $-\dfrac{2}{5}$

18. $\dfrac{5}{9}$
    $-\dfrac{1}{3}$

19. $\dfrac{6}{7}$
    $-\dfrac{2}{3}$

20. $\dfrac{4}{5}$
    $-\dfrac{3}{4}$

21. $\dfrac{4}{7}$
    $-\dfrac{1}{2}$

22. $\dfrac{11}{12}$
    $-\dfrac{5}{6}$

23. $\dfrac{3}{6}$
    $-\dfrac{1}{8}$

24. $\dfrac{4}{5}$
    $-\dfrac{1}{4}$

25. $\dfrac{7}{8}$
    $-\dfrac{5}{16}$

26. $\dfrac{5}{7}$
    $-\dfrac{2}{4}$

27. $\dfrac{15}{16}$
    $-\dfrac{1}{2}$

28. $\dfrac{4}{6}$
    $-\dfrac{3}{8}$

29. $\dfrac{3}{4}$
    $-\dfrac{5}{8}$

30. $\dfrac{9}{10}$
    $-\dfrac{4}{5}$

31. $\dfrac{1}{2}$
    $-\dfrac{1}{8}$

32. $\dfrac{10}{16}$
    $-\dfrac{3}{8}$

33. $\dfrac{8}{12}$
    $-\dfrac{1}{4}$

34. $\dfrac{2}{3}$
    $-\dfrac{1}{6}$

35. $\dfrac{5}{6}$
    $-\dfrac{3}{12}$

36. $\dfrac{8}{9}$
    $-\dfrac{5}{6}$

37. $\dfrac{3}{4}$
    $-\dfrac{1}{6}$

38. $\dfrac{5}{8}$
    $-\dfrac{3}{16}$

39. $\dfrac{1}{3}$
    $-\dfrac{1}{7}$

40. $\dfrac{6}{16}$
    $-\dfrac{1}{4}$

41. $\dfrac{5}{7}$
    $-\dfrac{1}{2}$

42. $\dfrac{5}{9}$
    $-\dfrac{1}{4}$

43. $\dfrac{5}{2}$
    $-\dfrac{3}{5}$

44. $\dfrac{9}{4}$
    $-\dfrac{3}{2}$

45. $\dfrac{8}{5}$
    $-\dfrac{1}{2}$

46. $\dfrac{5}{6}$
    $-\dfrac{1}{9}$

47. $\dfrac{7}{2}$
    $-\dfrac{3}{10}$

48. $\dfrac{10}{3}$
    $-\dfrac{5}{4}$

49. $\dfrac{3}{8}$
    $-\dfrac{1}{6}$

50. $\dfrac{16}{10}$
    $-\dfrac{6}{4}$

51. $\dfrac{8}{4}$
    $-\dfrac{2}{3}$

52. $\dfrac{11}{6}$
    $-\dfrac{3}{4}$

53. $\dfrac{13}{8}$
    $-\dfrac{1}{4}$

54. $\dfrac{6}{7}$
    $-\dfrac{1}{4}$

Solve.

1.

muffins	2			
cents	10			

2.

kilometers	20			
hours	1	2	3	4

3.

pencils	12			
boxes	1	2		

4.

bottles	12	24		
cartons	2			

5. You can buy 5 envelopes for 20¢. How many can you buy for 80¢?

envelopes	5	10	15	20
cents	20	40	60	80

6. A recipe calls for 1 package of meat for 4 people. 4 packages would serve how many?

meat	1	2	3	4
people	4	8	12	16

7. The ratio of lemonade to orange juice in a punch is 3:2. If you use 8 cans of orange juice, how many cans of lemonade would you need?

lemonade	3	6	9	12
orange juice	2	4	6	8

8. Map scale shows 1 cm = 10 km. If map distance is 3 cm, what is the actual distance?

cm	1	2	3	4
km	10	20	30	40

9. Rita rides her bike at about 30 km/h. How far will she travel in 2 hours?

km	30	60	90	120
h	1	2	3	4

10. A band has 10 clarinets for every 2 tubas. If there were 6 tubas, how many clarinets would there be?

clarinets	10	20	30	40
tubas	2	4	6	8

Add.

1.   32.6
   + 48.7

2.   53.9
   + 27.3

3.   61.8
   + 36.5

4.   29.4
   + 26.8

5.   74.6
   + 54.6

6.   82.5
   + 39.7

7.   67.4
   + 46.9

8.   27.7
   + 38.3

9.   43.7
   + 49.4

10.   56.2
   + 35.8

11.   24.5
   + 63.6

12.   84.8
   + 57.3

13.   75.7
   + 45.8

14.   94.4
   + 28.7

15.   66.6
   + 58.4

16.   37.6
   + 77.7

17.   26.2
   + 44.9

18.   85.5
   + 68.5

19.   52.1
   + 47.9

20.   73.3
   + 69.8

21.   93.8
   + 29.4

22.   87.6
   + 42.8

23.   33.9
   + 78.5

24.   23.7
   + 67.4

25.   55.8
   + 79.9

26.   62.53
   + 49.76

27.   98.27
   + 62.87

28.   59.36
   + 97.63

29.   86.47
   + 38.59

30.   25.69
   + 79.78

31.   34.72
   + 88.98

32.   64.64
   + 57.87

33.   49.56
   + 97.63

34.   95.78
   + 38.59

35.   55.64
   + 79.78

36.   75.62
   + 48.69

37.   97.17
   + 33.95

38.   56.78
   + 85.23

39.   73.56
   + 48.97

40.   98.95
   + 65.87

41.   96.3
     27.4
   + 31.7

42.   18.5
     36.4
   + 27.3

43.   46.5
     17.3
   + 65.2

44.   54.1
     37.8
   + 26.5

45.   72.1
     19.9
   + 34.2

46.   45.8
     26.3
   + 37.4

47.   81.2
     36.9
   + 44.1

48.   53.6
     28.2
   + 71.7

49.   94.6
     32.7
   + 25.6

50.   88.1
     56.7
   + 28.9

Subtract.

1. 15.3
  − 6.7

2. 22.1
  − 8.5

3. 17.2
  − 9.4

4. 11.3
  − 5.6

5. 13.5
  − 7.9

6. 18.4
  − 7.6

7. 12.6
  − 4.9

8. 23.3
  − 14.6

9. 31.2
  − 17.6

10. 14.1
  − 7.8

11. 24.5
  − 9.8

12. 32.1
  − 0.6

13. 51.4
  − 23.8

14. 41.3
  − 32.8

15. 67.2
  − 29.5

16. 43.6
  − 27.9

17. 62.3
  − 18.8

18. 34.1
  − 17.9

19. 25.7
  − 9.8

20. 53.4
  − 25.5

21. 33.2
  − 28.7

22. 56.4
  − 18.9

23. 42.3
  − 27.5

24. 61.5
  − 36.7

25. 74.8
  − 43.9

26. 75.1
  − 39.8

27. 48.2
  − 19.9

28. 64.5
  − 46.6

29. 52.4
  − 19.7

30. 35.7
  − 16.8

31. 57.31
  − 28.46

32. 73.24
  − 15.68

33. 81.45
  − 37.86

34. 92.53
  − 17.87

35. 26.31
  − 9.56

36. 61.84
  − 18.36

37. 81.32
  − 33.68

38. 75.65
  − 27.73

39. 43.27
  − 16.49

40. 52.43
  − 28.95

41. 45.13
  − 9.48

42. 63.26
  − 23.49

43. 94.51
  − 36.87

44. 85.68
  − 26.79

45. 71.32
  − 39.65

46. 61.32
  − 17.78

47. 53.27
  − 27.89

48. 81.12
  − 52.36

49. 98.32
  − 66.75

50. 43.81
  − 18.95

Table of Measures

Metric System	English System

— Length —

Metric System		English System	
1 centimeter (cm)	{10 millimeters (mm)		
1 decimeter (dm)	{100 millimeters (mm) 10 centimeters (cm)	1 foot (ft)	{12 inches (in.)
		1 yard (yd)	{36 inches (in.) 3 feet (ft)
1 meter (m)	{1000 millimeters (mm) 100 centimeters (cm) 10 decimeters (dm)	1 mile (mi)	{5280 feet (ft) 1760 yards (yd)
1 kilometer (km)	{1000 meters (m)		

— Area —

Metric System		English System	
1 square meter (m²)	{100 square decimeters (dm²) 10 000 square centimeters (cm²)	1 square foot (ft²)	{144 square inches (in.²)

— Volume —

Metric System		English System	
1 cubic decimeter (dm³)	{1000 cubic centimeters (cm³) 1 liter (L)	1 cubic foot (ft³)	{1728 cubic inches (in.³)

— Capacity —

Metric System		English System	
		1 cup (c)	{8 fluid ounces (fl oz)
1 teaspoon	{5 milliliters (mL)	1 pint (pt)	{16 fluid ounces (fl oz) 2 cups (c)
1 tablespoon	{12.5 milliliters (mL)	1 quart (qt)	{32 fluid ounces (fl oz) 4 cups (c) 2 pints (pt)
1 liter (L)	{1000 milliliters (mL) 1000 cubic centimeters (cm³) 1 cubic decimeter (dm³) 4 metric cups	1 gallon (gal)	{128 fluid ounces (fl oz) 16 cups (c) 8 pints (pt) 4 quarts (qt)

— Mass —

Metric System		English System	
1 gram (g)	{1000 milligrams (mg)	1 pound (lb)	{16 ounces (oz)
1 kilogram (kg)	{1000 grams (g)		

— Time —

Metric System		English System	
1 minute (min)	{60 seconds (s)	1 year (yr)	{365 days 52 weeks 12 months
1 hour (h)	{60 minutes (min)		
1 day (d)	{24 hours (h)	1 decade	{10 years
1 week (w)	{7 days (d)	1 century	{100 years
1 month (mo)	{about 4 weeks		

Multiplication Facts Table

×	0	1	2	3	4	5	6	7	8	9
0	0	0	0	0	0	0	0	0	0	0
1	0	1	2	3	4	5	6	7	8	9
2	0	2	4	6	8	10	12	14	16	18
3	0	3	6	9	12	15	18	21	24	27
4	0	4	8	12	16	20	24	28	32	36
5	0	5	10	15	20	25	30	35	40	45
6	0	6	12	18	24	30	36	42	48	54
7	0	7	14	21	28	35	42	49	56	63
8	0	8	16	24	32	40	48	56	64	72
9	0	9	18	27	36	45	54	63	72	81

Glossary

acute angle   An angle with a measure of less than 90 degrees.

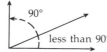

addend   Any one of a set of numbers to be added. In the equation $4 + 5 = 9$, the numbers 4 and 5 are addends.

addition   An operation that combines a first number and a second number to give exactly one number called a sum.

angle   Two rays from a single point.

area   The measure of a region as compared to a given unit, usually a square region.

associative (grouping) principle   When adding (or multiplying) three or more numbers, the grouping of the addends (or factors) can be changed and the sum (or product) is the same.

Examples: $2 + (8 + 6) = (2 + 8) + 6$
$3 \times (4 \times 2) = (3 \times 4) \times 2$

average   The average of a set of numbers is the quotient resulting when the sum of the numbers in the set is divided by the number of addends.

centimeter   A unit of length. One centimeter is 0.01 meter.

1 centimeter

circle   The set of all points in a plane which are a specified distance from a given point called the center.

center ●← circle

commutative (order) principle   When adding (or multiplying) two or more numbers, the order of the addends (or factors) can be changed and the sum (or product) is the same.

Examples: $4 + 5 = 5 + 4$
$2 \times 3 = 3 \times 2$

compass   A device for drawing models of a circle.

congruent figures   Figures that have the same size and shape.

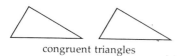

congruent triangles

coordinates   Number pairs used in graphing.

coordinate axes   Two number lines intersecting at right angles at 0.

count   To name numbers in regular succession.

cube   A rectangular prism (box) such that all faces are squares.

denominator   The number indicated by the numeral below the line in a fraction symbol.

Example: $\dfrac{1}{3}$ ← denominator

diameter   A segment that joins two points on a circle and passes through the center of the circle.

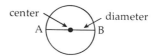

difference   The number obtained by subtracting one number from another.

Example:
$$\begin{array}{r} 48 \\ -25 \\ \hline 23 \end{array}$$ ← difference

digits   The basic Hindu-Arabic symbols used to write numerals. In the base-ten system, the digits are 0, 1, 2, 3, 4, 5, 6, 7, 8, and 9.

distributive (multiplication-addition) principle   This principle is sometimes described in terms of "breaking apart" a number before multiplying.

Example: $6 \times (20 + 4) = (6 \times 20) + (6 \times 4)$

dividend   The number to be divided in a division problem.

Example:
$$\begin{array}{r} 4 \\ 7\overline{)33} \\ -28 \\ \hline 5 \end{array}$$ ← dividend

division   An operation that is the inverse of multiplication.

$3 \times 4 = 12$ < $12 \div 3 = 4$
$12 \div 4 = 3$

divisor   The number by which the dividend is divided.

Example:
divisor → $$\begin{array}{r} 4 \\ 7\overline{)33} \\ -28 \\ \hline 5 \end{array}$$

edge   An edge of a space figure is one of the segments making up any one of the faces of the figure.

edge →

equality (equals or =) A mathematical relation of being exactly the same.

equation A mathematical sentence involving the use of the equality symbol.

Examples: $5 + 4 = 9$

$7 + \square = 8$

$n + 3 = 7$

equivalent fractions Two fractions are equivalent when it can be shown that they each can be used to represent the same amount of a given object. Two fractions are equivalent if these two products are the same:

$$\rightarrow 4 \times 6 \longrightarrow 24$$
$$\rightarrow 3 \times 8 \longrightarrow 24$$

equivalent sets Two sets that may be placed in a one-to-one correspondence.

estimate To find an approximation for a given number. (Sometimes a sum, a product, etc.)

even numbers The whole-number multiples of 2 $(0,2,4,6,8,10,12, \ldots)$

face The face of a given space figure is any one of the plane geometric figures making up the space figure.

face →

factor (see multiplication) In the equation $6 \times 7 = 42$, 6 and 7 are factors of 42.

fraction A symbol for a fractional number such as $\frac{2}{3}, \frac{3}{4},$ or $\frac{1}{2}$.

fractional number The one number we think about for each set of equivalent fractions. For the set $\frac{1}{2}, \frac{2}{4}, \frac{3}{6}, \frac{4}{8}, \ldots$ we think of one number, often expressed as one half or $\frac{1}{2}$.

graph (1) A set of points associated with a given set of numbers or set of number pairs. (2) A picture used to illustrate a given collection of data. The data might be pictured in the form of a bar graph, a circle graph, a line graph, or a pictograph. (3) To draw the graph of.

greater than (>) One of the two basic inequality relations.

Example: $6 > 5$, read 6 is greater than 5

hexagon A polygon which has six sides.

improper fraction A fraction in which the numerator is greater than or equal to the denominator.

Examples: $\frac{8}{5}, \frac{9}{6}, \frac{12}{3}, \frac{7}{7},$ etc.

inequality $(>, \neq, <)$ In arithmetic, a relation indicating that the two numbers are not equal.

kilogram A unit of mass in the metric system. 1 kilogram is 1000 grams.

kilometer A unit of length in the metric system. 1 kilometer is 1000 meters.

length A number indicating the measure of one line segment with respect to another line segment called the unit.

less than (<) One of the two basic inequality relations.

Example: $5 < 6$, read 5 is less than 6

line A line is a straight path (formed by a set of points) that goes on and on in two directions.

line segment See segment.

liter (cubic decimeter) The basic unit of capacity in the metric system. 1 liter is 1000 milliliters.

lowest terms A fraction is in lowest terms if the numerator and denominator of the fraction have no common factor greater than 1.

Examples: $\frac{3}{4}, \frac{5}{8}, \frac{11}{16}$

measure (1) A number indicating the relation between a given object and a suitable unit. (2) The process of finding the number described above.

meter The basic unit of length in the metric system. 1 meter is 100 centimeters.

minus (−) Used to indicate the subtraction operation, as in $7 - 3 = 4$, read 7 minus 3 equals 4.

mixed numerals Symbols such as $2\frac{1}{2}$ and $3\frac{1}{4}$

multiple A first number is a multiple of a second number if there is a whole number that multiplies by the second number to give the first number.

Example: 24 is a multiple of 6 since $4 \times 6 = 24$.

multiplication An operation that combines two numbers, called factors, to give one number called the product.

number line A line with a subset of its points matched with a subset of the real numbers.

0 1 2 3 4 5 6 7 8 9

numeral A symbol for a number.

numerator The number indicated by the numeral above the line in a fraction symbol.

Example: $\frac{3}{4}$ ← numerator

obtuse angle An angle with a measure greater than 90°.

90°

greater than 90°

octagon A polygon which has eight sides.

odd number Any whole number that is not even.

Examples: $1, 3, 5, 7, 9, 11, 13, \ldots$

one principle (for multiplication) Any number multiplied by 1 is that same number. One is the identity element for multiplication. $1 \times 8 = 8$

parallel lines Two lines which lie in the same plane and do not intersect.

pentagon A polygon which has five sides.

perimeter The sum of the lengths of the sides of a given polygon.

place value The value given to the place a digit occupies in a numeral.

Example:

$$3\ 5\ 6$$
hundreds' place ⟶
tens' place ⟶
ones' place ⟶

plus (+) Used to indicate the addition operation, as in 4 + 3 = 7, read 4 plus 3 equals 7.

polygon A closed geometric figure made up of line segments.

prime number A number greater than 1 whose only factors are itself and 1.

Examples: 2, 3, 5, 7, 11, 13, etc.

product The result of the multiplication operation. In the equation 6 × 7 = 42, 42 is the product of 6 and 7.

quadrilateral A polygon which has four sides.

quotient The number (other than the remainder) that is the result of the division operation.

Examples: 45 ÷ 9 = 5   6 ⟵ quotient
                        7)45
             quotient   − 4 2
                            3

radius (1) Any segment from the center to a point on the circle. (2) The distance from the center to any point on the circle.

radius

ray A ray is a part of a line consisting of a point and the part of the line on one side of the point.

line
ray

rectangle A quadrilateral which has four right angles.

regrouping A method of handling place value symbols in adding or subtracting numbers.

Example:
          1   3 13
        47 1 ten   4̸3̸
       + 29   16   − 17
        76 6 ones   26

remainder The number less than the divisor that remains after the division process is completed.

Example:
            6
          7)47
          − 4 2
             5 ⟵ remainder

right angle An angle that has the measure of 90°.

right triangle A triangle that has one right angle.

Roman numerals Numerals used by the Romans, primarily to record numbers rather than for computing.

Examples: I, V, X, L, C, D, and M are symbols for 1, 5, 10, 50, 100, 500, and 1000 respectively.

segment Two points on a line and all the points on the line that are between the two points.

A ⟵————●————————————●——⟶ B
              segment

set undefined; usually thought of as a group or collection.

similar figures Two figures that have the same shape.

skip count To count by multiples of a given number.

Example: 0, 5, 10, 15, . . . (counting by fives)

solve To find the number or numbers which, when substituted for the variable or place holder, make a given equation true.

square A quadrilateral that has four right angles and four sides that are the same length.

subtraction An operation related to addition as illustrated:

$$7 + 8 = 15 \begin{cases} 15 - 8 = 7 \\ 15 - 7 = 8 \end{cases}$$

sum The number obtained by adding any set of numbers.

Example:
            3
          + 2
            5 ⟵ sum

symmetric figure A figure that can be folded in half so that the two halves match.

times (×) Used to indicate the multiplication operation, as in 3 × 4 = 12, read 3 times 4 equals 12.

triangle A polygon which has three sides.

triangular pyramid A four-sided space figure that has triangular regions for all faces.

triangular pyramid

unit An amount or quantity adopted as a standard of measurement.

vertex The point that the two rays of an angle have in common.

vertex

volume The measure, obtained using an appropriate unit (usually a cube), of the interior region of a space figure.

whole number Any number in the set: 0, 1, 2, 3, 4, 5, 6, 7, 8, 9, 10, 11, 12, 13, 14, ...

zero principle (for addition) Any number added to zero is that same number. 0 + 5 = 5

Index

Prime numbers, 109
Problem solving
    addition and subtraction, 46–51, 110–111, 167, 174–175, 220–221
    addition and subtraction of decimals, 308–309
    addition and subtraction of money, 56–57, 310–313
    decimals, 304–313
    division, 214–217, 220–221
    estimation (addition and subtraction), 54–55
    estimation (multiplication), 169–171
    large numbers, 334–335
    multiplication and division facts, 102–107, 110–111
    multiplication of 2- and 3-digit factors, 168–170, 174–175, 220–221
    strategy, 47
Products
    estimation, 136–137, 171–173
    finding, 73
Pyramid, 60–61

Q

Quart, 342A–342B
Quotients
    checking, 196–197, 200–201
    estimating, 192–193, 200–201, 204–206, 208
    finding, 89, 191
    special, 138–139, 204–205

R

Radius, 66–67
Ratio
    problems, 280–281
    tables, 278–281
    writing, 274–277
Reasoning, 3, 305
Rectangle,
    area of, 316–317
    definition, 62
    puzzle, 315
Remainder, 189, 190–191
Right angle, 61, 64–65
Roman numerals, 293
Rounding numbers
    to nearest 10, 52, 136–137
    to nearest 100, 53, 136–137
    to solve problems, 54–55

S

Segment, 61
Similar figures, 225–227
Special products, 130–135
Special quotients, 138–139
Square
    area of, 316–317
    centimeter, 318
    definition, 62
    foot, 341A
    inch, 341A
    pyramid, 60
    yard, 341A
Subtraction
    decimals, 298–299, 300–302
    equations, 7
    facts, 6–7
    fractions with like denominator, 266–267, 270–271
    mixed numerals, 267
    money, 56–57
    number line, 3
    place value, 34–36
    regrouping, 34–43
    zeros, 40–43
    2-digit, 36–37
    3- and 4-digit, 38–39
Symmetric figures, 230–231, 303

T

Tangram, 101, 224
Temperature, 125, 219, 344A
Thousand
    reading, 18–19, 328–330
    writing, 16–17, 331
Triangle, 61–63, 209, 327

V

Volume, 320–321

Y

Yard, 341

Z

Zero
    in multiplication, 74–75
    in subtraction, 40–42